I0796887

Stop Holding Back

Stop Holding Back

An Honest Guide to Turning Fear into Action

JOZE PIRANIAN

Collins

Stop Holding Back

Published by Collins, an imprint of HarperCollins Publishers Ltd

FIRST EDITION

HarperCollins Publishers Ltd
Bay Adelaide Centre, East Tower
22 Adelaide Street West, 41st Floor
Toronto, Ontario, Canada
M5H 4E3

www.harpercollins.ca

HarperCollins Publishers
Macken House, 39/40 Mayor Street Upper
Dublin 1, D01 C9W8, Ireland
https://www.harpercollins.com

Library and Archives Canada Cataloguing in Publication information is available on request.

ISBN 978-1-4434-7226-5

Printed and bound in the United States of America

25 26 27 28 29 LBC 5 4 3 2 1

To every person who ever held back
out of the fear of being judged,
may this book be a mirror, a megaphone, and a map.
And to my younger self, hiding behind silence:
From stutter to stand-up, who saw that coming?

The cave you fear to enter holds the treasure you seek.

—JOSEPH CAMPBELL

CONTENTS

PROLOGUE

I never saw this coming. Me, Joze, writing a book about conquering fears? Not in a billion years. I genuinely believed I was destined to live a life punctuated by the rhythms of fear and discomfort. The truth is, dear reader, I avoided speaking for 25 years not just because of fear, but because of a debilitating stutter.

Growing up in Lebanon, I was terrified of being judged for sounding different. The moment I awoke, extreme social anxiety from dealing with a stutter flared up—and it lasted the entire day. Imagine you see a field that is full of explosive mines. Rationally you would avoid that field of doom altogether, right? Well, that field was my life. The mines were my speech blocks exploding with all the shame, embarrassment and anger caused by having a stutter. And although the explosions didn't cause physical damage, every time that I got stuck and stepped on a metaphorical mine, my self-esteem, self-confidence and self-love were destroyed.

Once, when I was about 11 years old, a teacher asked me to read a paragraph in front of the class. I started stuttering and I got badly stuck on a word. In fact, I must have repeated that same word five or six times. I felt utterly incapable of finishing that sentence. One of my classmates, thinking he was hilarious, loudly commented, "The record got stuck!" Everyone started laughing. Ouch. I not only instantly froze; I also bowed my head and shielded my face with my hands to avoid making eye contact with any of my classmates. I absolutely despised the fact that I had to be so different all the time, and that I was unable to say the words to express my thoughts and emotions.

Naturally, the sound of silence came to the rescue. Thanks, Simon & Garfunkel! I would often ask myself, why engage in the world and risk embarrassment when I could just hide in the isolating (yet comforting) cocoon of my silence? While I didn't make a conscious choice to "play it safe," avoidance was the only reliable way for me to get away from the scary experience of being judged for being different. As Maya Angelou eloquently said, "We do the best we can with what we know, and when we know better, we do better." At that time, I genuinely didn't know better. Unfortunately, playing it safe by chronically avoiding speaking proved to be the single-most-dangerous thing I could possibly do. This way of living constantly eroded my potential and filled my life with an ever-evolving folder of regrets.

Fast forward to today, and I can confidently say that my life would be utterly unrecognizable to the person I was back then. Quite frankly, he would be absolutely baffled to find out that the self-conscious young man somehow went on to perform stand-up comedy on three continents and in four languages. He would be shocked to hear that the guy who begged his university professors at McGill University in Montreal to exempt him from all presentations has since delivered five different TEDx Talks. Most importantly, he would not comprehend the fact that the man who once avoided speaking at all costs now speaks for a living at organizations, educational institutions and conferences around the world in places such as Dubai, Los Angeles, Madrid, Kuwait and Seattle—to name a few.

In fact, my younger self would have placed "professional speaker" at the bottom of any list of likely future professions.

In spite of the fact that I almost failed my grade 9 physics class, becoming an astronaut would have seemed a far more plausible future than the path I somehow forged. For a very long time, I would have gladly chosen to become a monk who takes a vow of silence over any career that involves the slightest need to speak at work. Why am I telling you any of this? To get you to start thinking about what you currently fear to do and then start imagining what currently unthinkable exploits might be possible for you, too. To be honest, moments before I step onto any of the many international stages where I have spoken, I sometimes pinch myself to acknowledge the hilarious absurdity of my life. "How did I get here?" I ask myself.

Although I might not know you personally, I believe you have picked up this book to find a solution to an obstacle that you are currently facing. No matter how similar or different our obstacles might be, our journeys share a fundamental commonality: We have held back from doing the things we wished to do. Whether you have held back due to the fear of judgment, rejection, failure or success, you may be dealing with your own "inner stutter" (more about this concept shortly). I want you to know right away that radical change is possible. Quite simply, the way your life is today does not have to dictate the way your life will be in the future. Former US secretary of state William Jennings Bryan said that "destiny is not a matter of chance; it's a matter of choice." Similarly, Ralph Waldo Emerson reminded us that "the only person you are destined to become is the person you decide to be."

If you hold back because of fear in areas of life that matter to you, *and if you have decided to do something about it,* this book is for you. If you have already started your personal growth journey and are looking to take yourself further into realms of outstanding possibilities, this book is also for you. However, if you are looking for rosy affirmations and empty platitudes about visualizing your way into success without doing uncomfortable things that currently scare you, we might not be the best fit. No hard feelings. While this might not be the book for you now, you might change your mind when you discover that the words *solution* and *action* are often two sides of the same coin. Indeed, the word *transformation* might as well be spelled transform*action*! As you embark on this journey with me, you will learn that with the right approach, mindset and action steps, your greatest fear might just become your greatest asset. This isn't a cliché—it's the wildly unexpected journey I've lived. This book is a blueprint containing all the concepts, mindsets and strategies that I've uncovered and discovered by direct experience and through academic research and conversations with people from all walks of life who have overcome a once seemingly insurmountable fear of their own.

I simply cannot wait to guide you on this path of conquering fear. It's time to stop holding back and turn your fear into action one micro-moment of bravery at a time. Why settle for "No way José" when the "Yes way Joze"* philosophy awaits. Ready? Let's go!

* "Yeswayjoze" is the name of my philosophy and my Instagram handle. You can access additional resources, including access to the Facebook group "Yes Way Joze," to connect with fellow humans on a similar journey of turning fear into action, at www.jozepiranian.com/stopholdingback.

Stop Holding Back

INTRODUCTION

Did I stutter?

In the sixteenth episode of the fourth season in the hit TV show *The Office*, Michael Scott, the well-meaning yet awkwardly gregarious boss, asks his employees to help him come up with an idea to reinvigorate the office. One of the salespeople, Andy Bernard, suggests that they change their answering machine message so that it has "a little more zing and a little more pep." His colleague Jim Halpert, known for being a prankster, suggests they come up with an *even newer* message that has "even *more* zing and pep." Naturally, Jim's very sarcastic response infuriates the painfully competitive Andy who is known for reminding everyone that he is a proud alum of Cornell University, the Ivy League college. (Having delivered a speaking engagement in Ithaca, I have walked through the Cornell campus and I can understand why Andy was so proud—it's gorgeous . . . I mean, it's "gorges."*) Looking for more input from other team members, Michael asks salesperson Stanley Hudson to participate in the group discussion. Hudson is regarded as a laid-back yet hardworking employee with limited patience for nonsense and useless meetings. Busy and committed to finishing his cross-

* The slogan for Ithaca, in upstate New York where Cornell is located, is "Ithaca Is Gorges"—a playful pun inspired by the abundance of gorges, narrow valleys between hills, running through the city.

word puzzle, Stanley initially declines the request. But his boss continues to try to draw him into the group. Finally, an annoyed Stanley erupts, boldly expressing his frustration: "Did I stutter?" he asks.

The conference room goes completely quiet.

Every time I've watched this episode—and *The Office* remains one of my all-time favorite shows—this scene has been uncomfortable for me to sit through. Fans might argue that no episode exceeds the cringe factor of "Scott's Tots," where Michael Scott has to face the consequences of a promise that he would pay university tuition for a whole class now that they're graduating high school, but all he's got to offer them are laptop batteries. But I naturally find myself being most affected by the aptly titled episode "Did I Stutter?" I've always felt the phrase indirectly implies that if someone does in fact stutter, their words would be worthless (or at least, *worth less*). And if the character did stutter, what would be so wrong about that? While I am fully aware that the writers were merely using a common idiom, I cannot help but feel stung by that line and what it implies about stuttering and people who stutter. As it happens, art does imitate life. And a year after that episode first aired, I experienced my own version of this scene during a summer internship in New York City.

In the summer of 2009, I had the opportunity to spend two months in Greenwich Village, right by New York University, with a group of 40 university students from the United States, Canada, Latin America, Europe, the Middle East and Australia. This internship program, called NYSIP (the New York Summer Internship Program*), was created by the Armenian General Benevolent

* This program is now called the Global Leadership Program (GLP).

Union (AGBU) to get young Armenians from around the world to connect with their roots and with one another. During the week, I was interning at a nonprofit run by Dr. Ani Kalayjian, a professor and clinical psychologist who studied post-traumatic stress disorder (PTSD) and post-traumatic growth (PTG) among refugees and other conflict-affected individuals. In case you are wondering about the difference, whereas PTSD is a negative reaction to an actual or perceived severe threat, injury or act of violence, PTG is defined as a positive psychological change in response to an extremely challenging life situation.[1] The concept of post-traumatic growth beautifully aligns with the premise of Nassim Nicholas Taleb's book *Antifragile: Things That Gain from Disorder*. According to the Lebanese author, antifragility refers to systems that do not merely withstand a shock; rather, they actually improve because of it.[2] In other words, exposure to adversity can, under the right circumstances, add an unexpected benefit to the individual's life that they wouldn't otherwise have gained. As you'll soon see, these concepts are deeply connected to much of what my book is about.

Coping strategies, resilience and social support, as well as making meaning out of the difficult experience and subsequently finding purpose, can all contribute to potentially turning trauma into triumph.[3]

When I was not assisting the Columbia university professor, I was enthusiastically enjoying my life in New York City. After work and on weekends, all the interns, who were placed at different organizations across diverse industries, congregated to explore the dining and nightlife scenes of one of the most exciting cities in the world. With over 25,000 restaurants, bars and nightclubs and only 60 days in the city, we would have to go to over 400 establishments per day to get through that entire list! While we didn't take on such an obscene goal, we discovered so many venues that I can't remember many of the names of the places we went to. And I typically have a great memory! One Saturday night, I was at some bar in the East Village with my fellow interns, who had now become good friends. Upon seeing a pool table, two of the guys from our group headed towards it and started racking the balls for a game. Moments later, I overheard their altercation with another group of young men who claimed they had been there first. After one of my friends let the group know that we would be playing our game first, whether they liked it or not, the other group pushed back. Not liking what he saw or heard, our other friend came to the rescue and loudly reminded the foes that our friend had already made it clear that we would be playing first. "He didn't stutter," he exclaimed. There was that line again.

While I know with utmost certainty that this comment was neither targeted at me nor indirectly meant to belittle people who stutter, I could not help but feel saddened by the truly negative implications of the phrase. I would have thought, perhaps naively, that the fact that they had all spent time with me over the past weeks would have made him a bit more sensitive. Stuttering has been my single-biggest source of insecurity. Why would one use that term as an insult? Whether it's Ken Pile being mocked by Otto for having a stutter in the movie *A Fish Called Wanda*, stuttering public defender John Gibbons being ridiculed by the judge and the jury in *My Cousin Vinny* or Billy Bibbit being manipulated by Nurse Ratched in *One Flew Over the Cuckoo's Nest*, I had to wonder, why does stuttering have such a negative connotation in society? Don't we all have a stutter in one way or another?

You read that right. I would argue that while you might not have a physical stutter, you, dear reader, might have your own version of a stutter that holds you back. We can call it your inner stutter. I know you're thinking "Joze . . . I picked up this book to get rid of an obstacle and not find out about an impediment I didn't even know I had." Stay with me for a minute and you will see how this metaphor not only makes sense but constitutes a helpful framework to think about your own obstacles and the best way to overcome them. If an actual stutter is hesitant speech with a chronic lack of fluency, an inner stutter could be described as not taking action due to fear and therefore experiencing a lack of momentum in your life.

Picture this: You are in a meeting at work and you think of an idea that could positively impact the way a certain project is done. This idea would not only improve the experience of your colleagues in terms of efficiency, but it might also get you noticed by the leaders in the room who are always looking for talent they can eventually promote to more senior positions. The person running the meeting asks if anyone has anything to share; you want to put your hand up but something stops you. Your inner monologue might include thoughts such as "What if they think the idea is stupid?" "What if they think I sound funny?" "I don't look great today. I should sit this one out and participate next time." Another one of your colleagues decides to share an idea that, let's face it, wasn't as brilliant as yours. The group reacts positively, and one of the leaders suggests that this person should be a presenter at the upcoming town hall, giving him more visibility and making him a great candidate for future advancement opportunities.

A good product with great marketing will always outsell a great product with good marketing. When we do not speak up during those critical moments, people will not know about us, and if they don't know about us, we won't come to mind when new opportunities arise. In moments like these, the fear of failure leads to an inner stutter that causes you to freeze, preventing you from doing something that you know you want to do.

Another scenario might be more relevant to my student readers: You are in your first year of university and you're taking an intro to psychology class. The professor starts by explaining a theory from the field of social psychology. You think of the perfect example that beautifully and humorously illustrates that theory, and you eagerly wish to share it with the rest of the class. Not only could that entertain and impress your classmates—you're in first year and keen to meet new people—it might also put you on the radar of the professor who might one day hire you as a teaching assistant. You only have a few seconds to put your hand up. Your heart starts to beat, you start to elevate your arm—but an unexpected form of gravitational pull keeps your hand down. The professor has now moved on to another topic and your opportunity has vanished. In that instance, the fear of being judged by your professor and classmates prevented you from speaking, thus inducing an inner stutter. Will you speak up next time or will you allow that inner stutter to prevent you from doing so again? I can think of countless times during my undergrad years in Montreal when I wanted to participate in class only to be met with the crushing gravitational pull of my fears, self-doubts and insecurities. While I deal with an actual stutter, I too have experienced the inner stutter—the more challenging one of the two.

Reflecting on my personal experience as a person who stutters, I can state with utmost confidence that the physical act of stuttering, while at times both inconvenient and tiring, pales in comparison with the internal turmoil that resulted from it.

Imagine I go to a café to order one of my favorite beverages: a rooibos tea latte. In the event that you are not a fellow tea enthusiast or a South African national, I will gladly inform you that rooibos is an herbal tea made from the leaves of the *Aspalathus linearis* plant, which is native to South Africa. I personally love having it as a tea latte with oat milk; in fact, I am sipping this heavenly hot beverage on a chilly February morning while I write this introduction. That most cafés have excruciatingly mundane selections of herbal teas is a definite pet peeve of mine. I've even considered starting my own line of tea ("Joiboos Tea"?) to fill this gap in the market. But back to the hypothetical story at the café. While ordering my beverage, if I were to stutter on "r-r-r-rooibos" and receive a neutral reaction from the barista who simply proceeded to make the beverage, the emotional difficulty of that interaction would be relatively negligible. If, however, I were to stutter on that word and notice that the barista and his colleagues were either laughing or visibly nervous because of my unusual speaking patterns, I would experience a high level of anxiety, shame and embarrassment. Those feelings would follow me around.

In fact, considering that I frequently experienced those emotions because I disliked being different, negative reactions from others would further validate and exacerbate the disempowering beliefs I held about myself. They would magnify my own inner stutter. Indeed, receiving a negative reaction while getting severely stuck on a word could, in my mind, reinforce the belief that I was weird and thus not worthy of fitting in with a group. The physical stutter without the psychological repercussions is merely a temporary block. It's the socio-emotional and psychological ramifications of the physical stutter (or other "unusual behavior") that largely shape the lived experience of the individual who grows up "different," whatever that difference might entail.

You don't need to be visibly or audibly different to have had the experience of feeling ostracized because of your unique characteristics. At my speaking engagements, I often ask the conference delegates to raise their hands if they have ever thought of themselves as being different. In most cases, the vast majority of the delegates answer yes. In other words, even if you do not stutter, belong to a community or group that has historically struggled more than others or deal with mental health-related challenges, it's highly likely that you have, at one point in your life, felt different. The primary source of my "feeling different" was my stutter. Yours could have been that you felt you were too short, too tall, too skinny or too large, or that your voice was too high, too low, too fast or too slow. As humans, we will never run out of things to feel insecure about. We often end up dealing with both the initial challenge and the subsequent inner stutter that gets in the way of us taking action in our lives.

Many of us have experienced these moments when our inner stutter—not our conviction, self-expression or dreams—dictated our fate.

At no time in my life did I avoid speaking more than when I was a teenager. Whether it's the struggle to find our identity, pressures from friends or the developing a sense of independence from our parents, the teenage years are challenging for many. At the time, one of my best friends was a girl at my school in Lebanon; let's call her LJ. I often phoned her—from my landline—to talk about our lives and, to be honest, to vent about my frustrations. If you're a member of Gen Z or Gen Alpha, it may be worth explaining that a landline is like a non-wireless mobile phone used only for making and receiving calls. Ironically, making and receiving calls are the two features that most of us probably don't use our phones for anymore. Later on, I'll talk about how tech—and or inability to escape it—affects our mental health and our ability to focus. But now, back to LJ. I'd tell her how my stutter made it impossible for me to socialize or to date. (While I struggled in these areas, let me say that I'm grateful to have always had a group of friends—from childhood on—that I remain close to.) The conversations with LJ were frequently lengthy, and not just because I stuttered. During one of those calls, she interrupted my tirade and planted a seed in my mind that only sprouted in more recent years: "You know," she said gently, "we all have something that makes us feel insecure." In my relentless fixation on stuttering, I quickly discarded her comment, interpreting it as a well-meaning gesture to console me in a moment of distress. Nobody else could possibly understand what it feels like to experience fear or to hold back, I told myself. Right?

Years later and while delivering keynote speeches at organizations around the world, I had countless conversations with people, either in person or online, who'd tell me about an obstacle that monopolized their lives and constrained their destinies. Whether they knew it or not, they were telling me that they had an inner stutter that held them back from becoming the best version of themselves. Far from being an abstract idea, this concept can be explained in a simple formula:

Fear + Inaction → Inner Stutter → Wasted Potential + Endless Regrets

Thankfully, it doesn't have to be that way. The wildly unexpected journey that I have been on over the past few years is proof. Over the next chapters, I'll share my thoughts and insights gained from my life experiences.

But first, let's go over some basic information about stuttering so that you understand where I am coming from in relation to the topic of fear.

Stuttering 101

According to the National Stuttering Association, stuttering is a "difference in speech patterning involving a loss of control of speech which results in disruptions or disfluencies."[4] It affects approximately one in 100 people and is up to four times more common among males than females.[5] In other words, 400,000 people in Canada, three million people in the US and 80 million people around the world stutter. If all stutterers lived in the same country, let's call it "Stutter Island," its population would be close to that of Germany. Getting through customs in the airport of that fictitious place would certainly take a bit of time. The stuttering lawyers on Stutter Island would, however, be exorbitantly wealthy . . . if they charged by the hour. Whether it was someone who stutters in the legal profession, customs or somewhere else, most of us have interacted with at least one person who stutters. Indeed, it could be someone in your class or at work, or perhaps you picked up this book because we know each other personally . . . and if that is the case, thank you for supporting my first publishing endeavor. If you're a resident of Gilbert, Arkansas (population: 26), Kaskaskia, Illinois (population: 23), or Tilt Cove (Newfoundland and Labrador, population 5), however, the chances of having met a person who stutters might be stacked against you. Worry not, I would gladly be your first stuttering friend.

Humans are wired for social connection, but disruptions in speaking capabilities can compromise our ability to connect with others. UCLA neuroscientist Matthew Lieberman said that our need to connect socially is as basic as our need for food, water and shelter.[6] It is no coincidence that solitary confinement is seen as the most extreme form of punishment for prisoners. Incidentally, both convicts and stutterers find it very difficult to finish a sentence. (Groan.) While what is most visible, or audible, to the outside world is the stutterer's speech blocks or disruptions, most of the stuttering experience actually resides in the unseen feelings of embarrassment, fear, anxiety and shame. Those emotions permeated much of my existence before I embarked on a transformational journey. Seeing that these negative experiences tend to be hidden from the people in the life of the person who stutters, Dr. Joseph Sheehan, a prominent expert in the field of communications disorder, coined the metaphor of the "stuttering iceberg" around 1970 to illustrate the dichotomy between what is seen and what is hidden.

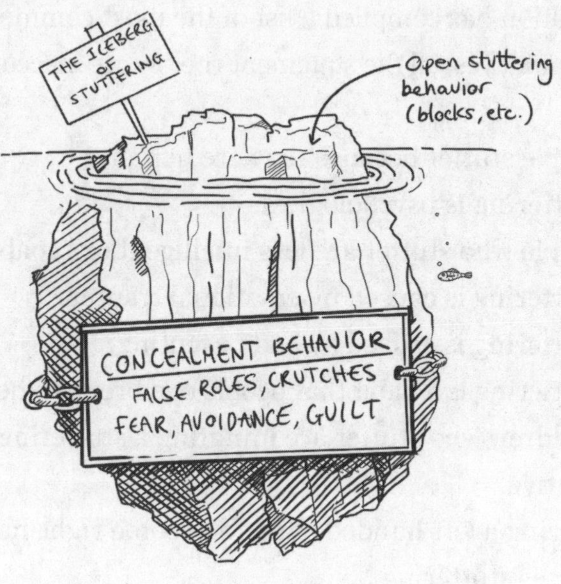

Before we address what stuttering is, let's make a crucial distinction between stuttering as a recurring condition and stuttering as a normal, occasional disruption in one's speech. When I hear a friend who is not a stutterer complain about the fact that they stuttered during their presentation or on a date, they are referring to the fact that stress temporarily disrupted their fluency. In contrast to occasions involving temporary and situational blocking, when I use the term *stuttering* or *stutter* in this book, I am referring to a condition that is far more severe and consistent than one's occasional linguistic fumbling under stress or anxiety. Moreover, while up to 8 percent of preschool-aged children experience stuttering, 80 percent will completely stop stuttering during childhood.[7] In other words, while many people will be familiar with the experience of stuttering, due to either having stuttered a bit during early childhood or being prone to getting stuck occasionally when under duress, these experiences are distinct from the stutterer, who can experience severe blocks whether or not they are anxious. Let's dispel some further myths about what stuttering is *not*. The National Stuttering Association has compiled a list of the most common myths about stuttering, and, yes, all the statements below are inaccurate:

- People stutter because they are nervous.
- Stuttering is psychological.
- People who stutter are less intelligent or capable.
- Stuttering is caused by emotional trauma.
- Stuttering is caused by bad parenting.
- Stuttering is a habit that people can break if they want to.
- Children who stutter are imitating a stuttering parent or relative.
- Forcing a left-handed child to become right-handed causes stuttering.[8]

While the precise cause of stuttering remains unknown, research has pointed to the fact that this at times inheritable condition is caused by differences in brain activity that interfere with speech production.[9] Contrary to a common assumption, stuttering is neurological and physiological; it is not psychological. That being said, emotional factors can amplify one's stutter. For example, I avoided speaking and avoided people for more than 25 years because I was afraid of being judged for being different. Not only did the fear make my stutter physically worse by disrupting my speaking process further, it mercilessly squandered my potential across various spheres of life: school and university, friends, romance and work. I had both a physical stutter *and* an inner stutter. Indeed, whenever I avoided speaking because of my fear of being judged or rejected, that was my inner stutter holding me back from doing what I most wished to do.

Holding back compromised my ability to express myself and fulfill my potential. If you picked up this book, it might have done the same to you. The time has come, dear reader, to tackle this conundrum by challenging your relationship with fear and elevating your life to a whole new dimension you might have never thought was possible.

1.

What are you waiting for?

You don't have to be great to start, but
you have to start to be great.
—ZIG ZIGLAR

In *Waiting for Godot*, Irish playwright Samuel Beckett tells the story of Vladimir and Estragon who endlessly wait for someone by the name of "Godot." As these two characters wait, and wait, they fill their time with conversations and activities to distract themselves from their angst. Vladimir and Estragon have every right to leave, yet they voluntarily choose to stay and wait. Why? What do they expect from Godot? Perhaps they assumed that the change they sought in their lives occurred on the outside through an external factor rather than from within. There are several explanations for their (and our) tendency to remain passive in life.

First of all, human beings prefer avoiding losses to acquiring gains of a similar value. For example, we would prefer not to lose a hundred-dollar bill that we currently have in our pockets over stumbling on a brand-new hundred-dollar bill. From the perspective of human evolution, this tendency makes sense because we are more likely to survive if we end up having fewer gains as opposed to losing everything until we have nothing else left.[1] Indeed, in prehistoric days, our ancestors found it advantageous to preserve their existing resources as a primary survival strategy rather than risk the loss of valuable resources and ultimate starvation. Unexpectedly discovering new resources is a welcome bonus, but preserving existing ones is imperative. So, returning to the two characters in the Beckett play, leaving before Godot's possible arrival would signify the loss of a potentially beneficial opportunity.

The second explanation is the fear of the unknown, which has long urged humans to err on the side of prudence instead of choosing the path of adventure. If Vladimir and Estragon suddenly stop waiting for Godot, they would *have* to abandon their comfort zone of waiting in that room and bravely venture into a new reality that might seem scary. In "Into the Unknown," from Disney's *Frozen 2*, Elsa sings about the risks of following the unknown, wisely saying that she's had her adventure and doesn't need something new. Not waiting for Godot is the "something new" that our two characters seem reluctant to engage in. Apparently, their reluctance is backed by science. In experiments that involved hooking up participants to electrodes that could deliver a harmless but somewhat uncomfortable electric shock to the skin, researchers uncovered an unexpected finding. Participants showed greater stress when there was a 50 percent chance of receiving a shock compared to a scenario where there would be 100 percent certainty of being electrocuted.[2] In other words, the uncertainty of a potential negative outcome was considered more threatening than a guaranteed one. We would rather *experience* a negative outcome that we assume inevitable than enter a situation that might or might not involve a similar negative outcome. In the words of director Alfred Hitchcock, "There is no terror in the bang, only in the anticipation of it." Leaving before Godot's arrival triggers the fear of uncertainty. To Vladimir and Estragon, waiting for Godot became the familiar, predictable and comfortable path; venturing into the unknown was the unfamiliar, unpredictable and uncomfortable one.

The third explanation is one that my readers who have taken an introductory psychology class might be familiar with. Leon Festinger, a social psychologist from New York City, posited that psychological tension is created when a person's behavior is inconsistent with their thoughts and beliefs. This underlying tension, referred to as "cognitive dissonance," is capable of motivating the individual to change their attitude in order to create greater consistency between attitude and behavior.[3] In other words, if you wait in line for an hour before getting into a famous brunch restaurant, you're likely to cognitively resort to justifying the wait by the fact that the cuisine is exquisite or that the ambiance of the restaurant is unique. I am not judging; as a brunch aficionado, over the years, I have waited in one too many endless lines for my eggs Benedict with salmon and avocado. Similarly, when Vladimir and Estragon wait endlessly for Godot, the thought that they might potentially be waiting in vain could create tension in their minds. An effective way to instantly resolve that tension would be to persuade themselves that Godot must certainly be arriving any minute, justifying the inconvenient or costly act of waiting. And the longer they wait, the more value they expect to get out of that encounter. If asked, the two incredibly patient gentlemen might have said, "Of course, Godot is coming, and our interaction with him will be phenomenal. We would not be waiting here if that wasn't the case." As a person who stutters and takes his time speaking, I am perhaps biased towards agreeing with the adage about patience being a virtue. Excessive patience, as demonstrated by Vladimir and Estragon, can, however, turn into passivity, complacency and an excuse for inaction. After all, why do anything else if Godot might be around the corner? In fact, why would we do *anything* if we believed that the solution to our obstacles was already on its way?

Are you currently waiting for a Godot to show up and change your life?

The Hollywood fallacy

It's a rainy day. Everything has been going wrong lately. You did not get that promotion at work. That promising juicy deal with the big account you've been working on for months—the one that was a sure bet—just fell through. That person you were interested in dating has rejected you. You have not seen your gym in weeks or months. In fact, you avoid the street corner that your gym is on so you won't be reminded of the monthly fee that's withdrawn from your bank account. Ignorance is bliss, right? Negativity keeps on piling up like the dirty dishes in your kitchen sink until . . . a magical inflection point is hit. Suddenly, *everything* changes. Like the Greek mathematician Archimedes who, while taking a bath, accidentally discovered a method to solve the king's physics question, you have your own breakthrough moment. Eureka!

You sprint out of your apartment and start running in the rain; it happens to be raining that day, of course. Katy Perry's fireworks shine brightly and loudly in the sky . . . J.R.R. Tolkien, writer of *The Hobbit* and the *Lord of the Rings* trilogy, coined the word "eucatastrophe" for moments like these. It is defined as "the sudden happy turn in a story which pierces you with a joy that brings tears."

From that day forward, your life was never the same. You have received multiple job offers with incredible packages, your entrepreneurial mind is brimming with ideas, your love life is flourishing, all those exciting international trips are racking up your frequent flier miles (hello, frequent cabin upgrades!), the receptionist at the gym knows your name (and not just because your membership card activates your profile on the computer when you check in) and you're meditating every day, thereby existing in a state of constant mindful presence. Could it be that *one inflection point* was exactly what you needed for *everything* to change? After all, the Pareto principle states that 80 percent of consequences come from 20 percent of causes. Could it be that 99.9 percent of outcomes actually come from 0.01 percent of causes?

While it truly would be magnificent if change occurred this way, I haven't found that to be the case. I know you won't want to read this, but . . . you might *never* have a breakthrough. I will write that phrase again just in case you're still clinging to an assumption about success that is not helping you in the slightest. You, dear reader, might *never* have a breakthrough. If I am sounding like a Debbie Downer, don't worry and do keep on reading. It's true what they say: Sometimes, things have to get worse before they get better.

Will *the* moment ever come?

Whenever we go through a difficult moment or emotion, it's tempting to distract ourselves with the fantasy of a future that is more favorable. This pattern is not dissimilar to a person who buys lottery tickets to daydream and temporarily escape their current reality. To put things into perspective, we have a one in 300 million chance of winning the Powerball jackpot. We are more likely to be crushed by a meteorite than to win the Powerball. Heck, we might even have a better chance of having shared the stage with Janet Jackson at the Superbowl than of winning the Powerball. No matter how wildly improbable the positive outcome might be, many find it tempting to hold on to the possibility if doing so makes us feel good for a little while. Not buying lottery tickets does not, unfortunately, exempt you from this behavior.

Taking a break from the stress of existence by imagining a better future that's one breakthrough moment away from becoming a reality is an alluring refuge for many of us. As a teenager, after school I went on many long walks and jogs in my neighborhood, replaying social scenarios that occurred that day and thinking about ways I would have preferred responding to them. For instance, one day while playing football (soccer in the US and Canada) at school in Lebanon, I told some players that their goal was offside and therefore should not count. Only, I stuttered quite badly while telling them that, and one of them replied, "Joze, you don't even know how to speak!" Later that day, while jogging, I was obsessing over that moment and thinking about what would have been an apt response. Post-event rumination is quite common, particularly among people who have social anxiety.[4] Referred to as "brooding," this subtype of rumination is a passive comparison of one's current situation with some unachieved standard.[5] In my fantasizing mind, I won every single one of those arguments with flying colors. In case you're wondering, I decided that I would have said, "Your football skills make my speaking look smooth!" This escapist pattern applies not only to lottery buyers or socially anxious individuals, but to anyone who spends days, weeks, months, years and even decades fantasizing about that rosy future. It's perhaps no surprise that Indian movie director Ashley Rodrigues said in an interview that "Bollywood's song and dance sequence has been a way for the masses to escape from the daily grind."[6] Surely, if we start thinking about all those times when we wanted to do something and yet held back because of fear, we might feel bummed out. So it's easier to fantasize about a "la la land" inhabited by a hypothetical Me 2.0—a new and improved version of yourself who has overcome the obstacles that are currently holding you back from living the life that you want to live.

That idealized future self will effortlessly do all the things that the current self is afraid of doing, such as:

» Speaking up in that meeting or in class? You got it.
» Having that uncomfortable conversation with a loved one? Let's talk.
» Asking that person out? Let's ask.
» Signing up for that class that is way outside your comfort zone? Done.

If you believe that one day a Me 2.0 will emerge and do all those things, why bother now?

» Once I solve problem X, Me 2.0 will finally start taking the action I want to take.
» Once I feel less overwhelmed, Me 2.0 will have that difficult conversation
» Once I lose 20 pounds, Me 2.0 will ask that person out.

- Once I feel more confident, Me 2.0 will participate in meetings or in the classroom.
- Once I retire, Me 2.0 will start traveling and discovering novel countries around the world.

The catch-22 is that the problem will not be solved unless action is taken towards changing the way that we perceive, interpret and react to our fear. Otherwise, we are merely beating around the bush. That pivotal moment cannot coexist with an unwillingness to take action. I used to tell myself, “Once my stutter goes away, everything will change.” Indeed, I had associated every shortcoming in my life with the fact that I dealt with a severe stutter. According to author and retired US Navy officer Jocko Willink, effective leaders exercise “extreme ownership” by owning everything in their world. Willink also loves reminding us that “there is no one else to blame.”[7] I was not taking ownership of my life. In fact, I was blaming my stutter for my lack of action. In a strange manner, my stutter protected me from ever having to take risks. Seeing that I was stuck in a prison that I had partially built, I was constantly missing opportunities to turn things around.

Mark Twain said, “Why not go out on a limb? That’s where the fruit is.” What assumptions are you currently holding on to? More specifically, what and who are you blaming for the current shortcomings in your life?

Can your desperation BE more quiet?

Henry David Thoreau wrote that “the mass of men live lives of quiet desperation.” To that, I would add that most people live lives of quiet desperation because they succumb to their inner stutter. Fantasizing about a better future instead of taking action can exacerbate the tendency to quietly exist without ever taking a leap towards building our dream lives. In fact, by merely going through the motions of our days and never doing something about our dissatisfaction with the current state of affairs, we guarantee that our lives will never change.

When I celebrated my birthdays as a teenager, I always wished for the same outcome when it was time to blow out the candles. The tradition of blowing out candles on your birthday is based on the idea that the smoke from the candles will carry your wishes and prayers to the gods.[8] As I held my breath just before exhaling, I secretly wished that my stutter would vanish. It never worked. Until very recently, I had never told anyone about this birthday wish. In fact, it took a set of cameras for me to finally tell my parents and my sister about that secret wish that I made every year on July 17. During the making of *Words Left Unspoken,** the feature film about my journey, I shared that painful moment with them. The fact that I had secretly led Thoreau's life of "quiet desperation" came as a genuine surprise to my parents and my sister. We have had a family life filled with love and pleasant memories, and hearing that I had been struggling in and through silence was a painful realization for them.

Whenever it occurs to us that someone in our lives has been suffering in silence, we feel the need to fix the situation by being more attentive and mindful of that person's patterns moving forward. People suffering from depression experience personality changes, including becoming quieter and more withdrawn.[9] These shifts in our loved ones are worth noticing and investigating. But since I was always quiet and withdrawn, it was less obvious for my loved ones to see the

---

* *Words Left Unspoken* was directed by filmmaker Josiane Blanc and produced by Rayne Zukerman at IGP Productions.

clues. There is, however, absolutely nothing wrong with being quiet if that is a person's natural disposition. In her bestselling book *Quiet: The Power of Introverts in a World That Can't Stop Talking*, Susan Cain tells us to "not think of introversion as something that needs to be cured." Many of you may be naturally introverted and your version of conquering fear will look different from that of the extroverted folks. Extroverts might thrive in their journey of overcoming a fear by involving their social circle, opting for goals that require diving into the deep end, as well as gravitate naturally towards bombarding their lives with novel experiences. An introvert, however, may spend a bit more time analyzing their fears and choose to approach novel and uncomfortable situations more gradually. Both roads can lead to accomplishments and fulfillment. Quietness can, however, be alarming if the person is *intentionally* dimming the light out of fear while feeling desperate about their current situation in life. While embracing quiet time is an essential ingredient of a balanced life, the quiet resignation stemming from fear-induced despair is not. In the corporate world, "quiet quitting" refers to doing the "minimum requirements at one's job and putting in no more time, effort and enthusiasm than absolutely necessary."[10] Quiet quitting might be socially acceptable, but one should not be quiet quitting life itself!

Being resigned to one's circumstances is linked to the concept of "learned helplessness." You might have heard of Ivan Pavlov and his popular experiments involving dogs, bells and salivation. Pavlov was not, as it turns out, a one-hit wonder in the world of science. (Take that, Cajal![*]) In addition to discovering the role of the nervous system in regulating digestion, which is the basis of the

---

* Santiago R. y Cajal was Pavlov's main competitor at the Nobel Prize awards in 1904, where Pavlov won.

modern physiology of digestion, Pavlov's research also influenced Martin Seligman. In the 1960s, following in Pavlov's footsteps, Seligman found that giving dogs electric shocks that were outside of their control caused them to experience anxiety and depression.[11] This next part gets even more interesting. Even when dogs *did* have the ability to stop the shocks by simply pressing a lever, they did not. They had internalized that lack of personal power from the first round and thus assumed that this powerlessness would apply to other situations—and, perhaps, to life in general. It's called learned helplessness[12] because when you repeatedly experience pain (in the form of rejection, failure, disappointment, a lack of fulfillment), you might "learn" that regardless of your actions, those outcomes will remain unchanged. If we expect those negative outcomes to happen anyway, our desire to take corrective action decreases gradually because . . . why bother? We no longer associate our personal volition with a capacity to shape, influence or dictate the outcomes in our lives and the trajectory of our destiny. In his book *Full Catastrophe Living*, world-renowned professor of medicine and mindfulness expert Jon Kabat-Zinn stated that "when you are feeling completely overwhelmed by the pressures in your life and you see your own efforts as ineffectual, it is very easy to fall into patterns of what is called depressive rumination, in which your unexamined thought processes wind up generating increasingly persistent feelings of inadequacy, depression and helplessness." The primordial difference between the previously mentioned canine experiment and the human experiment that is your life is the following: If you are aware of the forces that are currently shaping your behavior, you can bring about change.

Being aware that we are capable of shaping our path is the first step. What are some areas in your life where you are making self-limiting assumptions about the potency of your potential? Are you underestimating your ability to sway your life in a novel and more prosperous direction?

Chapter 1 takeaways

- The "Hollywood fallacy" is the expectation that change will occur in a singular breakthrough moment through which your life is instantly transformed.
- Will the moment ever come? Is it tempting to distract ourselves from taking action by fantasizing about an idealized version of the self—one who will do all the things that we are currently holding back from doing? You might think, "Once obstacle X goes away, everything else will flow."
- Living a life of quiet desperation guarantees that we do not take action, as we go through the motions of life under the misguided assumption that our behavior is unlikely to influence the outcome.

Meet Bobby Umar, 53

This engineer turned personal-branding expert had long dealt with a fear around body image. When he was six years old, one of his classmates made fun of the way that his outfit looked on him. "I felt so embarrassed," Bobby told me, his cheeks reddening slightly. Subsequently, whenever Bobby had swimming classes, he would rush towards the dressing room to avoid getting changed in front of the other kids. As he started gaining more weight, that self-consciousness was only made worse. Even when his shirt was off, he would still attempt to hide his body with his own hands. "I felt like I was the Michelin Man with all the rolls!" Bobby half-smiled, then dropped his gaze.

The last time he had taken his shirt off in public was in grade 9. Around that time, he decided that he would wear a T-shirt while swimming to protect himself from people staring. This fear continued to haunt him for decades. Bobby told me about a trip to Disney World in Florida with his wife, kids and some cousins. The home they rented had a pool in the backyard and everyone immediately went swimming on their first day there. Everyone except for Bobby. Perplexed, they asked him why he wasn't joining them. "I just don't feel like it," he said. As he recounted the experience, he shifted in his seat and his shoulders tensed up. He hadn't wanted to be the only person going into the pool with a T-shirt on. As he gained more weight and eventually became diabetic, Bobby became even more self-conscious about his appearance. When asked about his rock-bottom moment, he recalled, "I woke up one morning and I stared at myself and realized that I hated how I look."

Later that day, while he was waiting for his daughter to complete her music lesson, he pulled out his laptop and wrote a manifesto titled "What the F Is Wrong with Me?" In this document, he listed the things that he was upset about, namely being on five different diabetes drugs as well as his vicious binging habit that would often entail having two separate dinners, one with his family at 7 p.m. and an earlier one at 4 p.m., by himself. He published the manifesto on Facebook and forgot about it because of parenting duties. When he returned home and saw hundreds of likes and comments, his eyes widened in disbelief as he scrolled through the support he had received. In fact, people were unaware of the challenges that Bobby had been facing in silence all these years. While he initially expected his fear to go away once he had kids, the change had to come from within. What struck me as I listened to Bobby's story was how closely connected his struggles with body image and his patterns of binging were: two sides of the same coin, rather than separate issues. The shame he felt surrounding his body appeared to fuel the very behaviors that then enhanced that shame. His eating habits weren't just about feeling hungry; they were a way of coping with the emotional pain tied to how he saw himself. And yet, those exact habits reinforced the self-consciousness he was attempting to escape.

Thankfully, Bobby's story has a happy ending. On a family camping trip, his son wanted to go into the water. Noticing that his father was about to enter the lake with his shirt on, he asked his dad why he wasn't taking his shirt off before swimming. Bobby said that "the 10-second pause after my son asked me that question felt like hours." Knowing that he didn't want to transfer those fears and body image issues to his son, he took his shirt off and went in for a fun swim with his son. Although for 25-plus years Bobby had focused on what other people thought about the way he looked, now he realized that it wasn't as bad as he had always expected it would be.

The transformation did not happen overnight. Bobby consulted a therapist with whom he explored the origins of his body image issues. When he became a father, Bobby wanted to be a role model for his kids. He started getting changed in locker rooms with his kids to show them that it's okay to do so. Although the first time was terrifying, it got easier after 10, 15 and 20 times. His therapist also advised him to look at himself in the mirror after taking a shower in order to find something that he liked about his body. Gradually, Bobby was able to focus on the things he liked, such as having big arms, broad shoulders and nice eyelashes. He would often give himself a reassuring nod in the mirror, feeling his confidence grow.

Eventually, Bobby started being an active voice on the topic of body shaming on social media. When he hears people telling an individual who is overweight to "eat a carrot" or one who is underweight to "eat a muffin," Bobby's response is that everyone is beautiful. As with all transformational journeys, Bobby's has had its setbacks. Whenever he would regain some weight that he had lost, he suddenly didn't want to be seen in public anymore. In fact, he sometimes went through months of not wanting to be outside or be seen. Every time such a setback occurred, he had to regain control over his recovery, reaffirming his belief about being beautiful by using a support network and talking to his therapist, family and friends to re-optimize his mindset and get back on track.

Released from the shame of being who he is, Bobby has experienced unprecedented levels of freedom to go to the pool, enjoy a waterslide or get changed in the locker room at the gym. Not only does he feel empowered in his own life, he also gets to be a role model for his kids. He likes to remind them that their bodies are beautiful and that they can work hard towards being healthy. When I asked Bobby for any concluding remarks he might have for others, he smiled thoughtfully, his eyes soft with understanding. He said that while we might think people are focused on us, that is rarely the case. He added that people are often worried about living their own lives. According to Bobby, we shouldn't let fear prevent us from doing what we wish to do. He believes that the more we do the things that we fear, the easier they become. He also is a strong proponent of the idea that it's important to start. In his words, "While it might be awkward the first few times, do it and it's going to free you!"

The inner stutter corner

Bobby's inner stutter comes from a deep-seated insecurity around body image. This fear of how others will judge his body made him feel scrutinized in situations that other people would not bother thinking about twice. While many or most of us naturally associate swimming with joyful moments shared with family and friends, Bobby viewed it as a scary and uncomfortable situation. My inner stutter was the fear of being judged for sounding different and Bobby's, comparably, was the fear of being judged for looking different. While my stutter led me to hold back from speaking, his self-consciousness about his body led him to hold back from appreciating things like going to the pool with his family or wearing what he wanted.

Bobby's inner stutter around body image did not show up randomly; rather, it was shaped by early experiences of body shaming, which led to chronic self-doubt, hiding and discomfort in his own skin. This is not unlike me receiving negative feedback from the world when I stuttered, and therefore feeling deeply uncomfortable being myself. Bobby's journey of growth and healing did not simply entail changing his appearance. Indeed, as many people who have been on that journey can attest, the change that is truly needed occurs at the mindset level. It wouldn't be enough for me to work on my fear of speaking simply by implementing speech therapy techniques, and, similarly, improving one's fitness level is significant but not sufficient for counteracting years of negative emotions associated with the way you look. Through facing his fears and learning to like the way that he looked (while striving towards health and fitness), Bobby was able to achieve a sense of freedom and confidence, which enabled him to show up fully in his own life while being a role model for his kids. His personal transformation also empowered him to turn his inner stutter into a source of strength and empathy for others.

Recognize your inner stutter, stop holding back and be like Bobby!

2.
The appeal of avoiding

Avoiding danger is no safer in the long run than outright exposure. The fearful are caught as often as the bold.

—HELEN KELLER

Avoidance is protection. When we find ourselves experiencing a painful stimulus, survival instincts will kick in, motivating us to fight, flight, freeze or fawn. Whenever our body feels like it is in danger and believes that it can successfully deal with the threat, we will respond in fight mode.[1] For instance, if someone in a line cuts in front of you and you're unwilling to tolerate that behavior, you might choose to confront that individual by assertively telling them to terminate their unethical strategy and go to the back of the line.

If, however, we believe that we cannot face that danger but can avoid it by escaping the scene, we will respond in flight mode.[2] In this case, if the person cutting in line appears to be threatening, you might choose to wait in a different line or come back another day. Unlike fight or flight, which involve being proactive, the freeze and fawn responses do not. Indeed, we freeze when our body doesn't think we are capable of either fight or flight.[3] If you do not want to confront that person and yet you have to wait in line to complete an important task, your freeze response might involve staying in your position and accepting the situation.

Fawn, the lesser-known response, is used if we are unable to resort to any of the three primary stress responses.[4] We fawn by being overly agreeable, overly helpful and overly concerned with the well-being of others at the expense of our own. Instead of confronting the person cutting in line, your instinctive tendency might be to downplay the situation or attempt to appease the line-cutter to preserve social harmony and avoid tension. You might smile at the person and say, "It's okay, I'm not in a rush!" In that situation, your inner stutter might come from being a people pleaser to survive the stress that the situation has triggered in you.

If you have the fear of disappointing others and do not wish to deal with the consequences of being more assertive, you are less likely to state your boundaries. In that sense, the inner stutter formula here would be

Afraid of Being Assertive + Not Stating Boundaries = Inner Stutter

In this case, the inner stutter would mean accepting outcomes that are detrimental to your well-being, self-confidence and ability to reach your goals.

Those of us who are intimately familiar with the theory of learned helplessness might be more likely to opt for flight to escape that painful stimulus. If that doesn't work, we might end up freezing in the face of that fear, suffering embarrassment until we manage to exit the situation. Fawning can also come in handy as we attempt to mold ourselves to adapt to the pressures of the situation we're in.

As someone who dealt with a severe stutter his entire life, and still does at the time of writing this book, I used to alternate between the two equally constraining scenarios of flight and freeze, with the occasional fawning. For instance, when I stuttered and the person I was talking to reacted by making a disparaging remark, such as

"Dude, you can't even speak," my most common responses would be to flee by walking away or, if that was not an option, I would simply look down with a sense of defeat. In some cases, I might even have resorted to fawning by nervously laughing—my way of not challenging the status quo.

In more recent years, when I've received belittling remarks after a severe stuttering episode, I have thankfully dealt with the situation assertively by telling the person that I stutter and that their reaction is not okay. Growth and healing often require implementing a new, healthier response to an old trigger that once led to the maladaptive reaction of feeling disparaged, unfulfilled and unworthy.

In the past, my primary strategy was to flee by avoiding outright every speaking situation that I could. When that wasn't possible, I'd freeze and hope that people would shift their attention away from me once they realized that I would not manage to get the words out. For my misguided ego, not speaking at all was more favorable than speaking with interruptions and blocks. If I could choose between participating in a conversation and stuttering or avoiding that social situation and therefore not stuttering, I would consider the latter a superior outcome. Silence would protect me from the socio-emotional repercussions of sounding different. What would people say if they heard what I really sounded like? How will they feel about me when they find out the extent to which I can sound like a "freak"? When one successfully avoids doing something (e.g., presenting in front of an audience or saying hello to someone new) because of fear of judgment, the victory is always bittersweet. It's sweet because the immediate threat was mitigated; it's also (very) bitter because we know deep down that the threat will resurface. According to the National Health Service (NHS) in the UK, avoiding fears only makes them scarier the next time.[5] And the time after that. In the words of Jon Kabat-Zinn, most known for having created the eight-week Mindfulness-Based Stress Reduction program, "If escape and avoidance become our habitual ways of dealing with our problems, the problems just multiply." You probably didn't need the NHS or Mr. Kabat-Zinn to confirm this for you to know it is true. We might have won that one battle by avoiding; however, we certainly have not won the war. On the contrary, avoiding something that we wish to do because of fear is typically a sign that, unless we course correct, we will probably lose the war.

What if I were to tell you that facing the terrifying stimulus we avoid is precisely the gateway to achieving the outcomes that we wholeheartedly desire? Unfortunately, this piece of information will likely feel irrelevant while we are being ambushed by signals from our amygdala. In case you skipped the Psych 101 elective in college, the amygdala is an almond-shaped brain structure involved in the processing of emotions and memories associated with fear.[6] In fact, in that moment of processing, our brain and our "inner child" attempt to protect us, using the strategy of avoidance to survive danger. That danger might be physical or emotional, real or perceived.

The inner child is a metaphorical part of ourselves frozen in childhood, still clinging to the emotions, beliefs and memories we had at that time.[7] According to Shari Botwin, a trauma therapist and the author of *Thriving After Trauma: Stories of Living and Healing*, growing up does not imply that our thoughts, feelings or memories from childhood get automatically erased.[8] On the contrary. I have found the unmet needs of the inner child end up governing our reactions later on in life. Dealing with difficulties during that time in our lives when we were highly impressionable has a lasting impact on our adulthood. In fact, going through that adversity might have impeded our capacity to process feelings and make sense of the pain or suffering.[9] So, whenever we face a situation that reminds us of tough moments from our childhood, we are likely to resort to our stress response of choice.

Because I associated speaking in general with negative memories and emotions and fear of judgment, I chose to avoid speaking for over 25 years. It worked . . . to an extent. By not doing the thing that would have elicited a variety of negative outcomes, including being judged or mocked, I managed to protect myself from the world. I mean, who in their right mind would voluntarily speak if they knew they had a 50 percent chance of having to deal with a negative reaction that would make them feel inferior? At the same time, that also meant I was, unfortunately, protecting myself from experiencing life and the richness it has to offer. Avoidance is the ultimate double-edged sword. It is but a temporary solution to a recurring obstacle.

Are you currently responding to something you fear through the strategy of avoidance? If so, what are the opportunities that you are potentially squandering along the way?

Not doing the thing is great . . . at first

When we face the dilemma of selecting either action or inaction, we go through an internal calculus. We evaluate the potential costs and benefits that might result from taking action. If the perceived costs outweigh the benefits, it would only be logical to avoid them. For example, when I expected to be judged by others for being different, the costs of experiencing shame and embarrassment outweighed the potential benefits of connecting with other human beings. In a sense, I was being risk averse because I preferred the certainty of not losing over the possibility of winning. Stated differently, the prospect of getting mocked by one person influenced my behavior far more than the possibility of having several positive interactions. Not speaking up during that university class or the work meeting was therefore the most advantageous action I could take. Not speaking protected me from the world, in both its risk and glory. Through the lens of that one single battle, not doing the thing that I feared doing worked out great . . . at first. Until it didn't. To illustrate this point, let's go to Montreal, circa 2010.

When I was an undergrad at McGill University's business school, I majored in the now defunct psychology for management program. Although I was primarily a business school student, my multidisciplinary bachelor's degree gave me the opportunity to take up to 10 different courses in the social sciences. As I vehemently disliked my intro to accounting class, immersing myself in these courses was a breath of fresh air. As a confused first year business student, I took electives in philosophy, sociology and anthropology.

Because I always felt alienated from others on account of my stark stutter and associated fear of judgment, I was magnetically pulled towards the field of psychology. I had so many questions about people (especially myself) that I was impatient to explore. For someone who has faced a degree of adversity, studying psychology is appealing by nature. Indeed, it can provide both a respite and an opportunity to dive deeper into the theories that help explain one's own tribulations and the reasoning behind the plethora of interpersonal challenges. In a study entitled *Wounded Healers*, 40.2 percent of respondents reported experiencing mental health challenges before becoming helping professionals themselves.[10]

This statistic is contrary to what most people seem to think. (How many times have psychology majors been asked, "Oh, you're a psych major. Does that mean you can read my mind?" Trust me. Studying psychology does not equip you with such powers. But I digress. Back to the story.) One of the advanced psych classes I took towards the end of my degree was called Interpersonal Relationships. It certainly deserves its status as an upper-level class, considering that the complexities of interpersonal relationships have plagued human existence for millennia. Unsurprisingly, the existentialist French philosopher Jean-Paul Sartre claimed that "hell is other people" ("*L'enfer, c'est les autres*"). Hopefully, Sartre was not referring to his romantic partner, fellow existentialist philosopher Simone de Beauvoir. Otherwise, I hope French sofas were comfortable to sleep on in the 1950s. Either way, buckle up, because one *hell* of a story is coming your way. I would recommend curling up on the couch with a warm cup of coffee or tea.

As part of that class, we studied all types of human dynamics, including both platonic and romantic relationships. What made this course stand out was the anonymous forum that all the students could access. Think of it as a Reddit forum but exclusively for the students enrolled in this course. Seeing that the theme of the lectures revolved around the ageless question of how to make a relationship work, the forum was filled with daily threads eagerly started by students from all walks of life. On any day, you would stumble upon posts about how to make friends, tips for improving your dating life and even a thread or two about the best positions in the bedroom. For a student who had moved to liberal Montreal from relatively conservative Lebanon, I was initially surprised by the willingness of students to openly discuss these topics. While students might not have felt comfortable enough to ask those questions in the classroom, the anonymity of the forum liberated us from the shackles of societal and peer judgment. As a 20-year-old, I almost never spoke to any of my classmates unless *I* knew that *they* knew that I stuttered. Indeed, I was terrified of introducing myself to anyone because it meant my little secret would inevitably come out. They'd find out that I was different, broken and thus not good enough. These fearful thoughts were characteristic of my own inner stutter. Therefore, I always sat next to my friend Stephanie and her now husband, Jeff, who were both aware of my linguistic predicament. The mere thought of unexpectedly revealing my true self—a person who stutters—to the whole class was too scary to contemplate. But soon, an opportunity for me to begin facing that fear would emerge out of the ether.

One morning, a fellow student caught my eye. She was wearing a yellow hat and had short, dark brown hair and the sweetest demeanor. In the middle of a lecture on reciprocity in relationships, I was secretly developing a crush. Seeing that I would never allow myself to simply talk to her (and let her find out that I speak weirdly? No way!), I had to devise a strategy to communicate my interest in getting to know her better. If only there were some kind of bulletin board that I knew she'd be reading. Eureka! The anonymous online forum that every student was checking every day. As soon as I got home that day, I enthusiastically logged in and created a post with the following text: "Yellow Hat. You caught my eye today." To my surprise, *she replied*. My heart began to flutter. While I can't find the exact copy of the exchange on the anonymous forum, thankfully, I have a surprisingly good memory. Ask my sister and she'll gladly tell you about how I often remember events from her own life that she herself has forgotten. The exchange below is an approximate transcription of our interaction via the online forum:

ME: Yellow Hat. You caught my eye today!
HER: Oh, hey! Glad you liked it!
ME: How have you been enjoying the class so far?
HER: It's been an interesting one. I'm liking it! What about you?
ME: I never thought a class about relationships existed, let alone that I would be enrolled in it! By the way, I know this might sound forward, but would you be open to meeting up for coffee sometime?
HER: Sure =).
ME: Great. How about Second Cup near the Roddick Gates this Saturday at 4 pm?
HER: That works for me!
HER: Hey, I'm just confirming that we're on for tomorrow?
ME: [no response]
HER: Hey there, I never heard back from you, but I thought I'd let you know that some of the students from the class are organizing a group outing at the university pub on Sunday if you'd like to join us. It should be fun.
ME: [no response]

Before you jump to conclusions about my inconsiderate and spectral nature, you might already infer, based on what you've read so far, that this situation activated my flight stress response. I avoided responding because I assumed that as soon as we met and she found out about the stutter, it would be game over. Ironically, the inner stutter defeated me before giving the actual stutter a chance to be heard. Perpetuating the fantasy of what was possible was a more agreeable thought than actually taking the action that would unequivocally yield one of two fixed outcomes: acceptance or rejection. At the time, I was not aware of the fact that a rejection could be characterized as a victory because it implies that honest and purposeful action was taken towards a meaningful objective. Also, it has been said that rejection is redirection towards a person who or an opportunity that is a much better fit. Given the self-limiting beliefs that I held about how my stutter would be interpreted by both Yellow Hat and people in general, I equated taking action and revealing my true self with inevitable rejection. Therefore, complete avoidance of the situation was the most viable strategy I could employ to prevent myself from experiencing what was, in my mind, guaranteed rejection and, thus, failure.

I also considered taking a course in behavioral economics, which focused on game theory. While I ended up dropping that class because of scheduling conflicts, I learned about the difference between "one-shot games" (where there is only one interaction between the players) and "repeated games" (which consist of multiple interactions between the players over a longer period).[11] Much of life tends to fall under the category of repeated games. Most people's lives are regularly intertwined with those of others over extended periods. Whether it's your family and friends, your colleagues at work, the barista at that little café in your neighborhood or even that quirky neighbor with the cat, we tend to repeatedly interact with the other players in our lives. So, whether we like it or not, when it comes to our social lives, we tend to be in it for the long haul. By avoiding situations that could otherwise lead to positive outcomes, we create a pattern of avoidance. For example, if I choose to avoid speaking with the people I run into regularly, I am setting the tone for what our interactions will be like for years to come. And though we can win in the short term by avoiding the things that scare us, we end up both squandering our potential and diminishing our ability to confront obstacles in the long term.

We also deprive ourselves of fostering meaningful relationships that would otherwise contribute positively to our lives. *The Harvard Study of Adult Development*, the longest in-depth longitudinal study on human life ever carried out, revealed a simple, yet significant, result: The key to health and happiness is good relationships.[12] Human beings are social creatures, and there are seven keystones of support that we must get from our fellow human beings:

- safety and security;
- learning and growth;
- emotional closeness and confiding;
- identity affirmation and shared experience;
- help (informational or practical);
- fun and relaxation; and
- romantic intimacy.[13]

Avoiding people out of fear guarantees that those seven buckets remain unfilled, thereby depriving us of health and happiness. We've all heard the stories about people who pass away within a short time of each other, a phenomenon often associated with "broken heart syndrome." Whether it's Johnny Cash and June Carter, mother and daughter Debbie Reynolds and Carrie Fisher, Barbara Bush and

George H.W. Bush or people you knew personally, such examples remind us of the intricate link between our social connections and our health. I am not saying that Yellow Hat and I were going to be living in utopic suburbia with the white picket fence, the SUV and the 2.5 kids by now. However, I am saying that avoidance guarantees that we will never find out. When we do not speak in class, during a meeting or at that social event—despite wanting to do so—we victoriously protect ourselves from uncomfortable feelings in that one moment. Unfortunately, that "victory" is often misleading and (very) short-lived. It's a tainted pact that we make with our destiny: We trade our present comfort for future happiness. (For the sake of this argument, let's define happiness as a life of growth, fulfillment and connection.) Elizabeth Gilbert, author of the bestselling *Eat, Pray, Love*, reflected that "happiness is the consequence of personal effort." How might you currently be robbing your future self of relationships, health and wealth by not putting in the effort of doing the things you find uncomfortable? How many proverbial *yellow hats* (in your personal and professional life) are passing *you* by?

Games the mind loves to play

We often avoid situations that we fear because we feel imprisoned by what I refer to as the "tyranny of the worst-case scenario." Webster's dictionary defines a tyrant as a ruler who exercises absolute power oppressively or brutally. Whether it was Fidel Castro banning opposition parties and controlling the media in Cuba, Kim Jong-il creating an atmosphere of surveillance that limited individual freedoms in North Korea or Idi Amin ruling Uganda through terror and mass human rights abuses, tyrants thrive by using their authority to maintain control through fear and intimidation. In the same way in which a political leader might cruelly oppress their citizens without regard to their welfare, a hypothetical worst-case scenario can oppress the person imagining it by entrapping them in a self-imposed prison of inaction. The Sufi poet Rumi wisely asked, "Why do you stay in prison, when the door is so wide open?" This quote was shared with me by a student after I delivered a keynote speech at the Smith School of Business at Queen's University in Canada. I was invited to speak there after graduating, as I had maintained close relationships with the school. When we contemplate doing something we're afraid of, our inner stutter absolutely loves to remind us of all the ways the outcome of that action might damage our self-confidence, self-esteem and self-worth. What if people laugh? What if they mock me? What if they stare at me?

The fear of the worst-case scenario coming true is one that has prevented countless human beings from fulfilling their true potential in life. Motivational speaker Les Brown said it perfectly: "The graveyard is the richest place on Earth, because it is here that you will find all the hopes and dreams that were never fulfilled, the books that were never written, the songs that were never sung, the inventions that were never shared, the cures that were never discovered, all because someone was too afraid." So, is the solution to realize that the worst-case scenario has been blown out of proportion? Is it all "in our head"? Some may argue that we overestimate the likelihood of things going wrong and therefore should take action. I disagree.

You see, as someone who stutters, the fear of judgment was frequently not just "in my head." When I have gotten badly stuck on words, people have often laughed in my face, made disparaging remarks or simply walked away in a state of confusion. The fear I experienced was not something that I fabricated out of thin air. As a result of being different, I faced negative social outcomes. Far from being an unrealistic expectation, the worst-case scenario *has* happened, again and again and again. In other words, attempting to convince myself that I am overexaggerating the possibility of a negative outcome is likely to be pointless. Counterintuitively, voluntarily creating situations for me to repeatedly experience these worst-case scenarios has been one of the strategies I have employed for weakening the power they had over me.

Avocado toast and clickers

In economics, the law of diminishing marginal returns refers to the fact that after some optimal level of capacity is reached, adding an additional factor of production will result in smaller increases of output.[14]

Let's say your restaurant is making avocado toast and you start with one chef. The toast comes out smooth and creamy. You add a second chef and the toast comes out even faster, perhaps with some extra fancy toppings such as chili flakes and a poached egg. By the time you've got five or six people working on it, they're fighting over the avocado, one of the chefs dropped the toast and now there's food everywhere. Instead of more avocado toasts, you've ended up with fewer.

Now, let's suppose the avocado toast represents the fear that you experience, and the additional chefs represent exposure to the feared situation. After a certain number, the more chefs we have, the fewer additional avocado toasts are created. If we apply the law of decreasing marginal returns to the idea of exposing ourselves to the worst-case scenario, we can posit that after a certain point, every additional exposure to that uncomfortable scenario will generate smaller increases of stress and fear. In the same way that fewer additional avocado toasts will be created as more and more chefs are added to the kitchen, I have found that less fear is generated with every new unit of exposure to that scary situation. When you experience the worst-case scenario over and over again, it is by definition no longer the worst-case scenario. It also means that we have developed the capacity to withstand it. Exposing ourselves to that stimulus repeatedly, and surviving the situation, enables us to alter our perception of it. This phenomenon is aligned with the psychological theory of desensitization, which we'll get into in more depth a bit later. For example, one of the ways I work on my stutter involves going to the mall or to a busy urban area and asking 100 complete strangers for directions. You read it correctly. One hundred. Complete. Strangers. What the heck do I tell them, you might be wondering? Great question.

Allow me to describe what this exercise typically looks like: I head to a busy street or to a mall if it's cold outside. At the time of writing, I am based in Toronto and the exercise takes place at the mall more often than not. I typically show up with a clicker counter (like the one pictured here). I generally hide the counter in my pockets since I don't want my listeners to be suspicious. (My friends Nicolas and Choucri jokingly called me

the "Clicker King.") I use the clicker to keep count of my progress, with the aim of having 100 interactions.

That photo, by the way, may trigger some negative memories if you've ever waited in line to get into a nightclub on a cold night in February, only to have the bouncer, who's holding one of those clicker counters, tell you that you're going to have to wait even longer or that you won't be getting into the club at all. Having gone to university in two Canadian cities, Montreal and Kingston, I am no stranger to those long and painful lines. I eventually learned that discreetly slipping a twenty-dollar bill into the hand of a bouncer would save my friends and me an hour-plus of waiting. And before you ask what the point of this digression is, let me explain. As a person who stutters, I lose enough time getting stuck on words, so I need to find ways to win back that waiting time!

Here is a typical breakdown of one of my speech therapy challenges:

I like to start with easier interactions: On the way to the mall, I approach 10 individuals who are walking alone and ask for directions. "Excuse me," I have said tens of thousands of times to strangers around the world, "do you know the way to the mall?"

Once inside the mall, I *graduate* to 10 pairs (couples or two friends walking together) and ask if they know where a specific store is located. They either tell me that they know the answer and offer directions or say that they don't not know. We then part ways (after I thank them for their time, of course).

Next, I start asking for clothing stores with names that I find difficult to say. In fact, I'll often invent the names based on the words or sounds that I find most challenging. If you are reading this and I've stopped you on the streets of Madrid, Minneapolis or Montreal, you may remember someone asking about a "Status Apparel," "Williams Original" or "Spadina Cardigans." While the store names were fictitious, my intention of working on my stutter through this exercise was genuine. Funnily enough, I've approached a few highly fashionista types over the years who confidently told me that the store I was asking about does not exist. Clearly, they knew their boutiques and didn't like having their Fashion Intelligence questioned.

Next, I approach larger groups of people (something many people would find challenging, whether or not they have a stutter). I often do this exercise right before a stand-up comedy performance or a speaking engagement, and I find those group interactions to be somewhat similar to being up on a stage in front of an audience. And I have yet to find a better way to mentally prepare before a public-speaking engagement.

But, what happens if people start looking up the fictitious "Williams Originals" on their phones? Good question! Well, that is typically when I'll kindly interrupt their well-meaning assistance and explain the exercise as something along these lines: "Actually, I'm working on my stutter today by asking questions to a hundred people. The store doesn't really exist. This is part of an exercise. Thank you for your time." Sometimes, I modify the routine and disclose upfront that I'm a person who stutters and that I'm approaching strangers as a way to work on my speech and challenge myself. Some people are intrigued by the exercise and ask more questions. The FAQs, in case you are wondering, are

- How many questions have you asked so far?
- How have people been reacting to you?
- How long have you been doing this exercise for?

While not the objective, some of those conversations have led to full-fledged friendships. One of the first people who participated in this exercise, after I moved to Toronto in 2015, would invite me to his home in Ottawa eight years later to meet his adorable one-year-old daughter. Not only that, but Eddine's wife, Cyrielle, and her manager booked me to speak at a conference in Ottawa several years later. This story is a wonderful reminder of the serendipity that can happen when we put ourselves out there and do something uncomfortable or unexpected just by saying hello. And there's more to this story that readers might find interesting: One of the people attending the Ottawa conference told her spouse about my keynote. In turn, the spouse, a director at HarperCollins Publishers, advised his senior editor to consider me as an author. So the book you're now reading or listening to is a direct result of my showing up that day to face my fear. The more I reflect on my journey, the truer this statement proves to be: "Eighty percent of success is showing up."

Although I have had truly wholesome interactions over the years, I have also experienced countless negative ones, such as people laughing when I would hit a particularly bad block. As I write this passage, I am reminded of all the faces of the people who, on hearing me stutter, were physically incapable of holding in their laughter for more than a few seconds. As a somewhat wiser human now, I recognize that people respond to unexpected events differently, including with nervous laughter.

The Milgram experiment, conducted by Yale psychologist Stanley Milgram in the early 1960s, investigated an individual's obedience to authority by asking them to administer electric shocks to a fellow participant. While the shocks were fake and the fellow "participants" were actors, the study revealed the "shocking" result that 65 percent of participants continued to administer shocks all the way to the maximum voltage, simply because they were told to do so. This finding has often been used to explain how humans have historically been able to commit atrocious crimes. Another unexpected finding was that many of the participants who were asked to administer the shocks laughed nervously.[15] In fact, the higher the voltage, the more they laughed.

Nervous laughter is seen as a mechanism that our bodies use to regulate emotion as well as a defense against emotions that make us experience discomfort.[16] In other words, those individuals at the mall might have been laughing because they felt confused and uncomfortable, or simply because they lack awareness about what stuttering is. Every stutterer sounds different, so being familiar with one form of stuttering might not prepare someone for a particular stutterer's patterns of dysfluent speech. One of those unpleasant experiences unfolded a few days before I delivered my first-ever TEDx Talk, at Queen's University (Kingston, Ontario). To counteract the extremely high stress levels I was experiencing in the weeks leading up to the delivery of this talk in front of hundreds of people—truly a symbolic event for me—I decided to go to the mall and start desensitizing myself by asking for directions. While I have since delivered speeches before audiences of thousands, the prospect of speaking on the TEDx stage for 500 people was, at the time, an extraordinarily intimidating and challenging objective. The anticipatory nervousness was palpable in my voice; I was incapable of uttering a single word without severely stuttering for at least 20 seconds at a time for two weeks before the engagement.

I vividly remember the reactions from pedestrians that day. Many looked at me with a disturbed grimace—as though I were some kind of mutant. Some broke into laughter. Others, slightly more forgiving, spared me their reaction by simply walking away seconds into the first debilitating stutter. I was not having a good day.

And then, after one particularly negative reaction, I reached my tolerance threshold and felt the need to stand in a corner to process my feelings and emotions. Depending on one's state of mind on a particular day, it may take more interactions to reach the point where diminishing returns begin to take effect. I may have shed some tears. Okay, fine—I cried. While the tears quietly slid down my cheeks, I recall thinking, "Why am I doing this to myself? Why don't I just go home? Maybe I could pick up some of that delicious dark chocolate and raspberry Häagen-Dazs ice cream and binge watch *The Office*. After seriously entertaining these self-indulgent suggestions for a few moments, I abruptly snapped out of that soothing haze and decided I would not leave the mall that day until I had somehow shifted my state of mind towards a more positive and empowered one. With the TEDx event only a few days away and the social anxiety having overpowered every inch of hope I could muster, I knew that I had to get to work.

I stayed at the mall for nine hours that day, talking to over 300 people until the fear's gravitational pull had gradually lifted from me. By the time I returned home, I felt proud, at peace and pretty darn excited about the upcoming conference. The speech itself could not have gone any better and, on February 4, 2018, I received a heartwarming standing ovation from 500 delegates. While the initial reactions at the mall could have destroyed my morale before I'd even embarked on this journey of transformation and growth, now they had empowered me to desensitize myself to these so-called worst-case scenarios. Increased familiarity with the scenarios that we fear demystifies them to the extent that they are no longer capable of holding us hostage. Indeed, they lose their ability to prevent us from experiencing life.

Although my response has involved overcoming the fear of judgment by talking to hundreds of strangers, your strategy to overcome your inner stutter might look different. We'll get to how you ought to devise your personal strategies a bit later. What game is your mind currently playing with you? Is the tyranny of the worst-case scenario strengthening your inner stutter's hold on you and keeping you hostage?

Avoidance has consequences

Life is a decision tree. Every decision we make leads to an outcome that then offers a new decision to make, and the cycle repeats itself. Holding back from doing something we know we wish to do is a decision that we make. In the words of Laurie Buchanan, author and holistic health practitioner, "What you are not changing, you are choosing."

For example, if you are at a conference and there's an influential person in the room whom you'd like to meet, no matter how palpable your fear or anxiety might be at that moment, you are ultimately the only person deciding whether you'll approach that person. Although making your way towards them doesn't guarantee the conversation will happen or will go the way you're hoping, that step forward is the primary way you can control what is under your control: taking action. Taking action when you initially considered avoidance presents a different set of outcomes that otherwise would not have existed. As a keynote speaker, going out of my way to have conversations with the decision-makers in a room has often led to generating new speaking opportunities. What are the outcomes that you might be depriving yourself of because you choose fearful inaction over courageous action?

When you're in a meeting with senior leadership and do not speak up to share an idea, you deprive yourself of the potential to be seen and heard by influential colleagues who may have a say in the progression of your career.

When you do not say hello to that person at the conference whom you find very interesting, you may miss out on the opportunity to connect with them and strike up a friendship or mentorship or future collaboration.

That person you are interested in and yet never asked out could have been the love of your life, someone with whom you could have built a wonderful family and traveled the world.

Of course, taking action in those three scenarios could have also turned out to be fruitless. Whereas the thought of a worst-case scenario can act as a tyrant, the imagined best-case scenario ought not disappoint us if it doesn't come to fruition. "Peace begins when expectations end," said the Buddha. One thing that is almost certain, however, is that unless we are talking about a mindfulness practice (for example, sitting with your eyes closed and purposefully focusing on your breath while not doing anything else) or being cautious in certain situations that require vigilance, inaction is otherwise almost always fruitless. Taking action, however, is almost always fruitful in one way or another. Even a rejection is the world's way of communicating to you that there is a mismatch between your objective and the outcome. That mismatch might be a lack of fit: You may not be ready for this opportunity or there may be fundamental differences between the two parties that make this professional or personal union highly improbable.

This novel piece of information about the mismatch is useful because it helps us navigate similar situations in the future with more wisdom. If we are rejected from a role at an organization, we can generally assume there was a lack of fit between our profile and the requirements of the position. We thus either have to strengthen specific areas of our résumé or look at positions and organizations that are more aligned with our profile. In other words, while initially painful, this rejection can actually be a useful piece of the puzzle in the grander picture of our lives. In a viral TEDx Talk entitled "What I Learned from 100 Days of Rejection," Jia Jang shared his adventure of intentionally seeking out rejection by making audacious requests to strangers. For instance, he went up to the security guard at his place of work and asked if he could borrow a hundred dollars. He also went to a burger joint and, on finishing his meal, asked the cashier if he could get a "burger refill." Through this trajectory, not only did Jia desensitize himself to the pain and shame that typically come with rejection, but he also discovered that people are generally kinder than we assume and that rejection isn't as painful as we fear it is going to be. Having carried out, on a weekly basis, my exercise of talking to 100 strangers, I can say that I have come across countless kind individuals and that while a negative reaction or a rejection can initially sting, I had underestimated my capacity for handling that temporary pain. Ironically, going through those moments of pain made it more likely that I would feel equipped to tackle the next challenge. Voluntarily experiencing the worst-case scenario emboldens us to resiliently get back up and return to the arena.

And there's another interesting result. By challenging ourselves through the toughest variation of a challenge, the milder versions—those that we once considered terrifying—start to seem a lot more manageable. For instance, after delivering a speech in public or performing stand-up at the comedy club, I find it significantly easier to have a conversation with the barista at the café or with a group of new friends at a party. In Jia's TEDx Talk, he shared a particularly memorable story of knocking on someone's door and asking if he could plant a flower in their garden. The homeowner, understandably, responded with a no. Jia then asked him to elaborate, thereby uncovering the true rationale behind the rejection. It appeared the man had a dog who tends to eat or destroy things in the garden. Not only did the homeowner provide an explanation, which contradicted Jia's assumptions about being rejected as a result of the strangeness of the request or because of a lack of trust. The man also suggested that his neighbor Connie would be far more likely to welcome a flower to her garden. After successfully finding a home for the flower, Jia realized that he was rejected the first time because what he offered "did not fit what he wanted."[17] As writer Matt Haig eloquently said, "There is no rejection. Only redirection." And in the summer of 2012, I experienced clear proof of that hypothesis.

After graduating from business school at McGill University, I initially considered a research-heavy master's program at Queen's University that would potentially lead to a PhD. I visited Queen's and met with one of the doctoral supervisors. As a way of hedging my bet, I also applied to another graduate program* that included a semester in Mexico City. Although I didn't get accepted into the research program, my acceptance by the other graduate program shaped my trajectory in a highly positive manner. Indeed, while in Mexico, I not only discovered different places in what has become one of my favorite countries, including San Miguel de Allende, San Cristobal de Las Casas, Tulum and Puerto Escondido, but I also drastically improved my Spanish. I now deliver speaking engagements and stand-up comedy performances in that language too. Living in Mexico City for that semester remains one of the most memorable experiences of my life. I could easily see myself living there again, should the opportunity present itself.

Moreover, had I been accepted into the initial master's program, there is a strong possibility that I wouldn't have pursued stand-up comedy and public speaking. Indeed, I might have ended up working as a researcher at a university in a small town, never stumbling upon stand-up and, subsequently, keynote speaking. While that would have been a perfectly fine outcome, it might not have been the path destined for me. One path leads to possibilities that might not have become available otherwise—that's part of the decision tree of life. At this point in my life, a part of me remains open to the idea of getting a PhD and becoming a professor later

* The Master of International Business at the Smith School of Business at Queen's University.

on. That path would enable me to quench my curiosity for knowledge while still having opportunities to speak in public—in class and at conferences. Needless to say, becoming a professor one day would also be a wonderful outcome that my younger timid self would never have anticipated.

Contrary to the richness and variety of outcomes that can stem from having taken action, the consequences of avoidance are virtually always the same: They lead to a life filled with regrets. Whenever we avoid situations out of the fear of rejection, we fail to realize that rejection can be seen as a victory for two primary reasons: First, rejection implies that we have taken action, and, second, it tells us that there might be a mismatch between who we currently are and what we desire. Taking action, even when met with a rejection, constitutes reward in itself in the sense that it reinforces our self-confidence and our sense of self-efficacy. Self-efficacy refers to an individual's belief in their capacity to exert control over their motivation, behavior and social environment.[18] In other words, it is about whether or not we believe we can get things done.

Taking action is therefore a formidable way to prove the inner stutter wrong. If the inner stutter is based on the fear of being rejected, taking repeated action decreases the potency of the rejection stimulus in our minds and makes it more likely that we take action again in the future. At the same time, rejection provides us with invaluable insights into where we currently stand as well as corrective steps we may need to take to either choose a different outcome or adapt our profile to enhance our compatibility with that desired objective. For instance, getting rejected from a job might lead to obtaining a new certification, and getting rejected romantically might encourage someone to go to therapy and hit the gym. Unlike action, avoidance provokes endless ruminating: “What if I had done it? How would my life be different if I stopped avoiding?” As it turns out, it would be *very* different.

Chapter 2 takeaways

- When we avoid something out of fear, we protect ourselves in the short run while depriving ourselves from opportunities of fulfillment and growth in the long run.
- The fear of the worst-case scenario coming true has prevented countless human beings from fulfilling their true potential. Repeated exposure is a formidable way to gradually reduce the effect of that fear.
- Whereas taking action often leads to the enrichment of our lives, the consequences of avoidance frequently involve regrets and wasted potential.

Meet Elie Dagher, 34

Elie Dagher’s social anxiety was unmanageable. When he was younger, he experienced severe timidity, shyness and a fear of relating to other people. He was rarely comfortable when in the presence of others. His inability to find his voice and to own his space persisted until his early twenties. His wake-up call occurred through a near-death experience.

On a weekend in Beirut, Elie left a nightclub and started driving back to his family home in the mountains. There was only one problem: He was completely intoxicated. Having forgotten that he was driving at over 120 kilometers per hour, he opened his car door hoping to throw up. Naturally, his car started drifting to the left, hitting the pavement, but somehow, miraculously, he found his way back to the highway without any further issues. In that moment, he told himself, "This is it. If I continue down this path, I'll be gone in no time." The fact that Elie had just been accepted into Columbia University in New York further exacerbated the need for radical change. He stopped drinking that weekend, and when he consulted a doctor about the matter, he found out that he was an alcoholic. Indeed, one week after he stopped drinking, Elie started experiencing significant withdrawal effects, including mild seizures. His eyes dropped to the floor at the mention of his health scare.

With alcohol no longer an option for coping with his social anxiety, he knew he needed to take a different approach. Elie started reading about communication (including the timeless *How to Win Friends and Influence People* by Dale Carnegie) and he joined Toastmasters (public speaking club) to overcome his fear of interacting with other people. Every month, he then challenged himself to do something social that he was afraid of. He smiled as he shared some of the first steps he took. For instance, he would give three people compliments every day for a month. Then, he would say hi to five new people every day during the second month. By the third month, his goal was to help a new person every day. Knowing that his excruciating fear of rejection would not go away easily, he decided to take a job at a sales consulting company where he had to start selling on behalf of different clients. To further challenge himself, he even went on a 10-day silent Vipassana meditation retreat in addition to learning Spanish—a language he would use in his eventual journey throughout the world.

This transformation did not occur overnight for Elie. His voice softened as he recalled his first Toastmasters meeting. When he had to introduce himself in front of the group, all he could summon the strength to say was his name before sitting down. "In those moments, I just wanted to hide!" Elie said. In spite of that initial hiccup, Elie continued to challenge himself by returning to those sessions, where he would take on a new meeting role every week. When asked about his philosophy throughout the journey, Elie replied, "With progression, not perfection. A setback is a setback. If I fail today, I'll simply have to get up tomorrow." He leaned forward as he spoke, his determination evident. As an entrepreneur, he is no stranger to the fact that change occurs through A/B testing (a method of comparing two versions of something to see which one performs better, also known as "split testing"). He would go out, test something new and then either win or learn. When those lessons were painful, he would often go back home feeling sad, frustrated and wanting to give up. However, he kept on going, learning and, along the way, becoming exposed to more and more difficult situations. According to him, a setback is merely a learning opportunity and failure doesn't exist. His gaze shifted upward, reflecting his optimism.

Years later, his life would be unrecognizable to his old self. Elie runs his own business and travels the world while doing so. He has been to 60 countries, and his traveling path has included 10 months in Brazil, two months in Argentina, two in Mexico, two in Spain, and one in Italy, as well as time spent in the US, the UK including Scotland, France, Portugal and throughout Asia. His eyes lit up as he described his travels. At the time of our conversation, Elie was in Kenya where he was about to start climbing Kilimanjaro.

As a business owner, Elie has transformed his fear into his craft: He teaches others how to have a healthier relationship with their own emotions. In fact, when he was living in the US, he attended a Toastmasters meeting where he was greeted by a friendly woman. Not only did Elie end up coaching her husband for two years, but he was also asked to officiate at their wedding in Miami. His laughter filled the room as he recounted the unexpected turn of events.

When asked about what he would tell his old self or someone who is currently working through an obstacle,

Elie confidently replied that no fear is insurmountable. According to him, "We all know the answer; we simply have to reconnect with the power within ourselves." His voice conveyed a deep sense of purpose, encapsulating the essence of his journey.

The inner stutter corner

Elie's inner stutter came from the profound social anxiety that held him back for much of his life, acting like a barrier to self-expression and connection. Growing up, he felt intense discomfort around others, struggling to find his voice and space, much like someone with a stutter who feels trapped by their inability to speak freely. Unable to cope with his fears, Elie relied on alcohol to mask his anxiety. As someone who has used alcohol in the past to mask my stuttering-induced social anxiety, I can relate to that impulse. After Elie experienced a near-death experience, he realized he had to face his struggles once and for all.

Determined to reclaim his life, Elie began an incremental journey of self-discovery. He joined Toastmasters, challenged himself with small social tasks and gradually desensitized himself to the fears that once defined him. His approach of "progression, not perfection" allowed him to learn from setbacks and push his boundaries. He eventually took on even greater challenges, like traveling, silent retreats and even sales roles, embracing every discomfort as a way to reshape his relationship with fear. As Bill Wilson, cofounder of Alcoholics Anonymous, aptly put it in Chapter 5 of *The Big Book of Alcoholics Anonymous*: "Progress, not perfection."

Today, Elie's life is nearly unrecognizable from his past. As a business owner and world traveler, he has turned his former struggles into his life's work, teaching others to embrace their own emotional challenges. Reflecting on his journey, he advises others to connect with the strength within, saying, "We all know the answer; we simply have to reconnect with the power within ourselves."

Elie's journey from isolation to empowerment demonstrates how facing one's inner stutter can lead to a life of purpose and resilience. Recognize your inner stutter, stop holding back and be like Elie!

3.
Why do you hesitate?

The greatest mistake you can make in life is to be continually fearing you will make one.

—ELBERT HUBBARD

In 2006, I flew from Lebanon to the United States to attend a summer school program at Phillips Academy in Andover, Massachusetts. A prestigious boarding school whose notable alumni include the Bushes (father and son) and John F. Kennedy, Phillips Academy turns into a school for American and international high school students during the months of July and August. Over the span of five weeks, students enroll in classes with topics ranging from social psychology to mathematics. Surprisingly, I selected Public Speaking and Communication as the two courses I would complete that summer. Even then, I must have had the latent intuition that going towards what I feared was likely to be the best, if not the only, path forward.

Committed to empowering their self-conscious teenage son to come out of his shell through this international educational and social experience, my parents were excited about sending me to the United States for a summer they hoped would be filled with personal growth and new experiences. Although I had typically avoided social interaction while in the confines of my high school in Lebanon, this brand-new environment presented itself as an opportunity for me to reinvent my personality, devoid of the emotional shackles of my life back home.

When 16-year-old me stepped on that boarding school campus north of Boston, I instantly felt as though those shackles were lifted, and I thought I would have the power to determine the type of summer I would be experiencing. Would this be a summer like every past summer, during which I had allowed my stutter to hold me back from expressing my true self to the world? Or would this be the first summer that my true personality would finally shine through for all to see? I voted for the latter. Indeed, on moving into the dorm room that I shared with Ben, a student from California, I instantly told him that I stuttered. The fact that he reacted with so much empathy and understanding remains a highly positive memory to this day. Far from being a trivial matter, that moment constituted a major step towards embracing my differences and taking action in the face of discomfort. While Ben, or any listener, could have eventually figured out that I stuttered without me having to bring it up, a great sense of empowerment can accompany the act of revealing a source of insecurity to another person.

In her *Psychology Today* article "Why Self-Disclosure Powers Relationships," psychologist Tchiki Davis states that self-disclosure is beneficial for forming close and intimate social connections.[1] After experiencing the benefits of sharing my stuttering with Ben—a part of myself I had long hidden out of fear of judgment—I decided to take the same approach on a much larger scale later that night at the first general residence meeting with all the other dorm students. I did so not knowing the types of reactions I would receive. My heart started to pound. Wait! What will happen when I openly tell everyone there that I stutter? Will they all start laughing at me?

After the residence hall director shared a few words of welcome and went over the dos and don'ts of residence life, the time approached for the students to introduce themselves. While I generally despised moments like these, I knew deep down that this moment represented a rare opportunity to break free from the norm by doing things differently. Contrary to my general tendency to hesitate and shy away from telling the world who I was, I started my introduction this way: "Hello everyone, my name is Joze, and I . . . speak like sh*t!" Everyone started laughing. I then explained that I had a speech impediment and that I looked forward to getting to know my fellow dorm mates during the summer. Not only were people laughing *with* me, but I also felt a sense of liberation I had never experienced before. It was also, arguably, my first-ever stand-up comedy bit! While I might not use that same exact language today, that sentence is what my teenage self came up with at that moment, and it certainly landed with the audience!

Hesitation, however, can come back if we do not actively counteract it. Indeed, despite having taken that giant leap my first day on campus, my hesitation returned in the coming days. Over the next five weeks in Andover, I hesitated when it came to interacting with people beyond my initial group of friends. I also hesitated in showing students outside of my dorm that I stuttered. By attempting to hide my stutter, I gradually limited the depth of the conversations and thus of the friendships I would have with the other students. While I have plenty of positive memories of my time there, including friendships that have stood the test of time, I cannot emphasize enough that hesitation can rob us of experiences that will never reemerge. The riches that we deprive ourselves of when we do not take action might include missed opportunities to land a dream job, ascend professionally, start our own business or create genuine lifelong friendships.

In the same way that I constantly hesitated to speak or act out of fear of being judged, you might be hesitating because of fears of your own. If you picked up this book, that statement is most likely true. In fact, let's talk about your inner stutter.

You have an inner stutter

As a teenager, I wholeheartedly believed that I was the only person in the world who experienced such drastically overpowering levels of fear. I was once at a diner with friends in Beirut, and the waiter came to our table to get our order. I was terrified of revealing my stutter to the waiter and also of having my friends find out the real severity of my speech impediment in moments when I felt particularly anxious. Indeed, while I do stutter in all speaking situations, the degree of severity goes from medium to high depending on several factors, including whether the person I am speaking to knows me or is aware that I have a stutter. That night, I admitted defeat and decided just to point on the menu to the dish I wanted. While that tactic got the job done, it filled me with a sense of shame. I chose the safe yet degrading option over the challenging yet empowering one.

While in high school, I was so ashamed of being different that I discreetly gulped large amounts of alcohol from my parents' cabinet before attending some of the school's social events. Far from being a fun but forbidden ritual with close friends, these solo adventures fueled by liquid courage involved uninhibited imbibing strictly to neutralize my unmanageable social anxiety. At one of those social events, I was fiercely proud of myself for having gone up to the "cool guy" to introduce myself and chat. To my great disappointment and embarrassment, he replied with, "Dude, you reek of alcohol!" before shaking his head and walking away. While my social Achilles' heel was how I felt about my stutter, the main obstacle that held me back was the fear of judgment. More specifically, I was paralyzed by this ever-looming thought: "What will they say or think when my true self is revealed?"

Whether it is not meeting that person at the event, not speaking up in the meeting or class or not exploring new hobbies, the inner stutter can get in the way of genuine opportunities to enrich your life. You might consider theater, improv or music classes but then cringe at the thought of putting yourself in a situation where you could invite judgment for looking silly. "I'm not naturally talented at these things," you might think. You figure you'll stick to activities you're already accustomed to this year and decide to revisit those somewhat unconventional and yet growth-inducing hobbies sometime next year. "Next year," or as we saw in Chapter 1, the Godot that you await, may or may never come.

Beneath the surface of those instances of holding back are the hidden fears that stealthily sway the trajectory of our lives. It could be the fear of judgment, the fear of rejection, the fear of failure or even the fear of success. Fear of success is common among those of us who are prone to experiencing imposter syndrome—the difficulty of accepting that you are worthy of achievements in either your professional or your personal life.

Interestingly, research has shown that imposter syndrome is linked to perfectionism.[2] Indeed, we might not believe that we are worthy of certain achievements because we think that we need to be perfect before deserving them. World-renowned professor and Netflix-featured speaker Brené Brown said that perfectionism is a "self-destructive and addictive belief system that fuels this primary thought: If I look perfect, and do everything perfectly, I can avoid or minimize the painful feelings of shame, judgment and blame." Seeing that perfection is an unattainable objective and that perfect outcomes are impossible to guarantee, a perfectionist is likely to hold back from taking action that will advance their goals. Related behaviors include perfectionistic self-promotion by presenting a perfect image to others; non-display of imperfection by concealing any behavior that could be judged as imperfect; and nondisclosure of imperfection by avoidance of disclosing imperfection to others.[3]

As someone who chose to hide his stutter from others through my silence, I feared that they would find out that I was in fact *far* from being perfect. While being sensitive to the needs of others is an adaptive and emotionally mature approach to life, being overly sensitive to those needs can maladaptively turn into a fawning response, such as people-pleasing. A people pleaser is typically described as a person who consistently seeks to please others while sacrificing their own wants and needs along the way. In my own journey as a person who sounds different, my self-expression often leads people to feel uncomfortable when we first interact. This usually occurs in the initial moments of an interaction, while they attempt to figure out the reasons for my disfluency. I have often joked that in those moments, I routinely receive what I call the "WTF face" from my listener who confusingly asks themselves, "Is this person speaking this way because he's intoxicated?" or "Is he pretending to stutter to mess with me?" Therefore, choosing to openly be myself is inadvertently linked to some degree of discomfort, initially experienced by my listeners and then by me as a reaction to their confusion or lack of awareness and understanding. The ultimate question for me was often the following: “Do I choose silence and comfort or self-expression and discomfort?” On the *On Purpose* podcast with Jay Shetty, world-renowned mental health doctor, author and speaker Gabor Maté wisely said that “you can be yourself or you can be accepted, but not both at the same time.”

In the same way I have hesitated to speak because I have a stutter, you may be hesitating when you wish to act, which, as we’ve seen, is an *inner* stutter. This inner stutter exists in the gap between desire and action.

Thankfully, the principles that I have uncovered in my own journey of transformation will be relevant to yours. I learned to speak in the face of fear; you can learn to act alongside it.

My Vienna moment

When people meet me after a stand-up comedy show, they sometimes assume I have always been confident. Here is a man, they may think, who happens to stutter but has always been naturally outspoken. Otherwise, he’d never be going up on stage that often, right? The reality could not be further from the truth. Allow me to illustrate with a true story about the past inner workings of my mind.

When I was 13 years old, I went to Austria for a family vacation. We were in Vienna for three days. On day one, I saw a girl with red hair, and my 13-year-old self thought she looked adorable. A few seconds later, she got into a cab with her mother and they left. On day two, I was with my family at the Haus der Muzik, an interactive museum on the history of music located in the palace of Archduke Charles. And . . . *there she was*. She was cute *and* cultured? Clearly, my teenage self had *excellent* taste. I thought about saying hello to her because seeing her on two consecutive days in a big city is an astounding coincidence. As I was drowning in my own thoughts, she once again vanished. Day three arrived, and this was our last day in Vienna. I was having lunch on a patio with my parents, my sister and a lovely Lebanese couple we had met at the hotel. After ordering the schnitzel, my father began to tell the group all about the girl with the red hair. I looked away, embarrassed. (What teenager wouldn't be?) With incomprehensible statistical absurdity, I then saw her. Everyone at the table cheered for me. "Third day in a row!" they proclaimed. "You *have* to speak to her." Alas, the third time was not a charm. I just sat there, frozen with anxiety and paralyzed by one single thought: "What will she say when she hears me stutter?"

That was the self-limiting mindset that shaped much of my life growing up and all the way until my mid-twenties. My existence was plagued by "Vienna moments"—times when I wanted to do something and yet fear permeated my mind and dictated the outcome across all areas of my life. Years later, when I was in Madrid for a conference, I met up with the Lebanese couple, who had now relocated to Spain. While we were having a delightful dinner, Walid and Shireen vividly remembered the fact that I had stayed completely silent during the entire time we traveled together in Austria. You may be thinking that the Vienna story reflects a moment that most people would have not taken action in either. Now I'd like to share a different moment, one that the majority of people would not have worried about.

I was 18 years old. I had completed my first year of university in Montreal and was back in Lebanon for the summer. Upon finding out that my beloved late uncle Levon had organized a large family reunion, I immediately started to panic. Uncle Levon was one of my favorite relatives, but I was *really* dreading that day. While I have always loved my family, the thought of attending a large gathering where I was going to be asked plenty of questions terrified me. I knew I was going to get severely stuck on words and that my relatives were going to wait for me to somehow navigate the unpredictability of my communication disorder. I was going to feel small, unworthy and inferior. I also knew that my parents were going to have to "rescue" me by joining the conversation and answering these questions on my behalf. I had to find a way out.

As a licensed professional avoider, I began plotting a strategy to minimize the emotional damage, in the short term at least. A few days before the family occasion, I joined my parents and my sister on a weeklong cruise in the beautiful Mediterranean. With stops in Barcelona, Marseilles, Tunis and Capri, I should have been much looking forward to spending quality time with the family. But here I was, on a beautiful trip with my loved ones and, because of the upcoming family gathering in Beirut, I could not fully enjoy myself. I am certain that most of you can think of occasions where you were to be celebrating, and yet anxiety kicked in and took over.

One night, as we cruised the Mediterranean, I stood on our balcony right after showering, wearing only a towel. Completely drenched, I waited outside for 30 minutes, hoping to catch a cold so that I would have a valid excuse for skipping the reunion. Needless to say, I was not familiar with the Dutch Iceman Wim Hof (more about him in Chapter 9) and the immune-boosting properties of exposure to cold. And why didn't I just *think* of pretending that I was feeling under the weather? Did I really have to be such a hell of a method actor?

As it turned out, I went to the reunion, and while I struggled to express myself, my relatives were kind and patient. But my stint on the balcony shivering above the Mediterranean still qualifies as a Vienna moment (if not an honorary Oscar) thanks to the extreme efforts I made to avoid a situation.

I have thousands of Vienna moments, moments when I missed out on something that could have enriched my life. What are yours? How did you act then? How would you rather act in an ideal word? Well, let's turn this ideal world into reality.

Identify, believe, act

Once you recall some of your own Vienna moments, you can pinpoint the content of the fear and identify the inner stutter that is holding you back. Awareness is always the first step. For instance, I held back that day in Vienna because I was afraid of being judged and rejected by the young woman for being different. Once we know more about the fear that we are working with, it would be wise to dig a bit deeper by asking ourselves, "Is there a self-limiting belief that is causing this fear to repeatedly show up in my life?"

Growing up with a severe stutter, I often faced negative reactions when I would get badly stuck on a word. Some people would laugh when it was my turn to read out loud in the classroom. Others would make jokes about my irregular way of speaking. As you can imagine, all these negative experiences gradually shaped some limiting beliefs about my place in the world. I started believing that I was destined to a sad life filled with judgment, rejection and emotional pain. Even worse, I thought I was too damaged to be worthy of love, acceptance and all the good stuff that we humans hope to experience.

What we believe about ourselves undoubtedly shapes our later thoughts and the actions we engage in. In her *Psychology Today* article "3 Ways Your Beliefs Can Shape Your Reality," psychologist Dr. Juliana Breines shares the example of someone who believes they are competent and therefore is more likely to notice and seek out opportunities to help them get their dream job.[4] That positive belief can also translate into higher confidence during an interview, which will be interpreted positively by the interviewer.[5] In other words, not only would that belief lead to taking action, it would also increase awareness of opportunities for reaching a goal. This example ties in with the concept of self-efficacy, where believing that we are able to effectively perform a behavior increases the likelihood of performing it. In her article, Dr. Breines cites research suggesting that people are also more likely to engage in health-promoting behaviors, such as a following a healthy diet and exercising, if they have a greater sense of self-efficacy.[6]

Beliefs about who you are as a person on a fundamental level can also greatly influence your behavior.[7] If you believe that you are someone who goes after what they want, you will respond to opportunities proactively. Conversely, if you believe, through learned helplessness, that you are someone who passively submits to life's circumstances, you might not even perceive opportunities when they present themselves. According to the frequency illusion, also known as the Baader-Meinhof phenomenon, something that we have been thinking about will seem to happen more frequently.[8] For example, if you are thinking about buying a particular car, you are prone to start noticing that same make and model everywhere you go. Similarly, when I was spending time with my cousin Aram and his pregnant wife Sanan in Central Park, they kept noticing every single baby stroller that passed by. While we might initially assume that an item's frequency in the market has suddenly skyrocketed, something else is at play here. Professor Anina Rich, from the Department of Cognitive Studies at Macquarie University in Australia, explains that we just "weren't noticing it because our attention was not being drawn on it."[9] Through this top-down process, something that's on our mind will influence our perception and therefore our subsequent behavior. In other words, if we believe that we are not worthy of certain professional and personal accomplishments, or even of receiving love, we might simply ignore opportunities that could prove those beliefs wrong. Often, all it takes are a few negative experiences during a critical period of our development as children or teenagers for us to cement a self-limiting belief that will hold us back for years to come. Indeed, the beliefs that we hold about ourselves and the world around us will play a significant role in determining the actions that we choose to take.

Indian psychiatrist Dr. T.S. Sathyanarayana Rao wrote that the biggest misconception we have about beliefs is that a belief is a static, intellectual concept.[10] In his view, not only are beliefs a choice, but the biochemical potential for change and growth is also always there. He explains: "When we change our thinking, we change our beliefs. When we change our beliefs, we change our behavior." In my opinion, the best way to change our thoughts is through action that provides new evidence, thereby challenging our beliefs. We will be talking about this topic much more in Chapter 5.

After identifying both your inner stutter and your self-limiting beliefs, it's now time to devise an action plan. That plan must revolve around proactively creating situations where you can face that fear repeatedly—once, twice, thrice and a thousand times. In the timeless words of poet Robert Frost, "The best way out is always through." For example, in my second year of university, I begged my professors at McGill to exempt me from every single presentation. In my third year, however, I joined the public-speaking club Toastmasters International and the university's debating club—which absolutely *terrified* me—to voluntarily expose myself to that fear. Taking action constituted an irrefutably effective way to challenge the accuracy of the beliefs I held about myself and the world. Spoiler alert: The beliefs were deeply inaccurate. Humans are, on average, significantly kinder and more understanding than I had given them credit for.

We will be talking about the mindset and mechanics of how to take action later on in the book, but first, the next chapter will consist of a necessary expedition into the depths of fear.

Chapter 3 takeaways

» In the same way that I hesitate because of a stutter, you may hesitate because of an inner stutter caused by the fear of judgment, rejection, failure or success. What is your inner stutter? While you may have several, I would recommend focusing on the main one at first before tackling others.

» The fact that I went through a drastic transformation (remember the cruise ship story and the extent to which I went to avoid something) may remind you that drastic change is possible in your life, too.

» The way to overcome that fear begins by identifying what your inner stutter is, uncovering self-limiting beliefs that might cause that fear to repeatedly resurface and devising an action plan to engineer opportunities for growth.

Meet Denise Soler Cox, 53

Denise Soler Cox had a major fear: She wanted to make a documentary film but felt deeply overwhelmed by the grandeur of the goal. She was afraid not only because she had no experience making films, but also because she knew she wanted to tell a personal story about what it is like to be a first-generation Latina in the United States. In fact, she was petrified that the story wouldn't dignify the experience and that she would not honor this fragile, tender and nuanced lived experience. As she shared her feelings, her hands twisted together nervously.

Denise hesitated immensely before embarking on her filmmaking journey. When I asked her what motivated and inspired her to confront this fear, she started laughing and responded with "I got sick of hearing myself talk about the fact that I wanted to make a movie!" She smiled at the memory, shaking her head. Indeed, she had talked about her goal for 17 years, telling everyone with great certainty that she would be making this film. She frequently told people that one day she would finally do it, just not today. Not only would she share her goal with people in general, but she would also write it down every single January 1 on her New Year's resolutions for the upcoming year. In fact, every January 1, she invited her friends over and they would all write their lists of resolutions and intentions for the upcoming year. For 17 years in a row, she wrote "make the movie." "I felt like I was full of sh*t," Denise confided with a chuckle, her expression a mix of frustration and amusement.

That year, however, things were going to be different. She made a promise to herself that she would do whatever she could in one year to make the movie happen. If after one year, she had not made any progress, she would stop talking about this movie and would never again include it goal in her yearly resolutions list. On January 1, 2013, Denise committed to making significant progress on her film project—whatever that meant.

As a very organized person, Denise always includes a subcategory of tasks that are linked to the main goal she is planning to accomplish. However, when she wrote "make a movie," she did not know what sub-actions to write. In fact, all Denise had written was "call Claire." Claire was a casual acquaintance. Her child and Denise's had had a play date six months earlier. Claire had mentioned that her next-door neighbor was a documentary filmmaker. Perhaps, Claire, whom Denise barely knew, would be willing to introduce her to the neighbor?

Whenever Denise approaches a challenge, she likes to think about all the things she has to do, and she commits to doing everything she can, even if it feels uncomfortable. One day, as she was getting ready to drop her kids off at school, she received a voicemail from Henry, the documentary filmmaker, saying that he was busy with a film and didn't know when he'd have time to meet her. He then went on to say that even if had the time, it would be only 10 minutes.

With the possibility of her dream withering away, Denise started to cry. (Her voice wavered as she recalled the moment.) She then took a deep breath and reminded herself of an iconic moment in the movie *Dumb and Dumber*. The scene takes place when the two main characters, Lloyd Christmas and Harry Dunne are discussing Lloyd's romantic prospects with Mary Swanson, a woman he has a crush on. When Harry points out that the chances of Mary leaving her husband for Lloyd are "one in a million," Lloyd responds with the famous line "So you're telling me there's a chance!" Ignited and energized, Denise drove to Henry's office, called him and said she would love to take him up on his offer to chat for 10 minutes. This call led to a meeting that lasted well over an hour and subsequently to making the movie together.

One of the biggest lessons that Denise learned along the way was the importance of listening to her heart. From the first night the movie was screened, Denise was keenly aware that she wanted to make this film to make a difference in the Latin community. (At the time of my writing, it has been screened almost 500 times.) When asked to elaborate on that thought, Denise explained that she feels like she exists on the wobbly part of the branch of a tree, and that she must constantly trust herself because the fear is always there. Her hands gestured to emphasize the constant balance required. According to Denise, as long as she meets the fear with her purpose, and if she's willing to experience uncomfortable feelings, she knows she will manage to navigate the obstacles she might run into. In fact, she doesn't feel that she needs to *overcome* the fear. She invites the fear to stay because, in her words, "if I feel fear, it means I am doing something bold, and I want to live a bold life!"

Denise wants to do great things, and everything great that she has done seems to have been accompanied by lots of fear. Her face softened as she reflected on her relationship with fear. She has learned to be comfortable with the idea that she might be constantly living with a mild sense of fear. She no longer sees fear as an obstacle; rather, she will do the things she wishes to do while feeling afraid. For instance, she once stepped onto a stage thinking she would be speaking to 200 people, only to find out there were 4,200 people waiting to listen to her. Although she felt really scared, she believes the fear made her better. "Fear, you can come out on stage with me!" she jokingly recalls thinking to herself. Her eyes lit up as she shared this story.

When asked what she would tell her old self or someone currently facing fears, Denise instantly said that the number one thing is to trust your heart. She believes that as long as she trusts herself, as long as she believes in what she is showing up for, she will accomplish her dreams. Because Denise has such large goals in life, she values being clear about her purpose and working on trusting her heart in order to deal with the fear. Her voice was filled with conviction as she shared this final insight.

The inner stutter corner

Denise Soler Cox's inner stutter came from her longstanding fear of failure when it came to making a documentary. For 17 years, she dreamed of telling her story as a first-generation Latina in the United States, but her fear of failing to honor her community's complex experience kept her in a cycle of hesitation. Each New Year's Day, she wrote "make a movie" on her resolutions list, only to delay taking action. This pattern reminds me of my own journey, desperately hoping to go from shy to confident, yet never taking the required steps to reach that objective.

Finally, Denise grew "sick of hearing herself talk" about the movie without doing something about it. She gave herself a one-year ultimatum to make real progress—or else abandon the dream for good. This commitment propelled her forward. Her first step was a call to a filmmaker, Henry, who offered only a brief meeting. Instead of retreating, Denise seized the chance, turning the 10 minutes into an hour-long discussion and an eventual partnership. As I mentioned earlier, while avoidance is mainly fruitless, taking action is generally fruitful.

Over time, Denise learned to accept her inner stutter as a natural part of her journey. Instead of seeing fear as an obstacle, she took it as a sign of doing something bold. Even in nerve-racking moments, like speaking to 4,200 people, she invited her fear to "come on stage" with her. By embracing her inner stutter, Denise transformed her fear into fuel, allowing her to finally bring to life her dream of being a filmmaker.

Recognize your inner stutter, stop holding back and be like Denise!

4.

Taming the tiger within

The oldest and strongest emotion of mankind is fear, and the oldest and strongest kind of fear is fear of the unknown.

—H.P. LOVECRAFT

Born in 1962, Alain Robert, also known as the French Spiderman, has climbed Paris's Eiffel Tower, New York's Empire State Building and Dubai's Burj Khalifa using his bare hands without ropes.[1] On hearing about such exploits, it is tempting to conclude that the French Spiderman must have a neurological condition that prevents him from experiencing fear. We might initially assume that he is similar to S.M., dubbed by the media as the "woman without fear." The 44-year-old mother has a rare genetic condition, called Urbach-Wiethe disease, which has destroyed her amygdala, leaving two symmetric black holes where the fear center in her brain used to be.[2] Alain tells a different story. In an interview with *Forbes* in 2020, he said, "I was afraid of heights as a child." Most of us would *never* consider free climbing without any equipment. How can we explain the fact that someone whose inner stutter was caused by a fear of heights would intentionally gravitate towards overcoming and mastering the object of the fear? While Alain's example might seem extreme, I recently met a gentleman who applied the same principle to a different fear, one that you might relate to more than the fear of heights: the fear of being judged.

Eric Melis, a Dutch-born Canadian financier who works with institutional investors in the fields of infrastructure investing, fundraising and global equity markets, has echoed Alain's message of overcoming fear. Moving to Canada in the early 1980s, Eric was initially extremely self-conscious about speaking English with his strong Dutch accent. His inner stutter was caused by the self-consciousness over his accent. He also quickly observed that in North America, unlike in the Netherlands, public speaking was considered a necessary skill for success. He found it terrifying. "It's something you have to do. If you want to interact with people and society and have a successful career, you have to be able to speak in public," he told me when we met after I delivered a talk at an alumni event. When I asked about what empowered him to confront his fear, he compared overcoming fear to the simple procedure of getting a blood test. "The needle has to go in. It's unavoidable. You just have to get through it!" he exclaimed.

The metaphor of the temporarily painful needle illustrates Eric's journey of personal transformation throughout the 1980s. Indeed, he intentionally signed up to do things that were challenging. His first job in Canada was as a lifeguard, where he had to interact daily with swimmers and colleagues. He then volunteered to become a teacher, where he routinely had to speak in front of classes of both children and adults. The more he spoke in public, the less intimidating it became. "I was afraid that I would not be able to speak the way I wanted to. It was a mental block," he told me. Eric's description of the mental block is aligned with the concept of the inner stutter. Subsequently, he joined the student debating club (coincidentally, the same one I joined years later), and while he found the experience challenging, he felt a tremendous amount of growth. In fact, he ended up debating in tournaments against students from both Princeton and Yale.

Eric then decided to become a statistics tutor, where he was forced to stand in front of the class and explain complex concepts in English, which he still considered a foreign language. He believes he set himself up for success by over-preparing. "When you build your competence, you end up having fewer surprises," Eric explained. In the words of the Roman philosopher Seneca, "luck is where opportunity meets preparation." As a result of years of putting himself in situations that felt uncomfortable, Eric dramatically improved his public-speaking skills. When he was asked to speak at financial institutions in French, that challenge sparked another journey of personal growth, culminating in many successful public-speaking engagements in yet another language. "You have to embrace your fear and work with it," Eric shared with a smile. "Not against it. After all, you must swim with the tide, not against it, right?"

Eric's attitude did not stop there. He has inspired his daughters to conquer obstacles of their own. One of his daughters came across an ad seeking someone who spoke both French and Dutch to translate eulogies of members of the Dutch community in Montreal. She was initially reluctant to apply, since she had been born and raised in Canada and was not confident about speaking publicly in Dutch. Inspired by her father's philosophy, she decided to face that fear, applied and got the job. Gradually, through a proactive mindset and preparation, she overcame the inner stutter that she associated with speaking in Dutch in front of an audience.

"Unless you try, nothing is gained. We must embrace the cards we were dealt and make the best out of the inevitable," said Eric at the end of our conversation. Alain Robert, Eric Melis and Eric's daughter all intentionally leaned towards what they feared.

As you might expect, the journeys of all three of them resonate with me. I pursued public speaking and stand-up comedy, not in spite of the fear but *because* of it. Without this initial fear, I would have had limited incentive to pursue this interest. In the words of the Stoic philosopher Marcus Aurelius, "The impediment to action advances action, what stands in the way becomes the way." Without their fears, Alain might not have become a free climber and Eric might not have become a public-facing financier. When someone manages to "get by" with minimal effort, they might never ask themselves the questions that ultimately lead to a journey of self-exploration. In that sense, if you face it, your fear could end up being a valuable opportunity for growth, resilience and the uncovering of your potential. Once, in an Uber on the way to a comedy club, my friends A.K., Dana and Zein asked me if I had always gravitated towards the stage. "Astrologically, you're a Leo rising, so of course you'd be drawn to the spotlight!" Zein added. I laughed and responded that it was precisely because I was terrified of the stage that I was doing this. What I called "fear-induced curiosity," or FIC, led to my unlikely eventual exploration of this interest. Had I not experienced this seemingly insurmountable fear in the first place, I may have never embarked on this journey of understanding and conquering it.

So, what is fear anyway?

Good ol' fear

We have been talking about fear quite a bit. But what the heck is it? Webster's dictionary defines fear as an "unpleasant often strong emotion caused by anticipation or awareness of danger." This definition primes us to contemplate the indispensable role that fear has played in the development of our evolution as *Homo sapiens*. UCLA's professor of ecology and evolutionary biology Daniel T. Blumstein said that fear, honed by millions of years of natural selection, kept our ancestors alive.[3] Plagued by dangers everywhere, human beings—with their well-calibrated fear-oriented emotions and responses—were at a massive advantage compared to creatures who underestimated danger and fell prey to lethal fauna and flora.

The oblivious primate that routinely underreacted to potentially alarming stimuli in their environment was far more likely to enter dangerous situations and prematurely meet their maker. Their genetic makeup, including perhaps an underactive amygdala, would therefore be less likely to be transmitted to the next generations. Although overestimating the danger of a situation can cause unnecessary spikes in cortisol and adrenaline, it certainly beats underestimating danger, which can lead to perishing (and, thus, never experiencing any level of cortisol or adrenaline ever again). In other words, Tony the Tiger ate you and he thought you tasted *GRRREEAT!*

The lesson of taking danger seriously has been woven into countless tales handed down from one generation to the next. Anthropologist Jamshid Tehrani has spoken about the fact that fairy tales such as "Little Red Riding Hood," "Tiger Grandmother" and "The Wolf and the Seven Young Kids" contain "survival-relevant information" including the danger of strangers and the importance of following a parent's instructions.[4] Cautionary tales enable parents to leverage the potency of fear to protect their offspring, thereby preserving their genetic lineage.

American biologist Edward O. Wilson remarked that "genes hold culture on a leash." Although his phrase may be an overly reductionist analysis of human culture, it is worth noting that cultural practices often align with our biological objectives as a species. For example, fitness culture is directly linked to promoting physical strength, managing stress and engagaging in community bonding, which are all aligned with evolutionary objectives of surviving and thriving.

Similarly, my anthropology professor once reminded the class that the traditional formal and social event of a ball has historically served as an opportunity for members of the community to interact, make social connections and potentially meet romantic partners with whom to mate. In other words, a ball provides a structured environment for individuals to display their attractiveness and status, casting a metaphorical net for potential suitors. The fact that this activity facilitates the processes of courtship and, ultimately, mating and the spreading of one's genes, is yet another example of how what appears to be an innocuous cultural event is often driven by biological imperatives. And since the fundamental driving force behind natural selection is the replication of our genes, genetic predispositions that favor our survival and reproductive success are more likely to be passed down. Through that optic, fear has been a crucial ally when it comes to the survival of the individual, the tribe and the community. However, this ancient evolutionary alliance is a double-edged sword. Considering that modern scenarios differ from prehistoric ones, responses that were justified in the past may no longer be serving their purpose today. Professor Blumstein explained that, while fear is often a justifiable response to sources of threat, it can exact a high toll on health and productivity.[5]

So, what are situations in our lives today that are needlessly exacerbated by fear? Why and how does fear run amok?

Tiger 2.0 (or "the tiger trigger")

Today, as we navigate the twenty-first century, we can confidently assert that the sources of danger that most of us experience are qualitatively different from those faced by our predecessors. Whereas predators, poisonous plants and pale pastures constituted much of our daily fears as hunters and gatherers, in developed societies, the amygdala is mostly preoccupied with social fears. Indeed, according to psychologist Abraham Maslow's hierarchy of needs, once our most basic needs for survival and safety are met, our focus naturally shifts towards higher-level needs, including belonging, self-esteem and, ultimately, self-actualization.

Our modern-day tiger, "Tiger 2.0," is focused on being judged and rejected by the group. Prehistorically, being shunned, ostracized and abandoned by the tribe guaranteed your demise. Without the support and protection of the tribe, even the strongest member would have a difficult time surviving the unforgiving harshness of nature. For that reason, social rejection can feel like "pain to the brain."[6] Indeed, studies show that acetaminophen, the analgesic agent used to treat fever and pain in medications such as Tylenol and Panadol, can reduce behavioral and neural responses associated with the pain of social rejection.[7] Seeing that pain is one of the body's mechanisms to defend itself and promote survival, it typically shows up as a signal demanding corrective action.

When you fear public speaking, your evolution-shaped brain tells you that "if you mess this up, the group will reject you and thus you will be endangered as you navigate the wilderness all by yourself." In reality, however, even after the worst public-speaking performance, you'll likely get to go home, order takeout and watch something on Netflix.[*] Even if that one ineffective presentation at work costs you your job—a highly unlikely outcome—you'll be given a severance package as you hop over to LinkedIn and focus on finding your next opportunity. In other words, while the fear itself may be based on reasons that served a clear survival purpose prehistorically, its manifestation in the life of the modern human being contributes way more to the erosion of your potential than it does to protecting you from valid threats. But since we are subject to experiencing events and reacting to them through ancient mechanisms that once served a valid purpose, gaining awareness of these hidden processes can help us develop a healthier relationship with our "Stone Age minds."

The permanence paradox

Psychologist Leda Cosmides and her husband, the late anthropologist John Tooby, pioneered the field of evolutionary psychology and coined the saying "Our modern skulls house a Stone Age mind." Our brain circuits, Cosmides and Tooby explain, were not designed to solve the day-to-day problems of the modern-day human; rather, they evolved to solve the day-to-day problems of our hunter-gatherer ancestors.[8] For example, because of the lack of readily available calories in the wild, our ancestors had to maximize intake whenever food was available. While we can enjoy three meals a day, our ancestors were typically not guaranteed a schedule for

* This, of course, omits scenarios where a person does or says something deemed beyond reprehensible by most. If you are in that category, you might need a book about how to experience more fear in your life.

meals. The ancient form of intermittent fasting was unpredictable fasting! Gorging, whenever possible, was thus an effective strategy to sustain them while waiting for the next prey to hunt or edible flora to ingest.

Our Stone Age mind therefore leads to the gluttonous reality that our modern self is often tempted by the joys of overeating at a buffet. When I was a student in Montreal, my flat mates (Alex, Igor and Pierre) and I frequented an all-you-can eat sushi restaurant that offered unlimited nigiri, sashimi, maki and temaki for only $19.99. We flocked to that restaurant every Friday for lunch. To discourage patrons from ordering extravagant quantities of food, the restaurant charged a dollar per unconsumed piece. As university students who wished to make the most of that weekly feast, we ate eat every single morsel from our ungodly large orders until we were stuffed to the brim. I vividly remember us being unable to comfortably breathe or laugh thanks to the excessive pressure of the exquisite Japanese feast pressing against our diaphragms. In those moments, our prefrontal cortex, in charge of planning and rational decision-making, had lost control while our limbic system* emerged victorious.

Our anxious ancestral instincts can subtly influence us to maximize our caloric intake in moments of caloric abundance. As mentioned, our primitive self subconsciously reasoned that he, or she, might as well stock up because . . . who knows when the next meal might be? As you can imagine, that previously healthy instinct can have disastrous consequences when there are highly ca-

* The limbic system is a part of the brain involved in behavioral and emotional responses related to our survival.

loric food options at our fingertips. Although gravitating towards nutritional sustenance is an advantageous trait—evolutionarily speaking—being overly subservient toward and uninhibitedly enthusiastic about fulfilling that instinct can cause nefarious effects on our health.

In the aptly named book *Supernormal Stimuli: How Primal Urges Overran Their Evolutionary Purposes,* psychologist Deirdre Barrett argues that modern society allows us to gratify outmoded but persistent drives with dangerous results.[9] For instance, overusing social media instead of connecting face to face with a smaller number of people can lead to a large quantity of superficial and unfulfilling interactions. Similarly, overusing dating apps at the expense of building a meaningful relationship with a long-term partner illustrates how the otherwise crucial evolutionary instinct of finding a mate and procreating can lead us astray. Another example involves overusing food delivery apps to get junk food instead of cooking at home or having healthier alternatives, leading to both higher financial costs and negative health ramifications. While having access, in our pockets and at our fingertips, to all the food, friends and mates in the world can deceivingly seem like an "evolutionary victory," being overly obedient to these otherwise useful instincts causes shortcomings, both physically and psychologically (and perhaps also spiritually).

There are four Darwinian basal drives: survival, mating, kin selection and reciprocal altruism.[10] Whenever we engage in a behavior or social situation that involves one or more of these drives that have evolved over billions of years of evolution, a series of neuronal and physiological mechanisms can be triggered. If you have to speak up at a meeting in class, this seemingly innocuous moment is, in reality, linked to those Darwinian drives that have enabled the organism (you) to prosper.

Here is an example:

Wanting to speak up and share your thoughts during a university lecture might trigger the following internal responses in at least two of the basal drives in the Stone Age mind:

1. SURVIVAL: "If I speak up and share an idea that the other members of the tribe disagree with, they might decide to kick me out of the group, thereby abandoning me in the wilderness. I will likely be unable to survive on my own in the face of predators and without access to sustenance that other members would have hunted or gathered."
2. MATING: "If I speak up and share an idea that the professor or my peers deems foolish, I will instantly disqualify myself from being considered a viable mate by the members of the group. This compromises my chances of passing on my genes to the next generation. My genetic lineage might end with me."

I know some of you might be thinking, "Joze, I have *never* had thoughts like these before!" Therein lies the crucial distinction between proximate and distal levels of analysis. The proximate level refers to the immediate causes of a behavior or mental process, whereas the distal level addresses the distant, historical evolution of the psychological structures responsible for producing the behavior or mental process in the first place.[11] For example, while the voice of your proximal fear might say, "I do not want to ask a question in the meeting because I have a fear of public speaking," the distal fear, honed over a very long evolutionary period, thinks, "I do not want to ask a question because the group might judge me harshly and decide to abandon me, depriving me of my access to the resources that I need to survive." And where the proximal fear might say, "I hope I don't get rejected by her," the distal fear might think, "This woman's genetic fitness and pleasant disposition make her a highly desirable mate and potential mother for my future offspring. Do *not* mess up this opportunity." Expressed differently, the proximal thoughts are the ones that we have; the distal ones are the hidden instincts that often run the show behind the scenes.

When such drastic (distal) fears are triggered by the mere thought of engaging in a behavior, we normally experience the cascade of fearful and agitated sensations typically associated with the fight-or-flight response. Generally, the fight-or-flight response is linked to the following symptoms: increased heart rate and blood pressure, pale or flushed skin, dilated pupils and trembling.[12] With the exception of psychopaths, every human being, when experiencing a plethora of unpleasant physiological repercussions, will reconsider taking action. While opting not to act will rid you of that deep discomfort in the short term, succumbing to that defense mechanism inevitably robs you of potential rewards in the long term. It would be wiser for us to accept that those evolutionary neuronal and physiological processes are permanent and will likely always appear in certain situations.

Therefore, our objective is to commit to the habit of acting, regardless of the cacophony of the neurotransmitters and hormones that accompanies our inner stutter. While these reactions might have evolved to protect us in harsher environments, in most modern-day situations, we can acknowledge and act as if they were not there. The fact that the Stone Age mind's latent tendencies may never vanish does not imply that we are victims who cannot choose behaviors that will advance our goals in life. William James, one of the fathers of modern psychology, wisely said that "my first act of free will shall be to believe in free will." Whether it's speaking up in public, moderating our consumption at a buffet or asking someone out, all these behaviors involve attempting to take action while we are in a heightened state of evolutionary stress. The question is not whether we will experience strong emotions during those moments (we will); rather, will we leverage our free will to act, regardless? In the next chapters, we will dive into how to do so.

Chapter 4 takeaways

- Fear has been honed by natural selection and has played a crucial role in the evolutionary journey of human beings.
- While the fear itself might be based on valid evolutionary reasons that served a clear survival purpose prehistorically, its manifestation today contributes more to the erosion of your potential than it does to protecting you from real threats.
- The fact that the Stone Age mind's latent cognitive tendencies may never change does not imply that we cannot alter our behavior and take action.

Meet Ava Halvai, 27

Ava's fear of blood dates back to her preteen years, when she needed to have a blood test. Her face paled slightly as she recalled how, as soon as she entered the phlebotomy room and was made aware of what would be transpiring, she fainted. Following that one experience, the fear grew progressively and in relation to how much she avoided it. "The more I avoided it, the more the fear grew," Ava told me, her hands clenching briefly in her lap as she vividly recalled that stressful time in her life. Once focused on blood specifically, the fear expanded into a generalized anxiety related to anything associated with the medical field. From that one experience when she fainted in the phlebotomy room, Ava ended up developing a crippling fear of passing out. That fear was getting in the way of her life. Her shoulders tensed slightly as she described how it had. Indeed, it had grown tedious, exhausting and scary, like an infection spreading through her existence.

At one point, Ava decided to gather her courage and face the fear that had haunted her for years. "It was terrifying, but I decided to do it!" Ava recalled, a determined glint in her eyes. This decision to confront her fear was not made lightly. Ava recognized that it was a necessary step towards personal growth and reclaiming her life. Her voice softened slightly as she acknowledged the psychological toll her fear had taken and how overcoming it required a deliberate and committed effort.

Ava's chosen path to overcome this obstacle was through cognitive behavioral therapy (CBT), a therapeutic approach that systematically exposes individuals to their fears in a controlled manner. She explained how the process involved facing a hierarchy of fears, starting with looking at medical equipment, including needles and other apparatus. This structured approach allowed Ava to confront her fear in manageable steps, gradually building her tolerance and resilience. The culmination of her therapy was a visit to a blood test center, a setting that had been a source of immense anxiety. As a final test, Ava was expected simply to go to the center and watch a nurse take blood from other people.

A sense of relief passed across Ava's face as she described how, during this visit, she unexpectedly encountered the head nurse, Maryam, a strong Malaysian woman whose presence became a catalyst for Ava's breakthrough. Maryam not only encouraged Ava to witness a blood sample being drawn but she also asked Ava to be the one to draw a sample from *her*. After taking the sample, Ava's confidence grew and she even registered to become a phlebotomist herself. Her eyes brightened with pride as she said, "Can you imagine . . . I became the person who would help patients just like myself calm down!" As Eric Melis, the Dutch financier we met at the beginning of the chapter, said, "The needle has to go in. It's unavoidable. You just have to get through it!"

Ava's journey was not without its challenges. A brief look of frustration crossed her face as she recounted how the process of overcoming her fear was a gradual one, involving years of CBT, life interruptions and emotional setbacks. At times, Ava found herself embarrassed by her fear, attempting to conceal it, something that inadvertently caused the fear to deepen. It was during these moments that she learned to accept that it's fine to be scared of something and that overcoming fear is not an on/off switch but a continuous process. Indeed, recognizing that fear is a fundamental human emotion and that it is okay to feel these emotions empowered her to have a healthier relationship with it. A smile spread across her face as she added, "You wouldn't be a human if you didn't feel it!"

The impact of overcoming her fear was profound and far-reaching for Ava. It wasn't just about conquering a specific phobia; it was a transformative experience that shaped her perception of herself and her capabilities. The fearlessness she gained through this process instilled a deep sense of self-belief. Ava realized that she could navigate through the scary, unfamiliar and unknown aspects of life with courage and resilience. In fact, according to her, doing the difficult things in life, such as overcoming fear, is a courageous act of self-love. A confident gleam appeared in her eyes as she said, "If I can overcome this, I can overcome anything else." Going from fainting whenever she would see blood to voluntarily signing up to become a phlebotomist empowered her greatly.

When asked to reflect on her experience, Ava would convey a message of self-compassion and encouragement to her old self or anyone else currently facing fears. "Don't give yourself such a hard time!" Ava remarked. As a teenager, Ava always felt like she had to be perfect and in control of everything. Even though it is scary to overcome fear, she believes that we must do it because we owe it to ourselves.

As Ava looks back on her journey, she recognizes the transformative powers of confronting fears. It's not just about the specific fear itself but about the internal growth, resilience and self-discovery that emerge from the process. Ava's story serves as an inspiration for anyone facing fears, illustrating that with courage, support and self-compassion, it is possible to overcome even the most paralyzing fears and emerge stronger on the other side.

The inner stutter corner

Ava's inner stutter was caused by her fear of blood, which gradually grew into a debilitating anxiety surrounding anything medical. This inner stutter, much like a physical one, disrupted her ability to live freely and go through things that the average person would find mundane. Just as I feared how others would perceive my speech, Ava's fear of blood and fainting tainted her everyday life, making her feel powerless and limited in her choices.

For both of us, overcoming these obstacles required a shift in mindset and a large amount of courage. Ava's decision to confront her fear head-on through cognitive behavioral therapy was a gradual and painstaking process, just as my journey to embrace my stutter involved pushing myself into situations that felt uncomfortable. The fear wasn't magically overcome in a single moment; rather, it was a lengthy process. For Ava, each small step, such as looking at a needle, watching blood being taken, taking a sample herself and finally becoming a phlebotomist helped her reclaim control over her fear, ultimately transforming it into a source of empowerment. Similarly, each moment I confront my own fear of stuttering strengthens my confidence.

I can't think of a better parallel: a stutterer with a fear of speaking becoming a stand-up comedian and someone with a fear of blood becoming a phlebotomist! In both our journeys, facing our respective stutters led to profound growth. Ava's fear no longer controls her life, just as my fear of speaking no longer holds me back. We both found a way to turn what once felt like a limitation into a source of strength, proving that the courage to confront inner fears can empower us to achieve things that our younger selves would have deemed impossible.

Recognize your inner stutter, stop holding back and be like Ava!

5.

Act your way into new thoughts

Act the way you'd like to be and soon
you'll be the way you act.
—LEONARD COHEN

William "Bill" Wilson was born in East Dorset, Vermont, on November 26,1895.[1] A century later, Bill Wilson was named by *Time* magazine as one of the 100 most influential people of the twentieth century.[2] That list of remarkable individuals also includes Winston Churchill, Louis Armstrong, Bill Gates, Albert Einstein, Muhammad Ali and Mother Teresa. Bill's claim to fame can be summed up by the first letter of the alphabet repeated twice: AA. His own devastating personal experience with alcoholism ultimately led him to create the global peer-led program known as Alcoholics Anonymous. Most interestingly for the purposes of this chapter, Bill popularized an incredibly powerful saying that is capable of producing an instant shift in one's perspective of life. I know it did for me when I heard it recited by Giovanni Marsico, the founder of the Archangel Summit, at his annual personal development conference in Toronto: "You can't think your way into right action, but you can act your way into right thinking."

Conventional wisdom might (rightfully) ask us to think before we act. In fact, while I was in middle school, a school counselor taught us the "stop, think, act" framework. While this methodology is effective in many areas of life, I believe that sometimes we must act before we think. If the thoughts that we currently hold are not conducive to creating the life we want to live, a new and different path of action can be more effective for bringing about the change we seek. Indeed, our inner stutter thrives at the "stop" and "think" stages. But it's the "act" stage that is often the antidote to the hesitation and overanalysis of the other two stages. As Mark Manson says in *The Subtle Art of Not Giving a F*ck*, "Don't just sit there. Do something. The answers will follow." My personal experiences confirm the validity of this approach. When going through periods of depression, it was extremely difficult for me to focus on directly shifting my thinking. Instead, I would start by creating a list of nonnegotiable habits that I needed to complete every day in order to achieve a threshold of mental wellness that would effectively counteract my depression. Dragging myself to the gym, meditating, taking a cold shower, journaling and phoning a family member or friend daily gradually altered the way I experienced my day. While there are other resources and strategies to employ to overcome a dark night of the soul, including consulting a therapist (more about this topic later), deliberately shifting our behavior can bring about the first steps towards change. Unlike what some proponents of pop psychology might say, replacing negative thoughts with positive ones is not a straightforward task. Simply repeating positive affirmations in front of the mirror may not work for someone who is in the depths of a depressive or anxious episode. Would you be in the mood to recite rosy affirmations on a particularly difficult day?

I have often found that implementing the correct actions, even if it is alongside negative thoughts, can lead to noticeable improvements in thinking and feelings. As we enter the fifth chapter of our journey together, keep in mind the words of writer and civil rights activist James Baldwin: "Not everything that is faced can be changed, but nothing can be changed until it is faced."

Now pack your bags and don't forget your umbrella. We're going to the UK.

Does action cure fear?

At the age of 17, I attended a speech therapy program in England. At the time, my stutter was truly debilitating; I avoided speaking all the time. Research has shown that wanting to fit in and conform to our peers is highest during early and middle adolescence.[3] Unfortunately, if you sound different and wish to fit in, silence can quickly emerge as a viable survival mechanism. The only time that I could look "normal" as a person who stutters was when I did not speak. My strategy of silence as a method for social survival didn't go unnoticed by my parents.

One day, my father came into my childhood room in Lebanon and acknowledged that my sessions with some local speech therapists had proved ineffective. I agreed. He suggested that we look into other speech therapy program options abroad. After researching a few programs online, I came across an unorthodox one called the McGuire Programme. After further examination, I reached out to some of the organizers, and both my mother and I had a few phone conversations with some of the members. Interestingly, not only was this program founded by Dave McGuire, a man who stuttered, but all the coaches were stutterers who had gone through the speech program and found success with its novel methods. Finding out that some celebrities had gone through it, including the British singer Gareth Gates from the hit TV show *Pop Idol* and the Scottish guitarist Graeme Duffin from the band Wet Wet Wet, was the cherry on top. (In case you're wondering Wet Wet Wet, you've probably heard their iconic song "Love Is All Around," immortalized in the movie *Love Actually*.) Needless to say, my teenage self was excited about improving my speech while also hopefully getting to hang out with some celebrities.

After my mother and I had spoken with both the founder and some members, known as "grads," we decided that this was the right place for me. A few months later, I skipped a whole week of high school at the International College in Beirut to attend a four-day intensive McGuire course in Swindon, England. The city's claim to fame is its "magic roundabout," a confusing traffic circle that was voted the fourth scariest junction in the UK.[4] Unfazed by its scariness, I had fears of my own to worry about that week. As soon as I arrived at the hotel and saw over 100 people congregating in the lobby and bar, I started experiencing the familiar sense of social anxiety that had accompanied me every time I entered a setting involving people. But then, it hit me: "Wait a second . . . everyone here stutters, too!" My anxiety instantly evaporated. When I was no longer concerned that people would find my speaking patterns strange, I could finally relax and express my true self authentically. So I started socializing and getting to know fellow stutterers hailing from different countries and diverse academic and professional backgrounds.

Next I proceeded to learn a new breathing technique through which I would start gaining a certain degree of control over my stutter. Inspired by operatic singing, the technique I learned consisted of breathing through the mouth, speaking and then releasing the remaining air. Those of you who practice breathwork, such as the Wim Hof method or other types of conscious-connected practices, might notice some similarities. Indeed, the breathing technique that I use for stuttering somewhat resembles breathwork in the sense that the breath happens through the mouth rather than the nose, in addition to the fact that the inhalation tends to be faster than the exhalation. While the two approaches have drastically different purposes, I also practice breathwork and mindfulness techniques separately. I'll get into those a bit later, when we discuss the crucial necessity of cultivating mental wellness strategies in parallel to conquering fears.

Even though the technique I learned worked instantly, it took many (*many*) years to start feeling comfortable enough using it across different speaking situations. Seeing as I had not accepted that I was going to sound different despite having a speaking technique, I kept attempting to hide my true self whenever I was able to. While I had completed the speech therapy program before moving to Montreal for my undergraduate degree, I failed to use the speech techniques in my first few years at university. The fear of being judged by my peers in college superseded the desire to work on my stutter and express myself more effectively. Ironically, my inner stutter revolving around the fear of judgment for being different halted my ability to improve my outer stutter. I therefore resorted to the old and comforting method of opting for silence in place of speech. Indeed, not only did I request exemptions from presentations and in-class participation, but I also avoided socializing and interacting with people on campus—unless it was at a party where liquid courage could be imbibed. Unfortunately, sustainable change wouldn't happen without acceptance of the self. According to Dr. David Daniels's Universal Growth Process for Self-Mastery framework, the following components ought to exist for change to occur: Awareness, Acceptance, Appreciation, Action and Adherence (the 5As). Let's focus on Awareness, Acceptance and Action with a personal example:

As a child and then as a teenager, I often went to the speech therapist with my mother. Because I believed I would be worthy if and only if I could speak fluently by implementing the techniques I was being taught, I felt tremendous amounts of shame whenever I misused the techniques or got stuck on words. Those emotional circumstances did not offer a healthy milieu for change. For self-improvement to be sustainable, it is best, whenever possible, to add new behaviors on top of a strong foundation of self-awareness and self-acceptance. Those states rarely occur overnight; they are long-term processes that we must constantly work on in conjunction with the new actions we are implementing to improve our lives. Similarly, despite having learned effective techniques to control my stuttering, my lack of self-acceptance created severe internal tension that prevented me from applying these methods when interacting with people. As the proverb goes: "Tension is who you think you should be. Relaxation is who you are."

Seeing that I refused to accept I was going to sound different, I experienced ongoing internal tension in every social interaction. There are some similarities here to a person who wishes to lose weight. Let's call him Raj. If Raj focuses strictly on taking action by regularly going to the gym and changing his diet, it's likely that certain emotional triggers will easily drive him back to unhealthy eating habits as a way to soothe stress and discomfort. If, however, Raj also focuses on cultivating awareness of the thoughts and emotional patterns that kept him stuck and on fully accepting himself the way that he is right now, he would find it significantly easier to commit to beneficial behavioral strategies. Contrary to what some might believe, acceptance does not imply that Raj, or I, would be complacent or that we would be giving up. Acceptance is an effective way to meet ourselves where we currently are in order to alleviate counterproductive emotions.

In July 2023, I was invited to be a keynote speaker at the National Stuttering Association (NSA) conference in Fort Lauderdale, Florida. Although in the past I had been in environments where most people were stutterers, namely through my speech therapy programs, attending the NSA conference in the United States, as well the Canadian Stuttering Association (CSA) conferences in Canada, would prove to be a different type of experience. When I first arrived at the Fort Lauderdale Marriott Harbor Beach Resort on a beautiful summer day, I was instantly struck by the sights and sounds of hundreds of fellow stutterers roaming around the lobby. While some of them were using techniques to control their fluency, many were stuttering openly without a care in the world. Having been a shy teenager who avoided speaking at all costs and never dared to be seen (or heard) stuttering severely in public, I felt liberated witnessing individuals across age groups stuttering freely. At that moment, I wished I had attended a conference like this one when I was a painfully self-conscious young person. When you meet a group of people who all share your obstacle, you instantly feel a sense of connection. The NSA and CSA focus on acceptance of stuttering, both by oneself and by society. That is what contributes to such a positive and supportive atmosphere where every single stutterer feels like they are accepted—no matter how severe or mild their stutter is. When we accept, we halt our fruitless attempts at resisting reality.

It has been said that "what we resist, persists." While action that is devoid of self-acceptance is superior to not acting at all, the best-case scenario entails combining acceptance of our current situation with courageously taking uncomfortable actions to improve reality and make our future selves proud.

The IRS (inaction, regret and shame)

Action might not eliminate fear. However, it can effectively counteract the negative consequences of succumbing to our fear, namely inaction and regret. We can all think of countless moments when our failure to act in spite of truly wanting to was followed by a sense of shame. Unlike guilt, which tends to focus on the behavior itself, shame generalizes the focus onto the individual. In other words, it is no longer about the behavior that we failed to commit to; rather, we internalize that inaction as a sign of a personal and lasting defect. According to journalist and author Anneli Rufus, there are five ingredients to shame: regret, guilt, self-loathing, disgust and fear.[5] Here is an example of how this assortment of thoughts might permeate our cognitive landscape after we fail to act:

You're at a professional conference, a rare chance to connect with industry leaders and colleagues from influential companies. During a break, you see a senior executive from a company you've admired for years. They're standing alone, casually glancing at their phone—a perfect moment to introduce yourself. Your heart starts pounding, and you imagine how the conversation could go. But you hesitate, worrying that you'll fumble or come off as unprepared. Seconds pass, then minutes, and eventually, a group of other professionals approaches the executive, launching into an animated conversation.

You turn away, frustrated and disappointed, and spend the rest of the conference replaying the missed opportunity in your mind.

REGRET: "Why didn't I just walk over and say hello?"

GUILT: "That was my chance to build a connection that could elevate my career, and I wasted it."

SELF-LOATHING: "This always happens! I am a hopeless case. Sometimes, I hate myself."

DISGUST: "I'm disgusted with myself today. I'd better turn Netflix on and grab a couple of pints of Häagen-Dazs to feel better."

FEAR: "What if I never overcome this hesitation? How will I ever grow as a human if I keep holding back? How many chances will I squander if I don't get my act together?"

While guilt is concerned with one's responsibility for a harmful attitude or behavior, shame implies a negative self-evaluation.[6] Amplified by self-loathing and disgust, shame leads us to internalize the behavior that we feel guilty about, thereby turning it into a permanent feature of the self. Instead of focusing on changing the behavior, which is a realistic objective, we shift towards making the unhelpful assumption that we acted a certain way because we are incorrigible or flawed beings. In other words, you can feel guilty about having done something bad while still feeling like you're a good person. Conversely, if you feel ashamed about doing something bad, you feel like you are, by definition, a bad person. Research out of Queen's University and the University of Toronto has revealed a connection between "shame-proneness" and negative mental health experiences such as depression and anxiety.[7] While shame might sometimes be effective for tweaking our behavior in the short term, it rarely constitutes a solid foundation for sustainable change. For example, not only does fat-shaming, the act of making a person feel ashamed or inferior about their body size, not motivate people to lose weight, it also causes major harm.[8] Although in some rare anecdotal cases, fat-shaming might have worked, studies validate the opposite point of view. Indeed, body-shaming has been linked to eating disorders, alcohol misuse and chronic conditions such as high blood pressure and prediabetes, as well as shortened life expectancy.[9] While someone who is unhealthily overweight could be encouraged to form new, healthier habits that would gradually improve their health, shaming them is unlikely to lead to sustainable progress.

The same process applies to making other changes in our lives, including conquering the inner stutter that is currently holding us back from becoming the best version of ourselves. While shaming ourselves for our current shortcomings may light a fire under us for a short time, an approach based on awareness, acceptance *and* action will prove to be more effective.

As a child, I was constantly taken to professionals in order to find a solution for my stutter. My mother took me to speech therapists, psychologists, hypnotherapists and psychiatrists. This frantic impulse to "fix" me contributed to the belief that I was broken and thus in dire need of being repaired at any cost. That belief would cause many challenges in my personal life, including not recognizing my worth at times. At the time of writing this book, I am still working through these emotional ill effects by going to therapy. Naturally, it wasn't easy for me to accept the fact that I was different. It was by cultivating acceptance, amplified through meeting other people who stutter, and taking action, such as diving into stand-up comedy, that the trajectory of my life gradually shifted. When we meet ourselves where we currently are, we honor the path we have been on while recognizing that change will not happen overnight. As you embark on this journey of replacing inaction with action, remember to be kind to yourself. As I write these words, I am reminded of how crucial it is to show myself kindness and forgiveness as I imperfectly navigate the chaos of life. Equipped with a mindset based on acceptance, awareness and action, you will uncover the fact that life is full of possibilities to shape your destiny, every . . . single . . . day.

The power of experimentation

Seeing that I might be coming across as the poster boy for facing fears, it is my responsibility to state that facing fears does not grant instant rewards. Entering the arena does not guarantee victory. It is merely an admission to the fight. The good news is that you're in the ring. The bad news is that you're in the ring. You are simultaneously most likely to win and most likely to lose when in that position. In other words, you are *vulnerable*. Perhaps no quote is more apt to illustrate the metaphor of the arena than this one from Theodore Roosevelt, who wisely said:

> It is not the critic who counts; not the man who points out how the strong man stumbles or where the doer of deeds could have done them better. The credit belongs to the man

> who is actually in the arena, whose face is marred by dust and sweat and blood; who strives valiantly; who errs, and comes short again and again, because there is no effort without error and shortcoming; but who does actually strive to do the deeds; who knows great enthusiasms, the great devotions; who spends himself in a worthy cause; who at the best knows in the end the triumph of high achievement, and who at the worst, if he fails, at least fails while daring greatly, so that his place shall never be with those cold and timid souls who neither know victory nor defeat.[10]

Wow. When we look at fear through the lens of being in the arena of life, vulnerability is a high-risk and high-reward model. While sharing our authentic self with the world does open up the possibility of being judged or rejected, that very act also unleashes an array of delightful possibilities that would not have existed otherwise. For example, when you attempt to have a difficult conversation with your parents, you are instantly in a vulnerable position because you do not know how they will respond. When you sign up for a bachata or hip-hop dance lesson, you enter a space that might be unfamiliar to you, especially if you are rhythmically challenged, like me. You risk looking silly or weird as you strive to learn to maneuver the sequences taught by an enthusiastic teacher to whom dancing appears to be as natural as inhaling oxygen. Similarly, when you take on a challenging assignment that is outside your comfort zone at work, you are also instantly vulnerable in the sense that your current capacities will need to be stretched out and upgraded to achieve this goal. Thankfully, the metaphorical arena of modern life is much safer than the actual arena that the Roman gladiator would enter during the first century CE, facing a one-in-ten chance of not making it out alive.[11] While perhaps not a matter of life and death, the risk of the uncertain is one we must incur if we are interested in pursuing a new possibility that is aligned with our goals and dreams. In the words of bestselling author Brené Brown, internationally recognized for her research on vulnerability and shame, "When you shut down vulnerability, you shut down possibility."

For those of us who spent most of our lives holding back from taking action, we may have been under the impression that we were in a low-risk situation, when, in reality, we were in a high-risk one. Indeed, inaction can quietly have disastrous consequences. Quantifying inaction at work (by estimating a numerical figure that accounts for lost salary increases, promotions and offers from other organizations) certainly sheds light on the concrete consequences of holding back. Inaction often acts as a protective shell as we attempt to shield ourselves from vulnerability. Seeing that taking action implies that we are now "in the game," we must accept that our action can lead to either a desirable or an undesirable score. That conversation with your parents might not go the way you had intended. You may actually end up looking silly in dance class if you are not able to grasp the basic steps that are required before moving on to the more complex ones. The assignment or presentation at work might prove to be too challenging given your current skill set.

Mihaly Robert Csikszentmihalyi, the Hungarian-American professor who coined the psychological concept of "flow," warned us about the difficult emotions that can arise when the challenge of a task exceeds our skill level. Indeed, when we attempt to challenge ourselves, success is likely if we have the required skills; otherwise, we may experience mental states such as anxiety, worry and apathy.

In that sense, we have to use the valuable feedback we received by revamping our skills (if feasible) or by selecting a different challenge that is more compatible with either our current capacities or those that we can hone through deliberate practice and adequate mentorship or guidance.

Additionally, I will argue even an unfavorable outcome stemming from having taken action is generally superior to an unfavorable one stemming from not having taken action. Psychologist Carol S. Dweck popularized the idea that the "growth mindset" assumes that abilities can be developed through perseverance and learning from failure, whereas a "fixed mindset" assumes that abilities are unchangeable and that failure reflects an innate weakness. As long as we adopt a growth mindset, we can view shortcomings as mere stepping stones amidst the inevitable fluctuations of life. We can also feel empowered by the fact that we took action in the face of uncertainty and are thus more likely to do so again in the future, enhancing the probability of securing that favorable outcome the next time. Brené Brown defined vulnerability as "the willingness to show up and be seen with no guarantee of outcome." Exactly. There is no guarantee of outcome, but we must show up because 80 percent of success is showing up. Right?

Don't tell your mind, show your brain

Reading a self-improvement book is a great way to spark the top-down process of change. So is watching an inspirational documentary or even reciting positive affirmations. These behaviors are considered "top-down" because they entail starting with the mind or a strategy before implementing behavioral or tactical changes.

The proper mindset can go a long towards priming us for change. I must have watched Jim Carrey's *Yes Man* more than a dozen times while on flights to and from speaking engagements around the world. (As a side note, am I the only one who takes the solo, up-in-the-sky opportunity to shed a few tears during sappy movie moments that I'd totally eye-roll at on the ground? Just me?) *Yes Man* tells the story of a character called Carl Allen who is stuck in a negative and monotonous routine. After attending a self-improvement seminar led by a charismatic and eccentric cultlike guru, Carl makes the decision to embrace a new philosophy: saying yes to every single opportunity that comes his way. He ends up bungee jumping, taking flying lessons and learning Korean and Farsi, as well as running a marathon, among other achievements. The central idea of the film is that we can drastically change our lives by being more open to new experiences and opportunities. Whenever I go through a phase during which I am retracting from the richness of life instead of immersing myself in the ride, watching that movie serves as a wake-up call. Specifically, it's a reminder of the potential expansiveness of life's opportunities for growth and fulfillment, if and only if we say yes to challenges. Improv theater, in which the play is created spontaneously by the performers without a script, embodies that philosophy through the well-known tenet of "yes and." Explained briefly, this principle consists of saying yes to the premise or "offer" made by another person and then adding to it to co-create a scene. This approach, which encourages the performers to embrace mistakes, is also based on a philosophy of accepting reality as it is and building on it. Therefore, watching an inspirational movie like *Yes Man* and learning about the "yes and" philosophy are both effective ways to fine-tune our mindset, equipping us with an attitude that is more conducive to being proactive and willing to embrace new experiences.

Perhaps no activity elicits a mindset of adventurousness beyond our comfort zone and routine as effectively as traveling. Professor Julia Zimmermann from the University of Hagen in Germany and Professor Franz Josef Neyer from Friedrich Schiller University, also in Germany, attempted to solve that mystery in a 2016 study entitled "Do We Become a Different Person When Hitting the Road? Personality Development of Sojourners."[12] The two scholars looked at the impact of travel on personality, which was measured using the "Big Five" personality framework. The premise of the framework is that personality differences can be categorized into five major traits, or the Big Five: extroversion, conscientiousness, neuroticism, agreeableness and openness to new experiences. Accordingly, an individual's personality is a collection of different scores on these five personality traits. For example, someone could be low in extroversion, otherwise known as being more introverted; high in conscientiousness if they are studious or hardworking; high in neuroticism if they are prone to experiencing anxiety or depression; high in agreeableness if they are sociable or approachable, and high in openness to new experiences if they are imaginative and willing to venture outside their comfort zone. Keep in mind that all five of these dispositional traits exist on a spectrum. In other words, you don't have to be strictly extroverted or introverted; you might lean 62 percent towards extroversion and 38 percent towards introversion, reflecting a mix of both tendencies. In their study, researchers in Germany found that both short-term *and* long-term travel were associated with increases in openness and agreeableness as well as with a decrease in neuroticism.[13] Considering that the Big Five personality traits typically remain stable in adulthood, their malleability when exposed to travel is a fascinating insight. Having done a fair amount of solo travel myself, I can attest to the fact that travel *does* change you, usually for the better.

For the topic of embracing new and uncomfortable situations, the trait of openness to new experiences is most relevant. In a *Forbes* article, travel writer Jonathan Look Jr. wrote that "it is rare to meet a fearful traveler and it is even more rare to meet a traveler that grows more fearful as they gain experience."[14] As an avid traveler myself, I have experienced firsthand these benefits: the joy of learning about diverse cultures and the opportunity to reinvent oneself by going above and beyond my comfort zone. Now pack your swimsuit, goggles and towel. *Vamos a Colombia!*

In August 2015, I went to Colombia for 10 days. This was during my first year of employment in Toronto and I was looking forward to taking my first paid vacation. On researching potential dates for my trip, I found out that Medellin was hosting its annual flower festival, known by locals as "Feria de las Flores." Seeing that the timing worked out, I crafted an itinerary that included the urban centers of Bogotá, Medellin and the coastal city of Cartagena.

Arriving in Cartagena late at night, I went to bed right away with no specific plans for the coming day. I was, however, excited to discover the city that legendary Colombian author Gabriel García Márquez spoke so fondly about. When I woke up the next morning, I left my room to ask about breakfast and happened upon a group of people waiting in the lobby. Intrigued, I asked what they were waiting for, to which they replied that they were going to Isla Barú. So I googled Isla Barú, also known as Playa Blanca, on the lobby computer. I was instantly in awe of the beauty of the white beach in the photos. Boca Grande, on the other hand, the beach located in the city of Cartagena, is known for its black volcanic sand and murky water. Drawn to the turquoise Caribbean water of Barú, I asked the guests what time they were leaving. "The bus is arriving any minute," they told me. I rushed to my room and swiftly put on my swimming suit and packed my towel, a book by Malcolm Gladwell, 30+ SPF sunscreen, shorts, a T-shirt, some Colombian pesos and my phone. When I ran back to the lobby, the guests were just boarding the bus. I sorted out the payment for the day trip at the front desk and joined my new friends on their adventure. One hour later, we had reached Playa Blanca; the beaches were even more pristine than I expected.

After swimming for a few hours and having a delicious lunch featuring the freshest catch of the day, it was around three in the afternoon and time to go back to the hotel. While some of the guests were making their way to the bus, others seemed to stay put on their lounge chairs on the beach. When I asked whether they were heading back, they explained that they would be staying until the next bus arrived at 3 p.m. the following day. As it turns out, they had earlier booked a cabin at Hugo's Place, the hostel where we had lunch. Not wanting to leave paradise just yet, I ran to the hostel to ask about spending the night there. To my luck, they still had one available cabin with a gorgeous view of the beach. I confirmed the booking and alerted the bus driver that I would be returning the next day instead.

After enjoying the beach and socializing with the remaining travelers for a few more hours, it occurred to me that my phone's battery had run out. (I had not packed a charger.) While I initially considered asking around for a charger, it had become clear to me that not compulsively checking my phone was precisely one of the reasons why I was having such an incredible day. Indeed, by healthily disconnecting from the online world, I managed to connect with the offline world by fully immersing myself in both my natural surroundings and the social interactions. (The group I was spending time with included people from Chile, Spain and Argentina.) It also presented a great opportunity for me to practice my Spanish with a group of lovely people. While we were finishing our dinner at the hostel's beachside restaurant, a young woman came up to our table and enthusiastically asked, "*Quieren subirse a una canoa y ver plancton?*" If you haven't taken Spanish classes in forever (or ever), she wanted to know, "Do you want to get in a canoe and see some plankton?" Plankton, or more specifically "bioluminescent phytoplankton," are marine plants that possess the ability to emit light, thus creating the captivating sight of glowing waters in bioluminescent bays. Although I did not know much about plankton, the Argentinian travelers' excitement was contagious and we all decided to venture into the unknown. The guide led us to the rowboat, operated by a local guy in his twenties, and we embarked on what proved to be one of the most euphoric moments of my life. After sailing for about ten minutes, we reached a large surface of calm water, away from the crashing coastal waves. The young woman cheerfully explained that we'd be able to experience the luminescence simply by waving our hand in the water. I did just that and was instantly startled by the enchanting and magical experience of watching the plankton lighting up. After a minute or so, our amused guide told us, "*Pues, pueden nadar si quieren!*" which translates to "Well, you can swim if you'd like!" We jumped in and as we started moving around the water, we were blissfully surrounded by the sight of glowing lights.

The sudden bursts of bioluminescence in response to my movement created a dynamic and visually stunning interaction with the environment. BBC journalist Natalie Grice wrote an aptly titled article on the subject: "Bioluminescent Plankton: 'It's the Northern Lights of the Ocean.'" Psychologically, the experience evoked a sense of awe, harmony and connection to the natural world. The combination of not having checked my phone all day, spending quality time with lovely people and experiencing a stunning and interactive natural phenomenon all contributed to this being one of my favorite days on Earth. None of it would have happened had I not been in a mindset to say yes to the offer of going to Isla Barú that day.

This long story illustrates how the top-down process of adopting a mindset of openness and proactivity can create a milieu that is hospitable for taking action. Indeed, context is key. For example, planet Earth is inhabitable because it is situated at the ideal distance from the sun, shielded from harmful solar radiation by its magnetic field, kept warm by an insulating atmosphere and endowed with the necessary chemical ingredients for life, including water and carbon.[15] In the absence of those overarching conditions, the unicellular organisms that evolved into more complex life forms might never have existed. Expressed differently, the evolutionary processes of natural selection and genetic mutation that caused the eventual emergence of humankind might not have been possible in a different setting. If we think of Earth's favorable conditions (its conducive environment) as a top-down process, and the emergence of organisms with internal biological processes as a bottom-up process, we have a metaphor for how change and evolution occur. By referring to the hospitable environment as a *mindset* and to evolution as *action*, we can better appreciate the interaction between the two modes. Indeed, positive change is more likely to find a home in our lives when the proper mindset, motivation and method are in place.

However, it is key to remember this crucial nuance: Change will never occur in the absence of us *actually* taking action. In the case of conquering fear and overcoming the inner stutter, it is by challenging ourselves to *act* that we proactively gather new evidence that disproves self-limiting beliefs we might have been holding. For example, when I begged my university professors to exempt me from all presentations and in-class participation, it was because I was afraid of speaking up in class, since I expected others to laugh at me for sounding different. Someone else might similarly hold back for different reasons, perhaps because they think others will harshly evaluate every word they say and come to the conclusion that their ideas are foolish or not worth sharing. I could have read a million books about why what people think should not determine my self-worth. So long as I did not raise my hand and speak, however, no amount of positive thinking and mindset work could generate the outcomes I sought. Focusing on the action piece constitutes the bottom-up approach of executing the change.

As we take action, we also realize that our desired outcome is not the approval of others; rather, it's about being able to take action at all, regardless of whether approval ever emerges. Many of us get lost in the theoretical by placing too much weight on the cognitive piece compared to the significance of the behavioral. Author Mark Manson wrote an article about self-improvement "junkies" who feel the need to "jump on every new seminar, read all the latest books, listen to all the podcasts, hire all the life coaches and open all their chakras."[16] In his view, the junkie is constantly seeking some magic tip, technique or silver bullet of information that will create their next big breakthrough.[17]

While I would not have written this book if I did not believe in the crucial role that self-improvement literature can play in our lives, I have to constantly emphasize the irreplaceability of action. In my view, both the top-down and the bottom-up processes must exist simultaneously to provide us with the proper overarching guidance as well as the indispensable action that no amount of thought experiment and hypothetical tinkering can replace. When we develop the habits of courage and action, we are generating new memories that link fear to action as opposed to inaction. We also become strongly aware of all the positive outcomes and changes that may have occurred only because of direct behavior of taking action. These new memories then act as an updated database that will positively sway us towards acting more regularly and across different situations in the future.

According to the theory of operant conditioning, developed by psychologist B.F. Skinner, behavior that is followed by rewards will be repeated, whereas behavior that is punished will occur less frequently.[18] Keep in mind, however, that what constitutes reward and punishment is in part up to us. I have found that the rewards do not always have to be blatantly obvious for us to feel incentivized to repeat a behavior. For instance, if I'm at a networking event and I go up to a group of people to introduce myself, and one of them giggles when I begin to stutter, the pride I experience from challenging myself and doing something I find uncomfortable can supersede the temporary and minor setback (no matter how much it might suck in the moment). Seeing that action was taken in the face of fear, that moment is, by definition, a victorious one.

Research on motivation backs the idea that intrinsic motivation is more effective and sustainable than extrinsic motivation. Extrinsic motivation entails doing something with the hopes of receiving an external reward, while intrinsic motivation is a drive that comes from within.[19] Say, for example, you go up to introduce yourself to the group at the networking event with the goal of being rewarded by their validation, quantified by their positive reaction and their interest in staying connected via social media. You might interpret the experience without those outcomes as a failure. Conversely, if you've challenged yourself to face your inner stutter and you approached that group to introduce yourself and have a conversation, you would have, by definition, already achieved your objective. Indeed, intrinsic motivation is powerful because it can act as a continuous source of motivation.[20]

In his *Harvard Business Review* article "Understanding the Power of Intrinsic Motivation," Stefan Falk argues that one of the ways to tap into our intrinsic motivation is by understanding how one task fits into the bigger picture.[21] In my keynotes, I often speak about three mindset shifts that empowered me to change my relationship with fear: (1) desensitization through repeated exposure; (2) the insignificance of the moment through contextual gratitude (more about this later); and (3) connecting *why* this is a fear you wish to conquer. Whenever we manage to focus on the potentially amazing outcomes that might happen because we took action, we are less likely to feel overwhelmed by the temporary discomfort that is associated with the fear. For example, by viewing the act of introducing yourself to that group of strangers as a meaningful step towards the realization of your grand goal of conquering fear and fulfilling your potential, the relevance of the short-term feedback you received is drastically reduced.

While the reactions we receive in social interactions can be interpreted as data for refining our social intelligence and skills, they ought not be perceived as the ultimate reward. This distinction applies to other areas of life, including whether or not we will remain committed to our exercise routine. A study published in the *American Journal of Health Behavior* found that by looking at the participant's level of intrinsic motivation, we could predict whether or not they would commit to their exercise routine.[22]An individual motivated to go to the gym to receive validation from others, such as compliments or a growing number of likes on social media when posting progress photos, is less likely to persist in the pursuit compared to the person who derives joy from working out as well as improving strength and well-being. By the same token, if you see every session at the gym as an integral part of your journey towards becoming the best version of yourself, you are less likely to feel discouraged if you're not reaping the extrinsic rewards of getting praised for looking more muscular or leaner. Therefore, when it comes to conquering fear, focusing on the inherent victory of doing the thing we fear as opposed to ruminating about a disappointing outcome will lay the foundation for a more sustainable and prosperous journey towards the realization of our potential.

I know what some of you might be thinking. "Joze, that all sounds great in theory, but how the heck do we get ourselves to view humiliating moments as stepping stones as opposed to taking them personally *while* we are in the difficult moments themselves?" If I could go back in time and walk my old self through this cognitive rite of passage, I would remind the "old Joze" that the difficult moment is but *one* moment out of millions that we will experience in our lifetime. Interestingly, the monk Saint Bede defined "moment" as a period of time that spans 90 seconds.[23] Assuming the average lifespan in North America to be 80 years, that "moment" constitutes 90 seconds out of over 2,522, 880,000 seconds. Don't bother calculating that percentage; the answer is practically zero. Based on my personal experience, I have found that the duration of the most uncomfortable moment of fear is typically even shorter than a full 90 seconds. Once, I was in a two-minute ice bath at Othership, a mental wellness center that I regularly go to in Toronto. Ice baths have been shown to have a plethora of benefits, including reduced inflammation, immunity support and mood boosting.[24] The initial extreme level of discomfort lasted for about 30 seconds, during which my thought, on repeat, was "there is no way I am going to be able to handle it. I'd better get up and leave now!" Then, that state of agitation simmered down to a still uncomfortable yet more manageable mental and physical state. In fact, the thought of wanting to flee in the first 30 seconds pops up every time I go there, in spite of having had it many times before.

A similar phenomenon occurs almost every time I go on stage, with the bulk of the discomfort vanishing a few seconds into the beginning of my performance. In "Stage Fright," an article on WebMD, Hedy Marks confirms that "stage fright is usually worse before the performance and often goes away once you get started."[25] In other words, when we speak about a fear-inducing or very uncomfortable moment, we are often referring to *psychological pain* that lasts for just a few seconds. Keep this contextualization in mind as we consider the trade-offs of conquering fear. While that temporary moment of discomfort can be a painful one, research backs up the old adage of "no pain, no gain." Indeed, this philosophy, popularized by actress and fitness guru Jane Fonda, was scientifically validated in a bestselling book written by an addiction psychiatrist: *Dopamine Nation* by Anna Lembke.

In her book, Lembke, chief of the Stanford Addiction Medicine Clinic, pointed out that the same areas of the brain that process pleasure also process pain.[26] She added that pleasure and pain operate in balance through the body's self-regulating mechanism that strives to maintain equilibrium.[27] Every time the balance tips towards either pleasure or pain, this mechanism ensures that balance is regained through delivering either pain or pleasure. For example, the "pain" induced by doing something uncomfortable, such as going up on stage, talking to someone new, going through a tough workout or plunging into an ice bath, will be followed by a release in the neurotransmitter dopamine. Alternatively, pursuing instant gratification will unfortunately be followed by pain. For instance, compulsively checking our social media notifications tends to create instant pleasure followed by a negative state of mind such as anxiety or depression.[28] I am practically certain that both you and I, dear reader, have experienced firsthand the nefarious mental health effects of compulsively checking our phones. A 2023 study found that Americans check their phones, on average, 144 times a day.[29] By the time this book is published, that number will likely have grown. Whenever I'm going through a tough phase and slipping into unhealthy coping mechanisms, 144 times a day feels like a rookie number.

We'll discuss mental wellness later in the book, but for now, we are more focused on the fact that seeking discomfort (i.e., pain) proves to be an unexpected gateway to satisfaction. How awesome is it to realize that the discomfort of doing something scary is not only temporary, it can, potentially, transform our lives for the better in the long term. But it will also feel good in the medium term through our body's natural mechanisms of homeostasis. Hallelujah. I am, of course, not implying that changing our personal narrative around fear and discomfort is easy. While we are in the middle of those moments, our fight-or-flight response kicks in and we want nothing more than to escape. Taking a moment to respond instead of reacting is one of the most empowering lessons that you can incorporate into your personal philosophy. In fact, I am reminded of a pertinent story that I would like to share with you.

In my second year at McGill University, I moved into a new student building with three close friends I had met in the dorms the year before. Our United Nations-esque apartment included a Swiss-Colombian (Alex), a French-Ecuadorian (Pierre), a Serbo-Croatian (Igor) and a Lebanese-Armenian (Joze). When we were not engaging in lively discussions about Pablo Escobar, now former Ecuadorian president Rafael Correa, the Yugoslav wars, the Lebanese civil war, the Ottoman empire or the Armenian genocide, we were typical college students who talked about who we had crushes on. Once, one of my housemates had recently started dating a woman who lived in the same building as we did, and he wanted to introduce her to me. I agreed. When I first saw her and introduced myself,

I struggled while saying my name, as I often do, and got stuck on the letter J for about 10 seconds. She interrupted me and said, "J-j-j-j-j-j-j? What's that?" As a 19-year-old student hoping to come across as cool, that reaction hurt my feelings. My embarrassment and humiliation turned into resentment, and I instantly judged this woman. Indeed, I jumped to the conclusion that she must be a "bad" human being for having reacted that way to my stutter.

While my brash judgment might have felt justified in the moment, such a reaction was ultimately a lose-lose situation that nobody benefits from. A healthier response would have been to inform her that I am a person who stutters and that it takes me a bit of time to say certain words. Had she been made aware of the information she was missing, I am almost certain her reaction would have been a more understanding one. Thankfully, this healthier and more emotionally mature approach is the one I take in the vast majority of my interactions nowadays. Many of our initial reactions can be influenced by a lack of data and personal biases, as well as our own insecurities. While I am not stating that it is our responsibility to educate others about every condition, community or mental health challenge in the world, proactively advocating for ourselves minimizes unnecessary misunderstandings that get in the way of potentially favorable outcomes. If, however, the person remains ignorant or unwilling to meet you halfway after you have done your part, you are certainly not required to engage further. If it is someone you have to interact with in a professional or personal setting, then it would be crucial to address the conflict and identify a resolution. Otherwise, if they don't show good faith towards your genuine effort to create a positive social dynamic, I would suggest moving on. I have often said that having a stutter is like having a built-in assh*le-filtering device!

In spite of the uncomfortable interaction with my friend's new girlfriend, I believe it planted the seed for something I would realize a bit later in life. If I had a time machine and could go back a few years, I wouldn't tell my younger self to leave the premises to avoid that interaction before she arrived. That experience remained valuable from the standpoint of collecting life data and learning; it was a lived cautionary tale about the importance of deliberately responding to discomfort as opposed to impulsively reacting to it. It also taught me about resisting the urge to instantly judge the other person solely based on their initial reaction and giving them the benefit of the doubt instead. As my grandmother repeatedly said during my childhood and teenage years, "We should not judge others; we should understand them." Viewing an uncomfortable and potentially embarrassing situation as a portal for eventual growth is also aligned with the words of Nelson Mandela: "I never lose. I either win or I learn."

When we take action, we win.

Chapter 5 takeaways

- Fear and action do not have to be mutually exclusive. Fear and action can coexist.
- Whereas action might not eliminate fear, it can counteract the negative consequences of fear, namely inaction and regret.
- When we speak about a fear-inducing or very uncomfortable moment, we are often referring to *psychological* pain that lasts a few seconds.
- When we take action, we win, regardless of the outcome.

Meet Dan Shaikh, 33

"I was always the shy immigrant kid from Pakistan who didn't speak English well," Dan told me when I first asked him about his journey. His gaze dropped slightly as he recalled the past. Dan's language deficiencies made it difficult for him to communicate with his classmates at a school near Toronto. He experienced plenty of thoughts and feelings that he was unable to express, often appearing lost in thought. Instead of speaking, he simply nodded along to fit in, his shoulders hunched as if to make himself smaller. Indeed, he would hide from people whenever he could, a visible discomfort etched across his face. In gym class, when teams were being formed, he was terrified of being the last one picked, his face flushing with embarrassment. Dan vividly recalls that while he was trying to hide under the curtains, his classmates were still able to see his legs. Going into middle school, he dealt with the fear of standing out on account of his inability to express himself while also looking different from everyone else. As a way of dealing with the toxic shame that controlled his life for the decade that followed, Dan would often isolate himself and use his computer as a source of comfort. At age 19, he took a very first step to overcome his fear.

At university, Dan fell in love with a woman. Seeing that he was reading some literature about regret at the time, he felt encouraged to go for it, his eyes lighting up with newfound determination. While he did get rejected, he kept on reading about the topic of regrets. He found that many people had regrets linked to their career, passion and purpose. When he was in his early twenties, Dan started working at a large organization and he had disposable income that allowed him to explore different hobbies. In fact, he faced his fear of heights by jumping off a plane and skydiving, his exhilaration palpable. "If I could do this, what else could I do that I'm afraid of?" he recalls thinking at the time. He continued his adrenaline-fueled adventure by doing Toronto's CN Tower EdgeWalk, which consists of walking on a narrow ledge around the exterior of the tower's main pod, situated at a height of 1,136 feet. Then, he even signed up to take flying and hang-gliding lessons, his excitement tangible. On completing all these audacious goals, he gained more confidence in his abilities and decided that perhaps he could finish his bucket list by age 25.

Dan was doing five new experiences a week to constantly push himself out of his comfort zone. One of those experiences entailed a world travel solo trip. While he was gaining significant momentum on his journey of overcoming fear, he still experienced many setbacks along the way. He vividly recalls experiencing loneliness while he was at the hostel in Thailand. Indeed, Dan continued feeling inadequate because the other guests were not talking to him. This experience led him to check out of the hostel and book a five-star hotel instead. In his luxurious hotel room, he started to cry because he did not feel he had earned any of it. Tears streamed down his face as he confronted his self-doubt. He was simply avoiding the other location where he felt inadequate. That being said, the journey continued.

When asked about his strategy for conquering fear, Dan repeated the idea of the five new things he would be doing every week. He also felt it was helpful to tell people around him what he was doing to leverage the power of social pressure and accountability. To get the ball rolling, Dan kept his list relatively simple by including tasks such as ordering something new on the menu, trying a new restaurant, taking a different way home or even going on the Groupon app to try something new. One day, a friend suggested that he attend an event called Passion Search Competition. "Passion was such a foreign idea to me as an immigrant," Dan recalled thinking with a smile, a hint of amusement in his eyes. Not only did Dan say yes, but he also became a volunteer for the group, hosting the event. While he was there, he met someone who encouraged him to join a Toastmasters public-speaking club. Incidentally, Dan and I met at Toastmasters while we were both figuring out our respective lives. And that's where Dan met Rina Rovinelli, his future business partner. Just like Jim

Carrey in the movie *Yes Man*, saying yes changed his life.

Overcoming fear changed everything for Dan. In fact, if you went back to his school days, you'd see the shy kid who blended with the background, his presence barely noticeable. "I was not supposed to become the guy that I am now!" he told me, his pride evident in his tone. Having cofounded Speaker Slam with Rina, whom I also met through Toastmasters, Dan is now center stage at work and in his life. Members of the community regard him as a confident and influential person.

When asked about what he would tell his old self or someone who is currently facing fear, Dan likes to remind people that things can get better and that you have to believe there is a better version of you that exists out there. Instead of letting our past define us, he encourages people to decide to start becoming that better version today. "Transformation occurs when we start embodying that higher version of ourselves in the present," Dan wisely says.

The inner stutter corner

Dan's inner stutter, rooted in his feeling of being different as an immigrant kid with an accent, functioned much like a physical stutter. Just as a stutter interrupts the flow of speech, Dan's sense of being different interrupted his ability to express himself and connect with others. His limited English proficiency when he was a child as well as his immigrant background created an invisible barrier, making him feel separated from his peers and silencing him. In my conversations with immigrants or international students who speak their host country's language with an accent that makes them feel self-conscious, I've often found many parallels. Like me, they frequently avoided speaking for fear of being judged for sounding different. This inner stutter caused Dan to hold back, to nod along rather than speak and to hide rather than stand out—much like how a physical stutter can make a person hesitate to speak at all.

Over time, Dan worked to overcome his inner stutter, turning his fear and isolation into confidence by pushing himself outside of his comfort zone. Each new experience, whether skydiving, saying yes to volunteering or trying Toastmasters, was a step towards breaking through the internal barrier that once held him back. In the same way that someone with a stutter might work on it through speech fluency or control techniques, Dan actively tackled his inner sense of otherness by facing his fears. This journey empowered him to unlock his potential, ultimately becoming the confident, engaged person he had always wanted to be.

Therefore, Dan's inner stutter, his feeling of otherness, was as powerful an obstacle as any physical stutter, requiring courage and persistence to overcome. By confronting it head-on, he was able to go from a quiet, shrinking presence to someone who not only stands out with confidence and purpose, but who also empowers others to do the same.

Recognize your inner stutter, stop holding back and be like Dan!

6.

Micro-moments of bravery

It's not the big things that add up in the end; it's the hundreds, thousands, or millions of little things that separate the ordinary from the extraordinary.

—DARREN HARDY

In his popular TED Talk "Try Something New for 30 Days," Matt Cutts says, "I learned that when I made small, sustainable changes, things I could keep doing, they were more likely to stick. There's nothing wrong with big, crazy challenges. In fact, they're a ton of fun. But they're less likely to stick." Matt told the audience that he went from being "a desk-dwelling computer nerd" to "the kind of guy who bikes to work" before achieving the unexpected goal of hiking up Mount Kilimanjaro.[1] In other words, by focusing on the "micro-moments" of biking to work regularly, his life gradually shifted in ways that he could not have imagined. Focusing on those micro-moments ultimately led to the macro-moment of climbing the tallest mountain in Africa. In his iconic bestselling book *Atomic Habits: An Easy & Proven Way to Build Good Habits & Break Bad Ones*, James Clear identifies the three layers of behavior change: changing our outcomes, changing our process and ultimately changing our identity.[2] Changing our identity often involves changing the beliefs we hold about ourselves and the world around us. According to Clear, changing our beliefs is based on two steps: Decide the type of person you want to be and prove it to yourself with small wins.[3] One of my small wins is a daily meditation practice. It all started with 240 hours of silence.

In 2014, I completed a 10-day Vipassana meditation silent retreat in a peaceful center surrounded by luscious Lebanese mountains. But first, some context regarding how I ended up at that retreat. On completing my master's degree and deciding to return home, I started practicing Kundalini yoga, popularized by Yogi Bhajan, at a center called NOK Yoga Shala, in the Saifi Village neighborhood of Beirut, owned by New York financier and meditation practitioner Nigol Koulajian. Whereas the more commonly practiced Hatha, Vinyasa and Ashtanga forms of yoga emphasize physical postures, the Kundalini practice incorporates meditation, breathwork and chanting to a greater extent than its counterparts. The director of NOK Yoga Shala at the time, Hisham Hert, having sensed that I was drawn towards the meditational aspects of Kundalini, suggested that I look into Vipassana. *Vipassana* is a word in the Pali language that translates to "insight" or the ability to see things as they really are. One of India's oldest techniques of meditation, it was rediscovered by the Buddha over 2,500 years ago, who taught it as a "universal remedy for universal ills."[4] It was passed down through an unbroken chain of teachers. Until his passing in 2013, S.N. Goenka was responsible for appointing the current and future teachers in the tradition.[5] For those of you who have completed a Vipassana retreat, you would have heard Goenka's unique yet calming voice at the beginning and end of every one-hour-long meditation. Over the span of 10 days, the participants engage in what can only be described as a mentally and physically rigorous and challenging experience. A typical day starts with the first meditation at 4:30 a.m. Here is the schedule followed by all participants:

4:00–4:30 A.M.:	Wake-up bell
4:30–6:30 A.M.:	Meditate in the hall or in your room
6:30–8:00 A.M.:	Breakfast and rest
8:00–9:00 A.M.:	Group meditation in the hall
9:00–11:00 A.M.:	Meditate in the hall or in your room according to the teacher's instructions
11:00 A.M.–12:00 P.M.:	Lunch and rest
12:00–1:00 P.M.:	Rest and interviews with the teacher
1:00–2:30 P.M.:	Meditate in the hall or in your room
2:30–3:30 P.M.:	Group meditation in the hall
3:30–5:00 P.M.:	Meditate in the hall or in your room according to the teacher's instructions
5:00–6:00 P.M.:	Tea break
6:00–7:00 P.M.:	Group meditation in the hall
7:00–8:15 P.M.:	Discourse and instruction
8:15–9:00 P.M.:	Group meditation in the hall
9–9:30 P.M.:	Question time
9:30 P.M.:	Retire to your room; lights out

And then, you repeat that routine for nine more days. While the most common retreat format is 10 days, you can also do sessions that last one day, three days, 20 days or 30 days. On my tenth day there, the teacher advised us to maintain our new mindfulness practice daily, through one hour of meditation in the morning and another hour of meditation in the evening. After successfully completing the 10 days, I returned to my childhood home, where breakfast and the daily newspaper were waiting for me on the dining room table. Following this unique learning experience, I looked forward to attending my next Kundalini class at the NOK Yoga Shala center and to tell Hisham all about my experience.

As I took a sip of tea and started munching on my manoushe—a Lebanese flatbread made with za'atar, which is a blend of dried thyme, sumac, sesame seeds and salt—my Zen state came to a sudden jolt. The newspaper was opened to the obituary page and my jaw dropped when I read the name Hisham Hert. I sipped my coffee in a state of shock until my mother arrived and consoled me. She had read the obituary earlier and had left the newspaper open for me to read and process the news at my own pace. Aren't moms the best?

Having experienced the benefits of meditation while at the retreat, I was committed to making it a part of my life. While I managed to implement the recommended practice of one hour in the morning and one hour in the evening for the first six days, I unfortunately abandoned meditation altogether for the next five years. The goal of two hours of meditation every day was simply too rigorous. Five years later, however, in 2019, I started going to a mindfulness studio called Mindset Brain Gym in Toronto's Yorkville neighborhood. Completing a daily 20-minute meditation class proved more manageable than aiming for two one-hour-long meditation sessions each day. At the time of writing this book, I practice a Vipassana-style meditation for 15 minutes most mornings. Though I don't rule out the possibility of someday participating in another 10-day Vipassana retreat, being able to implement my current 15-minute routine occurred through small daily actions rather than a revolutionary overnight change. Indeed, most change tends to occur through micro-moments rather than major once-in-a-lifetime milestones. To understand change, let's consider biological evolution.

While I was studying at McGill University in Montreal, I enrolled in a fascinating course called Evolutionary Anthropology, taught by Professor Andre Costopoulos. We examined the role of evolutionary theory in social anthropology, archaeology, physical anthropology and linguistics. One of the lectures focused on the difference between "punctuated equilibrium" and "phyletic gradualism." According to paleontologists Niles Eldredge and Stephen Jay Gould, the punctuated equilibrium theory states that evolution includes long periods of stability with little activity, punctuated by bursts of activity.[6] Phyletic gradualism, on the other hand, a view that is more aligned with Darwinian evolutionary theory, states that transformation occurs through a "pattern of sustained, directional and incremental evolutionary change over a long period."[7]

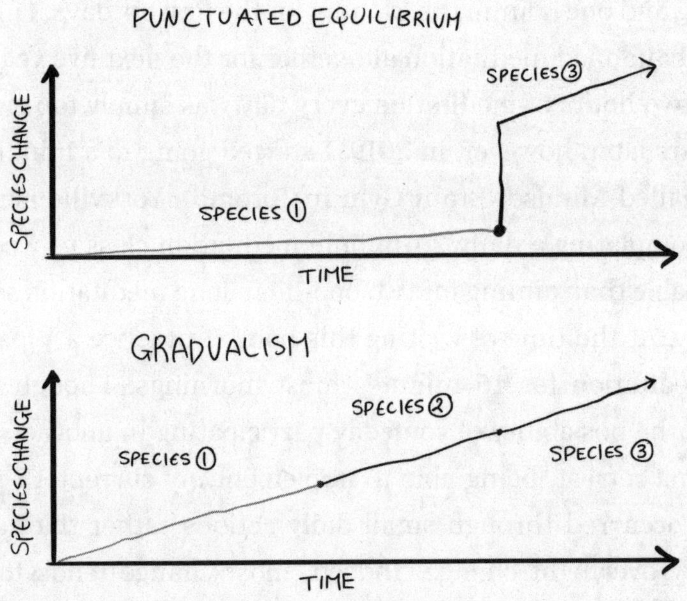

If you were to apply the theory of punctuated equilibrium to your personal evolution, you would focus on bigger, exceptional milestones, such as a major promotion, winning an award, meeting the love of your life or going on a 10-day meditation retreat. Those moments would constitute the bursts of activity occurring after long and stable, or boring, periods.

Alternatively, viewing personal transformation through the lens of gradualism would encourage you to prioritize smaller regular milestones, such as waking up earlier every morning to set yourself up for success, working at your craft for a half hour every day, saying hello to new people or starting each morning with a short meditation. Since there is no clear consensus among evolutionary biologists about which of the two theories is more accurate, why not apply the one that serves us the best when it comes to our personal lives? Regardless of the exact nature of reality, the beliefs we hold will often influence the outcomes we reap. According to psychologist Carol Dweck, students who believe they can get smarter and that effort makes them smarter will invest the effort that ultimately leads to higher achievement.[8] We can therefore *choose* to experience life as though it is governed by gradualism in order to cultivate the behaviors that will culminate in conquering our fears and realizing our fullest potential.

As far as personal growth is concerned, I believe that shying away from the punctuated equilibrium view, which depends too heavily on massive sudden changes in our lives, is the optimal strategy for us to follow. While we will certainly experience a combination of sudden and gradual changes in our lives, focusing on gradual change gives us a stronger sense of control and a greater ability to influence outcomes. Not only do we tend to overestimate the significance of the bigger milestones in our lives, but we also can forget that those huge milestones are often the result of the accumulation of a plethora of micro-moments during which we did something we found uncomfortable or scary.

Through repetition, we begin to associate the desired behavior with our new identity. Having performed hundreds of stand-up comedy sets, it would be safe to say that I'm the kind of guy who goes up on stage. After challenging myself to talk to tens of thousands of strangers, it would also be safe to say that I'm the kind of guy who socializes and enjoys meeting new people. After meditating on countless mornings, it would be safe to say that I'm the kind of guy who meditates. After all my professional speaking engagements at conferences around the world, it would be safe to say that I am an international public speaker. Tell me what kind of person you are trying to become, and I will tell you what micro-moments of bravery to implement in your daily life. But first, I hope you're hungry because we're about to talk about pies. In case you're wondering, lemon meringue pie is my favorite kind. What's yours?

The pie chart of your life

When we think about our accomplishments or defeats, our mind fixates on the most pronounced manifestation of those achievements or losses. When it comes to defeats, we often focus on big outcomes, such as getting fired, a relationship ending or a health issue emerging as opposed to recalling the series of negative micro-moments that may have led to those outcomes. For instance, we often focus on the day a breakup happened rather than the gradual drift and little conflicts that led there. When it comes to accomplishments, similarly, we tend to focus on the grand Instagrammable milestones that punctuate our years. For instance, if I wish to reminisce on my speaking journey of the past few years, a few key moments stand out: delivering a talk in front of 3,000 entrepreneurs at the Archangel Summit in 2018, a stage on which such notables as Gary Vee, Simon Sinek and Elizabeth Gilbert have spoken; speaking on the TEDx stages five times; performing stand-up comedy at the Queen Elizabeth Theatre in front of a thousand people; performing at the Beirut waterfront for 3,000 people; delivering keynotes at organizations worldwide, from international conferences in Kuwait and Dubai to organizations in Los Angeles, Vancouver and Seattle. I even had a speaking engagement at the FBI in Washington, D.C. While those are events of great personal significance, they constitute a minority of the total time of the overall journey I have been on. In fact, on a day when I have a speaking engagement, assuming I may be on stage for one hour, I am not on stage for the remaining 23 hours. If we created a pie chart to depict micro-moments and macro-moments, we'd find that the macro-moments or milestones make up a relatively tiny fraction of the pie. Anybody else suddenly craving a piece of key lime pie? I really like that one, too.

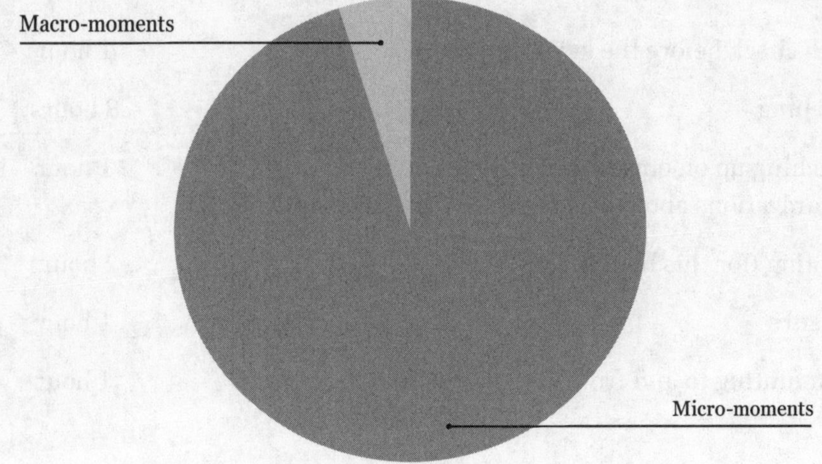

What am I doing during the remainder of the day of a speaking engagement? You can find an approximate breakdown of that day in the following chart. Welcome to a day in the life of Joze.

Macro-moment	**Duration**
Speaking engagement	1 hour

Remainder of the day	**Duration**
Rehearsing for the keynote in my hotel room	2 hours
Working on my stutter by going to a mall nearby and talking to 100 strangers	2.5 hours
Workout at the hotel gym and pool	1 hour
Meditation and breathwork	0.5 hours
Lunch	1 hour
Dinner after the speaking engagement with either some of the organizers or a friend or relative who lives in the city	2 hours
Tech check before the keynote event	1 hour
Sleeping	8 hours
Catching up on emails and having Zoom calls with organizations about other speaking engagements	1 hour
Writing (for this book!)	2 hours
Leisure	1 hour
Commuting to and from event	1 hour

To further illustrate the breakdown of the day of a speaking engagement with the macro-moment representing the time on stage and the micro-moments the time off stage, here's what a pie chart of a speaking day would look like.

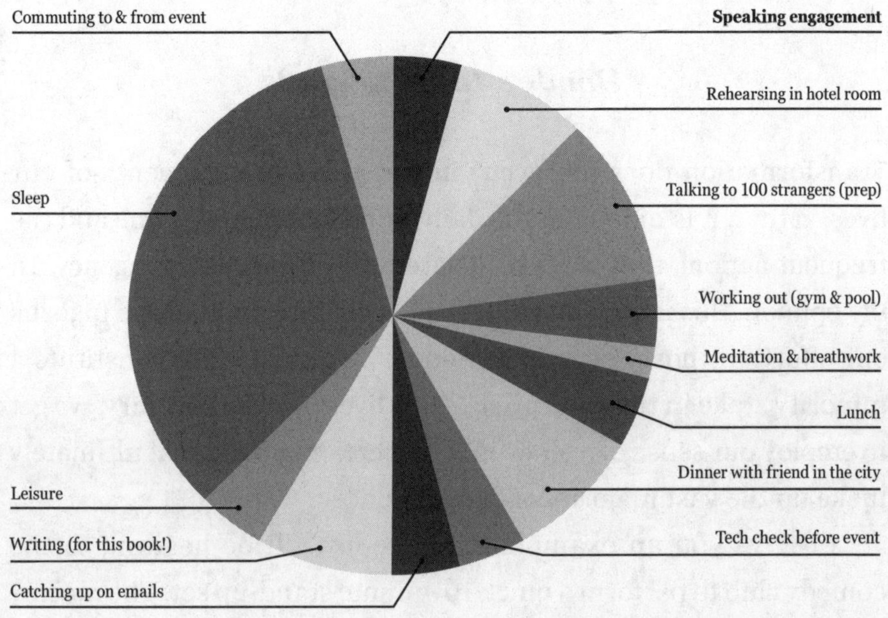

As the chart and the graph show, the "grandiose" macro-moment of being on stage in front of hundreds or thousands of people constitutes a tiny portion (about 4 percent) of a day filled with a plethora of activities that would not be considered extraordinary. In an era when glitzy social media posts aim to glorify our most significant milestones, we must remember that most of life occurs in the seemingly insignificant moments of our day. And note that if I skip one or more of the action-oriented micro-moments of my own day, the macro-moment may be affected. From experience, I have observed that my on-stage energy is compromised if I skip exercise, meditation and, of course, stuttering exercises.

So, how can we manage the destiny-shaping magical moments where the process of growth actually happens?

***Dónde está* the magic?**

Transformation does not occur in the grandiose moments of our lives; rather, it is hidden in the daily mindsets that we hone and the frequent actions that we take. Therein lies our sense of agency. In my opinion, this is good news. It implies that we do not have to focus our effort on those "once in a lifetime" moments that constitute a minority stake in the enterprise of our lives. On the contrary, we get to employ our sense of agency in the micro-moments that ultimately make up the vast majority of our existence.

I'll give you an example. Later today, I'll be heading to the comedy club to perform a quick 10-minute stand-up set. The macro-moment in this situation is being on stage for those 10 minutes. Before I make my way to the comedy club, however, I'll be going out to challenge myself by asking for directions from 50 or 100 strangers at the mall. In doing that, I prepare myself for the high intensity of the stage through the magic of desensitization. In spite of having been terrified of speaking in front of anyone for most of my life, the magic occurs in every single moment that I voluntarily expose myself to a dose of that fear. Whereas the audience sees only the macro-moment, I am aware of the micro-moments that make the macro-moment possible in the first place. My agency, or the *input*, occurs through the 50 or 100 instances of courage required to get through that exercise before going on that stand-up comedy stage—the *output*. People mostly see our output. A philosophical thought experiment accurately encapsulates this discrepancy; somehow, it involves bats.

Born in Belgrade in the former Yugoslavia in 1937 to German Jewish refugees, Thomas Nagel arrived in New York City as a two-year-old. He went on to study at Cornell, Oxford and Harvard universities before teaching at Berkeley and Princeton and ultimately landing at New York University, where he is currently the University Professor of Philosophy and Law Emeritus. The first time I heard of him was in 2010, while enrolled in a class on philosophy of mind at McGill University. This illuminating course was taught by Professor David Davies, a quirky and eloquent British man. I absolutely loved his class. Throughout the semester, we explored the nature of mental phenomena through the works of various philosophers, including René Descartes, Daniel Dennett and, you guessed it, Thomas Nagel.

At one point in the semester, the unsuspecting students of PHIL 306 were assigned to read a paper with one of the most unusual titles I'd ever come across: "What Is It Like to Be a Bat?" In his renowned 1974 paper, Nagel attempts to tackle the following question: Can a human ever truly understand what it is like, subjectively, to be a bat? According to Nagel, while we might know that bats perceive the external world through sonar or echolocation to make discriminations of distance, size, shape, motion and texture, their experience is not subjectively like anything we can experience or imagine.[9] In other words, we can never actually know what it is like to be a bat.

A similar question was tackled by Frank Jackson, an emeritus philosopher at the Australian National University. In his 1982 paper, "Epiphenomenal Qualia," Jackson proposes a thought experiment in which Mary, a brilliant scientist, is forced to investigate the world from a black and white room via a black and white television monitor.[10] Mary has never been outside of that room. Given that she specializes in the neurophysiology of vision, she learns all there is to know about what goes on in our brains whenever we come across ripe tomatoes and experience the color red. Jackson cleverly argues that when Mary is released from her monochromatic room and sees the color red for the first time, she will gain new knowledge about the world. In other words, her scientific understanding of red is different from the actual experience of seeing it.

No amount of objective perception can ever replace the subjective experience that one might have. If we apply philosophical insights to how we perceive other people's lived experiences, we can infer that no amount of objective knowledge about their behavior would paint a clear picture of what that person goes through. We will never truly know, with perfect accuracy, what it is like to be James, Ali, Sharron, Aysan, Jessica or Ping.

In *The Dictionary of Obscure Sorrows*, John Koenig invented words to express emotions that do not currently have English-language words associated with them. He defined *sonder* as "the realization that each random passerby is living a life as vivid and complex as your own—populated with their own ambitions, friends, routines, worries and inherited craziness—an epic story that continues invisibly around you like an anthill sprawling deep underground, with elaborate passageways to thousands of other lives that you'll never know existed, in which you might appear only once, as an extra sipping coffee in the background, as a blur of traffic passing on the highway, as a lighted window at dusk."[11] Except for when we deliberately sonder, our focus typically remains on the objectively perceivable macro-moments in people's lives. In other words, we tend to be oblivious to the micro-moments that shape both their daily subjective existence and the eventual exploits and setbacks that the world sees.

I attempted to dive into the magic of the micro-moments that enabled a refugee in the United States to become an Emmy-nominated journalist and author. Shall we go to Los Angeles?

When I first met journalist Silva Harapetian, I was curious to know about the journey she had been on to fulfill her professional dreams. Aware of the discrepancy between what the world sees and what the individual knows to be true, I asked her about the "input" that she implemented in order to bring about the "output" that others could see. Silva shared, a hint of vulnerability in her voice, that her fear was two-pronged: On the one hand, the fact that English was not her first language acted as a barrier given her primary ambition was to enter the public-facing world of journalism and media. On the other hand—her eyes flickered with a mix of determination and apprehension—she admitted that she also faced the fear of not being worthy enough to accomplish her dreams. Seeing that her parents escaped Iran during the 1979 revolution, Silva often felt the weight of expectation pressing down on her shoulders. She spoke softly as she reflected on the sacrifices her parents had made to ensure their children could build promising futures in the United States. When I asked Silva what inspired her to confront her fear, her expression shifted; a small smile appeared. "What if I don't face my fears?" she said, her tone firm. According to her, the consequences of not facing fear are much more significant than the fear of having done the scary thing in the first place.

This mindset shaped Silva's career since the early days. She recounted, her voice animated with excitement, how she moved, all by herself, to different cities, taking up a variety of jobs in the film industry. "I first went from Los Angeles to work in Fresno for five years," she shared, before she transitioned to being a producer in Bakersfield for two years. Even though she was initially working behind the scenes, she continually improved her presentation skills and put together a visual résumé to apply for TV and on-camera jobs. On an ordinary day in Bakersfield, she received a new job offer and moved to Lawton in Oklahoma for her first-ever on-camera reporter job. "That was a turning point," she said, her tone thick with nostalgic pride. Subsequently, she worked in Austin, Texas, before being recruited by an executive in Detroit, where she worked for three years, between 2006 and 2009, covering the Great Recession. Perhaps seeking warmer pastures, Silva then worked for 12 years as an on-air television journalist for CBS Miami, where she covered presidential campaigns, multiple hurricanes and several mass shootings, including the tragic events at the nightclub Pulse in Orlando in 2016 and at the high school in Parkland in 2018. When I asked her about where she found the relentless motivation to continue to take on opportunities that she found challenging and uncomfortable, she straightened her back and explained that she had identified strategies against the negative and critical voice in her head.

First, she periodically reminded herself to zoom out from a situation that is scary in order to gain a healthy distance and detachment from the fear. "I was always focused on the bigger picture," she exclaimed, her hands gesturing passionately. "I had a playlist with songs that had to do with believing in yourself, and whenever the inner voice of doubt crept up, I would start playing those songs." A smile of triumph broke through as she spoke. When she said that,

I instantly thought of Journey's iconic song "Don't Stop Believin'." BRB, I'm going to listen to it real quick.

Okay, I'm back and I'm feeling pumped! Second, Silva also used the method of reverse engineering, starting with the end in mind and identifying all the little steps that would have to go into the achievement of the final goal. "I had to come up with bite-size actions," she explained, her voice steady and confident. "Like working on my writing, improving my pronunciation in English and training for appearing on camera." Those were the micro-moments of bravery that enabled her to tackle her own inner stutter. Indeed, by breaking down the grand objective into these separate steps, she found it much easier to overcome the inner stutter associated with entering the media world as a foreign-born woman with an accent. Lastly, Silva knew about the value of having mentors and learning from those who had already gone further in the field. By asking them for advice, she managed to shorten her learning curve and reach her goals. "I was super focused. I had tunnel vision. I knew what I wanted to do and who I wanted to be. Nothing got in the way," she exclaimed with a sense of both humility and pride.

Any journey of transformation comes with both mountains and valleys. As the African proverb wisely states, "Smooth seas do not make skillful sailors." In other words, it is often in the rugged waters that our skills are sharpened. Subsequently, the sharpening of our skill set spills over into other areas of our lives, thereby empowering us to elevate our success further. Unsurprisingly, when I asked Silva about challenges she faced, she immediately said one word: *rejection*. "I sent out hundreds of résumé tapes and," she added with a genuine laugh, "I've kept, to this day, stacks of rejection letters from different TV stations!"

Silva's mood then shifted from lightheartedness to a more serious tone when she shared that some of the rejections were painful. "When they told me I sounded or looked too foreign or that my features were rough, I felt sad and angry because those were not things I could change." Additionally, she was perplexed by the fact that many of those stations did not appreciate her international perspective as a woman who escaped Iran and spent a few years in Germany as a refugee before moving to the US and learning the English language from scratch. "This was before being foreign or having a diverse background and perspective were considered cool!" she added, with a smile. According to Silva, at times her family and friends were worried about her and all the hardships she went through alone in a new city every few years. "My mom would call me and cry over the phone almost every day," she said, with chagrin.

Through this transformational journey, not only did Silva achieve her dreams, but she also ended up seeing the world, creating relationships with people she never thought she would meet and becoming aware of stories she would not have known about otherwise. As an independent journalist today, she wakes up excited about her work. "Having fulfilled these goals doesn't mean that I don't feel fear anymore," she said. According to Silva, while everything worth doing will make us feel fear, we have to decide whether or not we truly desire the outcome that awaits on the other side of that fear. She concluded our chat by saying that people should be encouraged to enjoy the process, no matter how challenging it might seem.

Through micro-moments of bravery, or "bite-sized actions" in Silva's words, truly unexpected, grander outcomes can emerge. Seeing that your agency will be most effective and influential in those micro-moments that precede the macro-moment, I invite you to consider ways in which you can deliberately add micro-moments of bravery to your daily life in order to prepare and generate the subsequent grandiose macro-moments that you desire.

Millions of moments

Not only are preparatory moments small in terms of perceived significance; they are also numerous. In fact, it is precisely this numerousness that creates the long-lasting change we seek. In the words of historian and philosopher Will Durant, "We are what we repeatedly do . . . therefore excellence is not an act, but a habit." Ultimately, a person's willingness to overcome their inner stutter by repeating those millions of micro-moments is also linked to their work ethic. Angela Duckworth, renowned author and professor of psychology at the University of Pennsylvania, popularized the term *grit*. Her 2013 TED Talk, "Grit: The Power of Passion and Perseverance," was viewed more than 30 million times. In that talk, Angela explained, "Grit is passion and perseverance for very long-term goals. Grit is having stamina. Grit is sticking with your future, day in, day out, not just for the week, not just for the month, but for years, and working really hard to make that future a reality. Grit is living life like it's a marathon, not a sprint."[12]

Seeing that, on average, 50 percent of our individual differences are genetic and 50 percent are environmental,[13] the individual will always have some degree of agency in shaping their environment in a way that can favorably impact their destiny. Unfortunately, you might not be able to jump into a time machine and retroactively alter the environment you inhabited during childhood and teenage years. Traumatic events during one's childhood are associated with greater rates of PTSD, depression, anxiety, antisocial behaviors and substance use disorders.[14] Such circumstances can pose challenges for individuals who seek to become the best version of themselves. Therapy and other types of support are crucial in such cases, and intentionally taking action to surround ourselves with supportive peers can also empower us to counteract a difficult start. While having a stutter caused emotional wounds while I was growing up, a sense of grit empowered me to gradually alter the fabric of my life.

Later on, I worked on shaping my environment in order to maximize the 50 percent of those differences that are more malleable than the genetic part of the equation.* This work ethic was built through deliberately completing tasks that contributed towards my objective, no matter how uncomfortable they were. By adopting a growth mindset, we are able to focus on enhancing our abilities through perseverance as well as by learning from failure. And who best to learn about the growth mindset from than champions at the top of their game?

When asked about Michael Jordan's athletic performance as a freshman, Dean Smith, the head coach at the University of North Carolina, commented that while Jordan was "inconsistent," his work ethic stood out.[15] That inconsistency might have been why Jordan was kicked out of his high school basketball team years before college. Can you imagine how silly the person who fired him must have felt every time Michael eviscerated his opponents by dominating one of countless games on live television? Jordan's UNC teammates

* While there is some promising research about epigenetics and the malleability of our genes, it's too early to tell how significant or practical its applications might be.

confirmed that he worked intensely to get better on the court while also continuing to practice after his other teammates were ready to head home.[16] His former UNC teammate James Worthy was quoted as saying, "After about 2.5 hours of hard practice, I'm walking off the floor, like, drenched [in] sweat, tired. And, here comes Michael pushing me back on the floor, wanting to play a little one-on-one, wanting to see where his game was."[17] That work ethic enabled Jordan to have an unimaginably successful Hall of Fame career and to amass billions of dollars in the process. While fans around the world witnessed Jordan's awe-inspiring *macro-moments* during televised games, the real magic occurred through the millions of *micro-moments* during the constant practice, working out and strategizing.

Overcoming your inner stutter might not require the extreme intensity that characterizes Jordan's work ethic; it will, however, require accepting the necessity of repeatedly doing, through plenty of micro-moments, what you might find uncomfortable, inconvenient and tiring. It's been said that insanity is doing the same thing over and over again while expecting different results. I can recall countless moments when I was genuinely confused by the fact that I kept on experiencing a negative outcome in spite of the fact that I was repeatedly engaging in the same behavior. For instance, I consistently avoided speaking—and people—thereby feeling desperate, depressed and unfulfilled. As I continued to avoid situations that triggered fear or discomfort, I was surprised when that negative emotional outcome repeated itself. The cure to that maladaptive thought process can be found in those micro-moments of bravery when we deliberately do what challenges us.

What sort of magical macro-moments might emerge unexpectedly merely as a result of repeated occasions to engage in micro-moments of bravery throughout the day, week, month and year? What is one micro-moment of bravery that you can take today?

Chapter 6 takeaways

- Not only do we tend to overestimate the significance of the bigger milestones of our lives, but we can also forget that those huge milestones are often the result of the accumulation of a plethora of micro-moments.
- That grandiose macro-moment that we might experience constitutes a tiny portion of a day filled with activities that would not be considered extraordinary.
- Reaching our goals will require accepting that we have to repeatedly do, through millions of micro-moments, what we might find uncomfortable, inconvenient and tiring.

Meet Melissa Bacha, 28

Born and raised in Algeria, Melissa had always feared meeting new people. A flicker of uncertainty crossed her face as she confessed a thought that often popped up and held her back: "What if I'm not interesting enough?" While her fear was not necessarily overwhelming, she simply knew that it stopped her from doing what she wanted to do and that it got in the way of the expression of her true potential in life. Passionate about teaching the French language, Melissa faced a lack of self-confidence about interacting regularly with new students, her hands often fidgeting as she explained this struggle. This fear continued to delay her from taking the first step towards reaching her objective. She knew it would be necessary for her to overcome this fear, but how would she go about it?

"I had to choose," she told me during our conversation, her eyes narrowing with determination. "Either I was going to overcome this fear or I was going to let it block me from achieving my goals in life." In other words, Melissa felt like she had no other choice besides doing it. She researched different platforms and stumbled on a website that enabled teachers to create a profile and teach a variety of languages to students from all over the world. As she browsed the website and came across an abundance of teachers who were earning revenue by working remotely, it became clear that if others could succeed, why not her? "I can try, and if I don't manage, so be it. But I should at least try," she wisely stated, her tone growing more confident as she spoke.

When asked about what strategies she employed to overcome the fear of putting herself out there and interacting daily with students from around the world, Melissa commented on the fact that she engaged in what she humorously referred to as "self-manipulation." In other words, she would constantly push herself to do something about the fear.

The journey of conquering this fear was not a straightforward one for Melissa. Reflecting on the path she had been on, she realized that whenever we experience fear, we tend to find excuses to not do "that thing." Her voice softened as she admitted that in her case, she initially told herself that her plan would not work because her laptop was too old and she didn't have a webcam. How many of us have resorted to the silliest excuses instead of just doing the thing?

Instead of focusing on the final goal of teaching French online, however, Melisa found that creating many small tasks towards the completion of her objective was more advantageous. Those were her micro-moments of bravery. "Slow is better than stop!" she said with a smile, her eyes gleaming with radiant confidence. The gradual accumulation of smaller goals ultimately led to her reaching her desired objective of being a full-time online teacher.

Conquering that one fear drastically changed Melissa's way of thinking. She realized that she would be able to accomplish other objectives if she dared to try. She confided that she is now significantly less afraid of failure and much more open to new experiences. And her posture was more upright, her energy calmer yet more assured. Her new attitude has served her well: By teaching online while in Algeria, she earned enough revenue to move to Ottawa, pursuing her lifelong dream of moving to Canada. In the process of moving to a new country by herself, she has experienced a tremendous amount of personal and professional growth that might not have been possible otherwise.

When asked about what she would tell her "old self" in Algeria or what advice she would give to someone currently looking to overcome fear, Melissa shared that the most important thing in life is to try and not to fear failure. Her gaze softened with empathy as she also encouraged people not to abandon their goal and to keep walking, no matter how slowly or quickly, towards the objective that resonates with their life purpose. Whenever her friends tell her that they are afraid of trying new things or applying for a new job that's outside their comfort zone, or that they don't feel good enough for something, Melissa reminds them that the outcome is not up to them.

"We can do our best," Melisa explained, her voice steady. "And let the chips fall where they may."

The inner stutter corner

Melissa's inner stutter had been tied to her fear of meeting new people, a hesitation that interrupted her confidence much like a physical stutter disrupts the flow of speech. Every time she thought of introducing herself, self-doubt held her back, echoing the pause and struggle of stuttering. This inner stutter surfaced in thoughts like "What if I'm not interesting enough?" that kept her from fully embracing her passion for teaching and limited her growth.

Over time, Melissa found ways to work through this barrier. She broke her goals into manageable steps, facing her inner stutter bit by bit, whether by creating an online profile on the teaching platform or starting with just one student. Much like I learned to work with my fear of speaking, Melissa reframed her inner stutter as something she could gradually overcome, showing that the path forward isn't about eliminating hesitation but moving ahead despite it.

Eventually, Melissa took an even bigger step: moving to Canada, where each interaction became a chance to expand her world. Where her inner stutter once held her back, she now saw new possibilities. Today, Melissa meets her students with confidence, proving that even an inner stutter can be managed and transformed.

Recognize your inner stutter, stop holding back and be like Melissa!

7.

From moment to momentum

It does not matter how slowly you go
as long as you do not stop.
—CONFUCIUS

On June 13, 2019, the Toronto Raptors played against the Golden State Warriors in Game 6 of the NBA Finals. Given the electrifying level of competitiveness displayed by the two teams following five lengthy games, the fate of the 2019 championship game involved one hell of a battle. By halftime, for the Golden State Warriors, with a promising score of 57 points, a 14-point advantage over the Raptors' score of only 43, victory looked probable.

The turning point in the Raptors' momentum came in the second half when Kawhi Leonard, their star player that season, acted with sheer brilliance through both offensive prowess and defensive fortitude. For starters, Leonard's scoring ability and crucial plays on the defensive end helped his team overcome the worrisome double-digit halftime deficit. His leadership and playmaking also empowered his teammates to maximize their own performance. Then, the game's most iconic moment happened in the final minutes when Kawhi Leonard attempted a three-pointer, now known as the "Kawhi shot," which bounced on the rim several times before going in. I vividly remember being at a Toronto pub when the three-pointer went in; the ambiance exploded with pure exuberance. That legendary shot solidified the Raptors' comeback, thereby swinging the momentum firmly in their favor until they secured a 114–110 victory over the Warriors.

For the first time in the history of the franchise, the Toronto Raptors, the only NBA team not based in the US, victoriously secured the championship. It was through resilience, tenacity and the subsequent momentum that the Raptors unexpectedly and forever altered the course of their history as a badass team that is not to be reckoned with. In spite of a terribly challenging setback at the halfway point of the game, the team emerged victorious.

When we face a setback in our own journey, we must choose between succumbing to defeat or slowly building momentum in order to maximize our chance of transforming the final verdict. Research has confirmed that the "hot hand" in the NBA is a real phenomenon.[1] Looking at 34 years' worth of NBA data, researchers found that players who hit three or more shots in a row had a 6.3 percent higher chance of hitting the next one.[2] How can we generate momentum? How can we create the conditions for having hot streaks in our own lives? Your very own Kawhi shot could be happening any moment now, momentum-permitting.

Why must we repeat, repeat

Repetition is often praised as the key to mastery. Malcolm Gladwell popularized the idea that it takes 10,000 hours to develop true expertise (the "10,000 hours rule"). The originator of that idea, psychologist Anders Ericsson, has since challenged Gladwell's oversimplification, seeing that it left a crucial part out of the equation.

According to Ericsson, those hours of practice are valuable only when we include *deliberate practice*: paying close attention to specific improvement targets while constantly expanding one's comfort zones.[3] Given that this book focuses on doing the things we fear, this journey is inherently one of repeatedly stepping outside of our comfort zones. Paying attention to how we do each time is also a crucial part of this journey. When I go to the mall and challenge myself by talking to 100 strangers, I often quantify this exercise and track my performance in terms of the extent to which I was able to apply my speech therapy techniques in these high-pressure situations. For you, it might be writing down the fact that you've said hello to one stranger each day, perhaps engaging in small talk about the weather. (Right now, as I write this chapter, I live in Canada. And trust me . . . talking about the weather is a national sport here.) Alternatively, you might be using a spreadsheet to track the number of times you've challenged yourself to speak up in a meeting, even if it's simply to share one or two ideas with your peers. Or you might use an app to track your meditation with a goal of adding one minute to your daily practice every month until you reach 15 minutes each day.

While we might never become world-class experts in most of the things we do, nor should that be a goal, the 10,000 hours rule clearly conveys the following undeniable fact: The more we do a certain task, the closer we get to mastering it. In the case of facing fears, this means that the more we face our fears, the better we get at . . . facing our fears. According to neuroscientist and world-renowned podcaster Andrew Huberman, neuroscience research on willpower has shown that our anterior mid-cingulate cortex (aMCC) is activated by engaging in behaviors that we do not want to engage in, leading to the growth of that brain area and of willpower.[4] As mentioned earlier, this does not suggest that the fear will go away. Rather, this simply means that we can hone our capability of confronting these obstacles on a daily basis while enhancing our ability to do so over time. Although the positive outcome is never guaranteed, through repetition, the statistics of serendipity are more likely to be on our side. Repetition also enables us to familiarize ourselves with the worst-case scenario, thereby gradually liberating us from its pull. For example, repeatedly exposing ourselves to a fearful stimulus increases our comfort level with it, freeing us from its power to hold us back. In his book *The Brain That Changes Itself,* Dr. Norman Doidge tells us that thoughts and actions can physically alter the structure of the brain itself. Through neuroplasticity, change occurs by forming new wiring, habits and behaviors.[5] In fact, repeating an activity builds thicker, stronger and more hardwired connections in the brain.[6]

So, why don't we feed the brain the information it wants *in there* so that we get the outcomes that we want *out here*?

The informavore diet

Humans are informavores: beings that produce and consume information.[7] Naturally, the information that we consume will influence our mindset and subsequently our thoughts, feelings and behaviors. Information, however, is not consumed merely through "passive information sources" such as reading a book, listening to a podcast or watching a documentary. Information is also consumed through "active information sources" in the real-world situations that we participate in. In my last year of university, I decided to attend an open house session organized by the McGill Debating Union at the beginning of the semester. A few weeks earlier, my mother had told me that the son of an old family friend was an active debater in that very club. As soon as I arrived, I felt overwhelmed by the eloquence of virtually every person in the room. Saro Setrakian, the family friend who went on to become a partner at a corporate law firm in Toronto, was one of the people called up to demonstrate his debating skills.

In this room, words bounced like lively tennis balls in a match where thoughts were served with dynamic precision and returned with playfully vindictive gusto. How was I, a person with severely compromised linguistic rhythms, to survive in this ferociously rapid world of words? Despite enjoying the experience as a spectator, I was deeply reluctant about joining the club. On my way out of the room, I quietly waltzed over to the desk of one of the organizers to thank him and say goodbye before leaving. When he asked me what I thought about the event, I explained that I was initially interested in joining the debating club to work on my stutter and my fear of public speaking. I then proceeded to admit that on witnessing the speed and wit in the endless repartees of the members of the club, I did not feel like this would be a great idea after all. The organizer, a friendly male student debater with blond hair who might have been a year or two older than I was, paused, smiled and responded, "I think you should do it." That one unexpected act of kindness empowered me to join the debating club and compete in various tournaments throughout my last year of undergrad.

Had I not entered that room, I would not have gathered the inspiring information that nudged me towards a once-in-a-lifetime growth-inducing experience. In a sense, the information I acquired by watching the debate and especially by engaging with that one student positively altered my path. Had I passively glanced at the debating union's webpage instead of actively showing up, I might not have accessed the information that empowered me to join the club. After graduating, I continued to challenge myself not only through public-speaking clubs but also various interests-based meetups, with the sole purpose of channeling a seemingly insurmountable social anxiety into challenging yet rewarding social activity. I often checked www.meetup.com to find out about local meetings with like-minded individuals, where we would discuss philosophy, embark on a fun group activity to discover the city or practice foreign languages with people who were native speakers. As a polyglot who can communicate in six different languages, I rejoiced in the ability to simultaneously work on my stutter and on my languages in an enjoyable setting. Two birds with one stutter?

Introducing myself to countless strangers across all types of meetup events and in novel settings also contributed to the revamping of my relationship with fear and discomfort. What was initially terrifying became gradually more manageable. Interestingly, it also enabled me, through the bottom-up process (see Chapter 5), to accumulate new information about the world that contradicted the self-limiting assumptions that held me back in every imaginable way. I had so many examples of my stutter being associated with negative social reactions while growing up that it became imperative to proactively access real-world information that would generate a bank of new positive memories to gradually replace self-limiting beliefs with self-expanding ones. According to the "positivity ratio theory," developed by Dr. Barbara Fredrickson, experiencing three times as many positive emotions than negative ones leads to optimal levels of well-being and resilience.[8] While the mathematical accuracy of the 3:1 ratio has been challenged by some researchers, we would certainly benefit from tilting the balance of the emotions we associate with our fear from negative to positive. For example, assuming I had accumulated 10,000 negative experiences linked to speaking, the positivity ratio, also known as the "Losada ratio," would imply that I would have to generate 30,000 positive experiences in order to have an optimal relationship with the obstacle. Far from being intimidating, that figure is achievable through daily interactions with the barista, the neighbor, family and friends, and through my occasional speech therapy exercise of talking to 100 strangers in one day. That number doesn't have to be exact, of course, but the idea of focusing on generating novel positive data to counteract negative past experiences is an effective attitude to have.

In *Rewire Your Anxious Brain: How to Use the Neuroscience of Fear to End Anxiety, Panic and Worry*, Catherine M. Pittman and Elizabeth M. Karle state that to reduce anxiety, we ought to rewire the amygdala, the brain's alarm system, by forming new associations that compete with the old ones.[9] Inevitably, this exercise involves voluntarily exposing oneself to the anxiety trigger, the source of the fear or your inner stutter in order to prove to the brain that you can survive the moment. According to Pittman and Karle, this is an "activate to generate" process, in the sense that we have to activate the anxiety or fear in order to generate new neural pathways.[10] For instance, by proactively entering various situations that require me to speak, I voluntarily activated my fear and started the process of rewiring my amygdala. The new information I gathered stemmed from diverse social, cultural and professional settings, which drastically enhanced the journey of learning and growth. Furthermore, traveling and living in multiple cities over the years played a crucial role in diversifying my informational diet in a way that deepened my perspective and understanding of the world. After living in Lebanon until the age of 18, I went on to study at McGill University in Montreal, intern in Manhattan, attend graduate school at Queen's University in Kingston (equidistant from Toronto and Montreal), complete a semester abroad at IPADE Business School in Mexico City and work in Toronto. While traveling is not a prerequisite on this journey of personal transformation, I encourage those who can to take advantage of the opportunity to discover the world and yourself along the way. Unsurprisingly, travel has been linked to lowering depression, rewiring the brain, boosting creativity and optimizing personality.[11] As Mark Twain said, "Travel is fatal to prejudice, bigotry and narrow-mindedness, and many of our people need it sorely on these accounts."

As a result of having moved to Montreal for undergraduate studies, I formed a strong and lasting relationship with McGill University. Years later, McGill invited me to speak to students, staff and alumni about my journey. At one event, a recent graduate came up to me and shared that she resonated with the path that I had been on. Brittany, a 24-year-old management consultant, was experiencing a massive amount of social unease during and right after the isolation of the COVID pandemic. Whenever she'd find herself in a crowd, whether of people she knew or complete strangers, Brittany experienced drastic levels of anxiety. "I no longer knew what to say in conversations," she told me. "It was as though I had forgotten how to talk to people, what questions to ask them." The young consultant's fingers fidgeted with the edge of her sleeve as she explained how this new anxiety caused her to hold back and therefore experience an inner stutter.

Before the pandemic, Brittany was a highly social person who moved around a lot as a child and was always ready to jump into new social situations and make new friends. When she joined the rugby team at university, however, very different patterns emerged. Brittany knew that socializing with her teammates would lead to benefits on the field. Even though she wanted to form connections with the other players, she started avoiding interactions and uncovered a new and yet subpar way to deal with the anxiety and loneliness. More specifically, she adopted a daily habit of binge-watching TV, replacing real human interaction with a series of comforting virtual friendships. "I became friends with the people on the screens," she said with a subtle smile, her eyes reflecting a fusion of amusement and regret. "I would repeatedly watch *Friends* and *The Office*, and I just found comfort in hanging out with the characters without the need to experience any form of anxiety. Monica and Jim were my two favorites from those shows," she said with an honest expression, recalling those "bad old days" with a sense of relief.

I could relate. While those coping mechanisms worked for a while, the worsened isolation made her realize that she needed to bring about change. First, she started seeing a therapist with whom she could talk about how she was feeling and identify specific steps that would empower her to gradually alter her social anxiety. Second, she started watching YouTube videos about social skills, charisma and the importance of getting out of her comfort zone. Whether for gaining tactical tips or mindset shifts, a strategic informavore consumes the information that will move the needle forward. Seeing that Brittany started this journey at a low point, she intuitively understood that she had to start with small, consistent steps. "A lot of TV shows and movies make it feel like you need a big group of people around you to feel supported," she explained, with a tone that was both lighthearted and concerned.

According to Brittany, prioritizing important relationships and focusing on one-on-one conversations proved to be an effective way to work on her social and conversation skills, in addition to becoming comfortable with silence again. Indeed, unlike in virtual interactions, in-person conversations involve a certain rhythm and inevitable moments of silence throughout. As a person who stutters, I understand that there can be even more moments of silence in between. By stepping back, temporarily, from the group settings that she found overwhelming, Brittany spent her time building authentic relationships.

By working on conquering her fear one conversation at a time, Brittany's cumulative efforts towards overcoming her inner stutter successfully crescendoed during a family vacation in Portugal. Halfway through the family's time together, Brittany announced that she would be spreading her proverbial wings by leaving her family for a few days to go on a mini-trip all by herself. As soon as she checked into her youth hostel, she noticed a large group of people chatting outside. With dinnertime approaching, Brittany considered her two options: She could either go have dinner by herself or she could introduce herself to the group and see how her evening would unfold. After carefully analyzing the pros and cons of the two options, Brittany snapped out of the cognitive back and forth by reminding herself that this was a low-stakes situation with a group of strangers whom she might never see again. Not only did the introduction go smoothly, but she also ended up hanging out with the group the entire week. Together, they shared wonderful times, including going to the beach at 2 a.m., and enjoying delicious dinners and highly memorable dance parties. "In the working world, we tend to meet up with friends over dinner to talk about experiences we've had as opposed to cocreating those experiences together," she shared, her eyes lighting up as she recounted the joyful memories from her mini-holiday. One of her biggest takeaways from the Portugal trip was that life's greatest moments occur when we push ourselves. "When you feel discomfort, it means you're about to learn something new . . . you'll be a stronger person coming out of it," she added as her face filled with pride. After the transformational experience she experienced, both through the small, consistent steps she took as well as her time in Portugal, Brittany went on to successfully interview with and join one of the largest management consulting firms in the world. She is now able to implement the skills of networking, meeting new people, supporting colleagues and asking the right questions as she navigates her role and the complexities of her industry. While the social anxiety does occasionally return, she now knows how to lean on the skills and mindsets she has developed in order to conquer the fear.

Engaging in self-acceptance was also a crucial part of Brittany's trajectory in the sense that she no longer believes that the only way to express herself is through a loud, extroverted voice. "Everyone is different . . . I can express my voice in my own way. I don't have to be friends with everyone or worry about always pleasing people," she said with a quiet conviction. According to Brittany, surrounding herself with the right people who act as a support system made a large difference, too. When I asked her what she would tell someone who is currently facing a fear, she quoted James Clear's *Atomic Habits* by saying, "If you master continuous improvement and get one percent better each day for one year, you'll end up 37 times better by the time you're done." In her view, consistently experimenting with little changes, building skills through consuming the right information and practicing a bit every day all empowered her to boost her confidence in order to overcome her inner stutter.

So, what are some ways for you to expand your informavore diet and initiate actions to go above and beyond your own inner stutter?

Oh well, or what if?

We ought to occasionally reflect on whether our accumulated behaviors will prove beneficial or detrimental to our future well-being and to the fulfillment of our potential. This holds true regardless of the specific outcome of a single incident. Imagine you're at a book signing event for one of your favorite authors. (As I write this, I'm excited to attend Ryan Holiday's live talk in Toronto this evening; his book *The Obstacle Is the Way* is deeply aligned with my message.) At the end of the talk, the author opens the floor to questions. You have a burning question but hesitate because your inner stutter holds you back. You go home replaying the moment, wondering, "What if I had asked my question? How would I have felt? Could my question have positively impacted others in the audience? Might the author have been impressed and suggested we connect via email?* How could that single moment have shaped the trajectory of my life?"

* In case you are wondering, I did end up asking Ryan a question in front of thousands of people at the Elgin and Winter Garden Theatres on November 20, 2024. This also led to corresponding via email! You can watch the full video at www.jozepiranian.com/stopholdingback.

In an academic paper entitled "The Temporal Pattern to the Experience of Regret," researchers showed that we regret the things we did not do much more than the things we did do.[12] While action can be more uncomfortable (i.e., psychologically painful) in the short term, inaction tends to elicit far more regret (arguably more psychologically painful) in the long term. Had you asked the question at the book signing event only to receive a brief, unemotional answer, you would have done your part while allowing the chips to fall where they may. That sense of closure, whether it is positive or negative, would have prevented the endless rumination that many of us experience on having missed an opportunity that we deemed favorable. When we don't endlessly wonder about the "what if?" we are more likely to find peace by surrendering to the consolatory "oh well." In fact, whereas "what if?" halts momentum, "oh well!" is a clear indication that momentum is brewing. In other words, when we find something that scares us and we do it once and yet do not experience the desired outcome (i.e., "oh well!"), we can still build momentum. That's because taking action galvanizes us while reducing the pain of inaction-induced regret.

The best way to turn a moment into momentum is not by fixating on the results and the sought-after outcomes; rather, it is by realizing that taking action, regardless of the immediate outcome, inches us closer to the grander outcome of self-actualization than fearful avoidance and overly cautious inaction ever will. In *Atomic Habits*, James Clear encourages us to "focus on the process, not just the outcome." When it comes to conquering the inner stutter, the process revolves around taking action; the outcome, however, has to do with whether the action we took leads to the achievement of the desired objective. In other words, we ought to focus on the action we can control, rather than the results, which are often beyond our influence. Furthermore, the momentum generated by our action is often a more powerful focus than the outcome of any single effort. For example, a Raptors player missing one shot during that momentum-driven second half of the final was far less important than the collective energy generated by the players' resilience, tenacity and creativity. As the theologian Reinhold Niebuhr famously said in what would become known as the Serenity Prayer, "God, grant me the serenity to accept the things I cannot change, the courage to change the things I can, and the wisdom to know the difference."

Chapter 7 takeaways

- Repeating an activity builds thicker, stronger and more hardwired connections in the brain.
- The information that we consume will influence our mindset and subsequently our thoughts, feelings and behaviors. Information is not merely consumed through reading a book, listening to a podcast or watching a documentary. It is also consumed through the real-life situations that we deliberately participate in.
- Action, regardless of the immediate outcome, inches us closer to the grander outcome of self-actualization than hesitancy and inaction ever will.

Meet Dr. Roberta Pellant, 58

Dr. Roberta Pellant is a professor of management who has taught in leading business schools. While she grew up in a wealthy family in Wisconsin, her father abruptly lost his job when Roberta was 14, leading to their gradual descent into poverty. A hint of discomfort crossed her face as she recalled her fear that people would find out she was poor. Her jaw tightened as she talked about how that fear created an obsessive drive to overachieve, which led her to complete several college degrees and write multiple books. Roberta figured that if she had prestigious titles, people would not judge her for not having had running water at home in Wisconsin. Her shoulders would tense as she described doing everything she could to become somebody she wasn't in order to please people around her and to be accepted by society.

As a teenager, Roberta's fear of judgment was so rampant that she pretended to live at her grandmother's house, waiting for the school bus in front of that house instead of her own. Whereas some people's strategy in the face of fear is to shut down (like mine was), hers was the opposite in the sense that she wanted to overcompensate for what she perceived as a source of shame. Her eyes briefly brightened as she recalled becoming a star athlete at the school and selling paintings she created.

When she turned 50, Roberta realized that she was not happy. Her gaze fell to the floor as she admitted that as soon as she would achieve one milestone, she'd anxiously prepare to accomplish the next one. She was fed up with her constant need to achieve as a way to prove to the world that she was no longer that poor girl from Wisconsin. In fact, even her good friends had no idea that she grew up in poverty. According to Roberta, it was about time that she forgave herself and let go of the past. "Secrets make us sick!" she told me, her voice wavering slightly. She went on to share her story publicly, which she found cathartic and which turned out to be an effective way to help others overcome their own fear of failure.

When asked about the practical steps that she took to overcome her fear, Roberta shared a plethora of strategies, including talk therapy, breathwork, cold therapy, talking to her inner child, writing letters to her deceased parents, yoga and meditation. Her expression shifted when she explained that FEAR gives us a choice: "Fear Everything And Run" or "Face Everything And Rise." Ultimately, she had to make herself a priority. "If people are going to judge me for how I grew up 40 years ago, so be it!" she exclaimed, her eyes flashing with self-acceptance. She simply no longer wanted to live her life according to other people's expectations instead of her own.

Roberta's journey is one that has fluctuated tremendously. She was born into a wealthy family, grew up poor, became wealthy again with her husband until they divorced and then proceeded to build her life up again. Her lips pressed together as she discussed how her fear had always been poverty as well as the judgment and shame that came with it. She did not believe that no matter what happened to her, she would find a way to navigate the adversity. After going through ups and downs, however, she learned that nothing is permanent in the world and that there is nothing to fear. Her eyes became gentle as she reflected on how, initially, she felt as though she was the only person going through fear. Once she started opening up about her journey, however, it became clear that it was not uncommon for other people to have similar experiences.

When asked about what she would tell her old self or someone else who is currently dealing with fear, Roberta replied that the key is to stop caring about what other people think. Instead of feeling triggered or uneasy, she now uses fear as a learning curve to expand beyond her comfort zones. A smile crept across her face as she described how she is opening herself up to new horizons she never thought possible. After experiencing pain and shame from the age of 14 to 50, everything has now changed for the better.

The inner stutter corner

Dr. Roberta Pellant's inner stutter was linked to her deeply ingrained fear of being judged because of her childhood poverty, a fear so powerful that it fueled an obsessive drive to overachieve. Like my physical stutter, her inner stutter was a persistent, unshakable part of her life, one she had to navigate carefully to avoid feeling exposed. While my stutter represented an involuntary loss of control over my words, Roberta's inner stutter was caused by feeling compelled to prove herself over and over, to compete with the shame of her past by achieving more, accumulating accolades and hiding her true self. Whereas many of the other inner stutter examples have to do with not taking action in the face of fear, hers manifested itself through not knowing when to stop. Indeed, the action in her case came from an unhealthy fear-driven place, which got in the way of her ability to experience fulfillment and joy.

I avoided speaking, fearing the moment I would get stuck and be judged, while Roberta hid her background, fearing it would undermine everything she had accomplished. Whereas I would often shut down in fear, she reacted in the opposite way, trying to overcompensate for what she perceived as a flaw. Her inner stutter was a relentless need to stay one step ahead of potential judgment, as if constant success could mask her past.

When I began openly speaking about my stutter, it allowed me to face it head on, no longer avoiding what made me feel vulnerable. For Roberta, sharing her truth about growing up poor offered a release from the pressure to pretend. In telling her story, she no longer had to overachieve to silence that inner stutter. Both of us learned that vulnerability has its own power: It's not about eliminating what makes us different but about embracing it.

Through these parallel journeys, we have come to see our stutters, both inner and outer, as gateways to self-acceptance, growth and connection. Just as my speech journey has allowed me to inspire others who hold back from fear, Roberta's story resonates with those who feel they have to hide parts of themselves. By embracing her past, she learned that what she used to see as weaknesses was simply a part of who she was. Owning those parts has opened doors she never thought possible.

Recognize your inner stutter, stop holding back and be like Roberta!

8.

Will you stand up for your life?

You gain strength, courage, and confidence by every experience in which you really stop to look fear in the face. You are able to say to yourself, "I lived through this horror. I can take the next thing that comes along."

—ELEANOR ROOSEVELT

Born on the 11th of October, 1884, in New York City, Eleanor Roosevelt had a privileged and yet deeply difficult childhood. Though born into a family milieu of prominence and wealth, she was not shielded from difficulty: young Eleanor lost her mother to diphtheria when she was eight years old and her father to suicide when she was 10 years old. She was a "shy, awkward child starved for recognition and love."[1] Eleanor faced many obstacles, including being afraid of the dark and people's disapproval. She also had a fear of public speaking.[2] Years later, she forever changed the perceived role of a First Lady, while her husband, Franklin D. Roosevelt, was president, by developing a reputation for being fearless and unconventional.[3] Indeed, not only did Mrs. Roosevelt embark on a top-secret mission to the Pacific in an area under enemy attack, but she also became a spokesperson at the United Nations. In fact, in 1946, she was appointed a delegate to the United Nations General Assembly, served as their first chairperson of the Commission on Human Rights and played a key role in drafting the Universal Declaration of Human Rights.[4]

It is through her deliberate efforts to overcome her fears that Eleanor was able to lead a fulfilling life of advocacy, service and impact. Political life is rife with examples of leaders navigating adversity and ultimately confronting the obstacle through courage, perseverance and determination. Whether it is the story of Franklin D. Roosevelt, paralyzed from the waist down at a time when disability awareness and inclusion were nonexistent and who faced both the Great Depression and World War II, or King George VI, who fulfilled his royal duties and delivered important wartime speeches in spite of dealing with a severe stutter, there is no shortage of tales of courage in public life. While we may not have at our disposal the resources that a publicly prominent life offers, we can still choose to turn fear into the fulfillment of our potential. Tales of bravery exist in vast quantities in the private lives of individuals around the world. One of those people is Nora.

Born and raised in Giza, the third-largest city in Egypt, Nora Armani was an extremely outspoken child. Her father and grandfather frequently reminded her of a story that illustrates her confidence in social situations at the tender age of three. One day, while at the café that her family frequented every Sunday, Nora ran into a classmate. When she noticed that her friend, who was only a couple of months younger than she was, had a light bruise, Nora immediately decided to take the matter into her own hands by saying with a serious tone, "Look, little one, if you don't behave, you will hurt yourself again in the future!"

However, the once gregarious Nora became excessively shy in the years that followed. When I asked her if she knew why that change occurred, she recalled an incident at school. "I was ranked first in my class," she told me, a hint of anticipatory sadness glimmering in her eyes. "And one day, the teacher asked me a question and I didn't know how to answer. He told me it was incorrect and, suddenly, I went into my shell and didn't come out." Throughout adolescence, Nora's shyness grew further. "During basketball training, I would observe all the other girls who were very sure of themselves . . . and they looked so confident in their own skins. I, on the other hand, did not feel like I was enough." Her shoulders slumped slightly as she described how, instead of interacting with her team members, Nora would stand in the corner by herself.

A few years later, Nora left Egypt to pursue a master's in sociology at the London School of Economics. When I asked her about the impact of the different cultural landscapes, she said, with a thoughtful expression, "I grew up sheltered in the Middle East, especially as a girl. I was often told what to do, where to go and what to say." Once, while listening to a lecture by the German sociologist Ralf Dahrendorf, Nora heard him say, "You shouldn't accept anything that is given to us until you research it for yourself. Always question everything." That liberating insight planted a seed that would soon bear fruit.

A few weeks later, during a seminar, Nora was brimming with enthusiasm about an idea that she wanted to share with her class. As she prepared to do so, she found she was unable to raise her hand. "It was physical . . . my hand just wouldn't go up!" she told me, her voice tinged with both despair and humor as she carefully described this powerful inner stutter moment. A few seconds later, one of her classmates raised her hand and talked about the exact idea that Nora had planned to share. The other students were so impressed by the idea shared by Nora's classmate that they spent the remainder of the class discussing it. "I could have shot myself at that point!" Nora said, bursting into laughter. "I wanted to share the idea, but I didn't dare." On the way home that day, frustrated and committed to change, she told herself, "STOP! You will never be shy again."

While making that decision, cognitively, was the first step, Nora agreed with me that change rarely occurs overnight. Initially, she started to challenge herself to participate whenever she could, no matter how uncomfortable it felt in the moment. During this personal revolution, as in any political or social revolution, she initially gravitated towards the other extreme. "I was interjecting a lot . . . and it took a while to adjust and find the optimal middle ground," she admitted, slightly embarrassed. Today, Nora practices and teaches the concept of "presence," which she defines as being in the right moment at the right time. According to her, it is only when we are fully immersed in the present moment that we do not worry about what people are thinking about us. Thoughts such as "Did I say the right thing? Will they laugh? Will I impress them?" are not helpful, she added, especially when one is attempting to overcome shyness. She believes that our shyness can resurface if we start placing ourselves at the center of the interaction. Indeed, when we start wondering "Why are they not asking me a question?" or "Do they not think I'm interesting enough?" we revert to a state of shyness. However, Nora warns us that when we initially attempt to counteract that tendency and start seeing some success in our behavioral changes, we may end up being overly forward or imposing in a social setting. The ideal balance, in her view, is to cultivate a sense of presence in the moment without always making it about ourselves (i.e., our ego).

Nora went on to explain that overcoming fear has to do with

taming the ego. When we fear that we might be hurt, it's the ego's fear. Nora concluded her thoughts by saying that it is through connecting to something outside of ourselves instead of dwelling on our ego that we make fear less relevant. Although I understood what she was getting at, I asked her to provide a concrete example of a situation where she managed to successfully overcome shyness by not placing the self at the center of the equation. Generously, she offered two distinct examples that are aligned to her professional life as the founder of the Socially Relevant Film Festival* in Manhattan as well as a performer who does one-woman shows.

"Through the film festival, we have programmed 700 films from over 40 countries," Nora explained, sparkling with both pride and enthusiasm for her work. "I know that I have made a small difference by empowering international filmmakers to showcase their work at a film festival in New York City, which is no small feat." Nora then added that putting all the time and effort into something bigger than herself was one of the ways she got rid of the control that fear had over her.

When she is not behind the scenes, Nora performs on stages around the world. According to her, when she is on stage, she sees herself as a conduit for the message to the audience. Instead of thinking, "How do I look?" "What will they say?" or "Do I look fat?" she focuses on the fact that what she is doing at that moment is helping make a difference in the lives of the audience members. "Seeing that the story that I'm telling might affect them in a positive way, the shyness vanishes because I no longer feel, ironically, like

* *Words Left Unspoken*, the film about my journey, had its US premiere at the Socially Relevant Film Festival in March 2025.

I am the center of attention," she explained, gesturing animatedly. Whenever she teaches students, she often reminds them to "dare to be dull." I smiled and asked her to elaborate. "You don't always have to say something interesting," she answered. "There is nothing more beautiful than a human who is just *being*." I was certainly feeling calmer and more in the present moment as a result of my conversation with Nora.

Towards the end of our chat, I asked about what advice she would give people who desire to overcome their own fear. Her initial response was simple: "Break it down." If someone were to ask her to write a book, she said that she might initially panic. I can relate to that. She explained that once we break things down into smaller components, the objective becomes far more manageable. With the example of the book, this might involve starting with creating an outline and naming the different chapters and subchapters. She believes that once we break something down, we gradually notice that it is not the insurmountable mountain that we might have once considered it to be.

Nora encourages people to do the work and find out where the fear or inner stutter is coming from in the first place: Is it societal pressure? How do you feel about what people think of you? Are you succumbing to what people think you should do? By reducing the fear to a series of current attitudes and beliefs, Nora believes that we can tackle the components individually. "You don't get up the mountain through one big jump," she exclaimed, her eyes widening. "Today you might reach level one, tomorrow level two, and when you look back, you might feel amazed by how far you've come. At the end, without even noticing, you'll find yourself at the top of the mountain."

Nora's analogy cleverly illustrated the sometimes surreal journey that I have embarked on over the past few years. If the macro-moment constitutes the top of the mountain, the micro-moments make up all the steps towards that grand milestone. Nora applies a similar logic to memorizing her one-hour performances by focusing on one paragraph before moving on the next one. "Discipline, repetition and sticking to what you said you would do are all crucial ingredients on this journey of overcoming fear and fulfilling our potential," she added.

Nora, who now shares her time between Manhattan, Paris and Yerevan, concluded by saying that given her theatrical training, she learned to "play a character" of the person she wished to become. "Play it until you make it," I thought to myself. Even though the changes—from being excessively shy to becoming a stage performer and the founder of a film festival—did not occur overnight, a drastic transformation can become a reality through gradual exposure to the stimuli that we dread the most.

So, are you ready to stand-up for your life?

Gradual exposure effect

Momentum sounds exciting in theory; in practice, it's simultaneously scary and boring. It's scary because it requires doing something uncomfortable, and it's boring because it requires doing that thing over and over and over again. When I tell people about my pre-stage exercise of talking to 100 complete strangers, they are initially a bit confused. Some ask me, "Can't you just practice in front of a mirror" or "Have you tried practicing a longer conversation with one person?" Phoning my grandmother for a conversation is an impeccably wholesome endeavor that nourishes my soul in so many ways. However, seeing that the level of discomfort associated with that task is relatively low, it cannot by itself directly contribute to the goal of overcoming the fear of speaking. (And, may I add, let this be a reminder to call your grandparents if you are able to.)

While one conversation certainly helps me counteract the negative habit of looking for ways to avoid speaking, which pervaded most of my existence, there is no getting around the fact that deep change requires deliberate repetition of a challenging task. In *The Talent Code: Greatness Isn't Born. It's Grown. Here's How.*, bestselling author Daniel Coyle explores the question of what makes certain people excel in particular areas such as sports or music and other artistic pursuits. According to Daniel, the recipe for success includes "deep practice" that pushes people just beyond their comfort zones, "ignition" of a spark that catalyzes passion and motivation and "master coaches" who can accelerate the learning process.[5] The key idea of the book is that these three ingredients can contribute to the development of "myelin," a fatty substance that insulates nerve fibers and enhances signal transmission in the brain.[6] While we can experience "ignition" by listening to an inspiring speech and access "master coaching" by working with a coach, we have to be willing to withstand the emotional journey that inevitably comes with "deep practice."

By the time I've finished my exercise of talking to 100 strangers before many of my speaking engagements and stand-up comedy performances, I've often experienced wildly varied responses, ranging from the blatantly negative all the way to the unimaginably positive, with a bunch of neutral ones in the middle. In other words, it's a good ol' normal distribution. Counterintuitively, all types of reactions have played crucial roles in my transformational journey. Whereas the positive reactions act as a source of encouragement, the negative ones serve to remind me that I can emotionally survive the worst-case scenario. In the past, the mere thought of that worst-case scenario could have prevented me from even considering taking action. Today, bringing about that very outcome is an empowering strategy that builds resilience and helps me to take ownership of my journey. In the words of Jim Morrison from the Doors, "Expose yourself to your deepest fear; after that, fear has no power, and the fear of freedom shrinks and vanishes. You are free."

According to the American Psychological Association, resilience is the "process and outcome of successfully adapting to difficult or challenging life experiences, especially through mental, emotional and behavioral flexibility and adjustment to internal external demands."[7] Expressed differently, resilience is about bouncing back while hopefully experiencing some growth along the way. By having 100 interactions with strangers and potentially receiving some negative reactions while I stutter, I have honed the capacity to bounce back. While resilience is often an inside job in the sense that we have to take ownership of our obstacles, it is not a solo job. For example, I often communicate with other members of my speech therapy program via a quick call before or during the exercise. Our ability to bounce back is indeed related to the extent to which we have honed a supportive entourage. Where would Vincent Chase from the hit HBO series *Entourage* be without the constant support he receives from his friends Eric, Drama and Turtle as he navigates the challenges of the entertainment industry?

According to psychologist Elaine Shpungin, there are four Ps to building resilience: purpose, practices, possibility and *people*.[8] Whereas the first three have to do with introspection and mental wellness, the last one reminds us that it often takes a village to realize difficult goals. By cultivating deeper and more nurturing relationships, we can better protect ourselves from the harmful effects of stress, thereby enhancing both our physical and our psychological health.[9] Equipped with the optimal mindset and people around us, we are ready to create these micro-moments of bravery during which pure magic can occur. I have often felt as though having 100 of those interactions, when I typically ask for directions from groups of people, is sensorially (that is, connected to the five senses) analogous to imbibing a generous serving of spirits. Consuming alcohol reduces social inhibitions by suppressing inhibitory neurotransmitter systems.[10] When our social inhibitions are reduced, we are more likely to say hello to that stranger at the party or introduce ourselves to a group of people at a wedding. An alternative way to reach a similar outcome (without requiring liquid courage) is to prove to ourselves that we can tolerate the discomfort of that social situation. Every new data point shows the brain that it can survive these moments of discomfort. Desensitization essentially means getting your reps in. In clinical psychology, "systematic desensitization therapy" is commonly used to treat anxiety disorders through exposing yourself to fears in stages in order to gradually get more comfortable dealing with those fears.[11] Desensitization is based on the premise that we must expose ourselves to our fears in order to reduce our sensitivity to the stimulus that otherwise induces anxiety or fear in our mind. Psychologists recommend exposure and desensitization therapy to help break the pattern of avoidance and fear.[12]

What is one behavior (or more than one) that you are currently avoiding even though your intuition is saying that this very behavior represents the portal to the life that you seek the most? More importantly, how can you engineer an exercise that (1) is challenging, (2) can be done regularly and (3) can provide you with valuable feedback?

My surreal progress

The Joze from just a few years ago would never (*ever*) have believed any of the milestones that have been materializing in my life over since then. Many of those moments have felt like scenes from Hollywood films. In October 2022, I had the opportunity to speak at the Federal Bureau of Investigation in Washington, D.C. That's right, I was invited to give a talk at the FBI. When I arrived at the J. Edgar Hoover Building on that rainy fall morning, it took me a few seconds to process the magnitude of the moment. After going through security and officially entering the building, I was escorted to the auditorium where I would speak. The planning team told me the director would arrive shortly. I assumed that they were referring to their manager. When the director arrived, I remember thinking that this man did not emanate the energy of a regular manager. He said, "Hi, I'm Christopher," and we exchanged niceties. We then proceeded to our seats in the front row. When he went up on stage to deliver opening remarks and introduce me as the keynote speaker, it occurred to me that the man I met was actually Christopher A. Wray. In other words, I was introduced to the stage by the director of the entire FBI!*

How the heck did I end up there? This was one of a multitude of milestones that occurred simply as a result of my willingness to continually expand my comfort zones. Had I not taken the first steps to overcome what was at the time a seemingly insurmountable fear of speaking, none of the subsequent events would have happened. Whether it was speaking at major conferences and sharing the stage with CEOs worldwide, or attending the world premiere of *Words Left Unspoken*, the movie about my journey, I've experienced surreal events that once felt impossible. These moments would not have happened if I had continued living the way I always had, holding back because fear. Trust me, I fully understand any level of skepticism you may feel when considering the achievements possible in your own life. As someone who avoided speaking, and avoided people, almost entirely for more than two decades, I would have said that anyone who told me that I would one day speak for a living had a deranged sense of humor. And yet, it happened. It happened not because I am special; rather, it happened because I adopted a certain approach to an obstacle that others might have responded to differently. Accepting the limitations that an obstacle presented at times would have eliminated so many accomplishments. Self-acceptance is a fundamental step that you must embrace, but it does not preclude proactively taking action in order to gradually rewrite

* Christopher Asher Wray was the director of the FBI at the time of my event and until January 2025.

the story that you tell about . . . yourself. Your life today does not have to dictate the nature of your life tomorrow. Radical change is possible. I have lived it, and so can you.

No input, no output

In the words of Joe Strummer, lead singer of the Clash: "No input, no output." Complacency is defined as being satisfied while also being aware that one is underperforming or might easily lose momentum. Interestingly, complacency can occur at any stage of your journey. Indeed, it can occur *before* you start taking action by admitting defeat right away. However, that complacency can also occur *after* one or more positive milestones are achieved. I recall that a few days after my first-ever stand-up comedy performance in New York, I was back in Toronto and had a highly counterproductive week. I was binge-watching Netflix, consuming unhealthy food and, quite frankly, resting on my laurels. The experience of a high after a given accomplishment can, if we're not careful, serve as justification for unnecessarily creating a low.

The inevitable ebb and flow of life will naturally bring about a regression following a deviation in either direction. But we shouldn't become complacent when that happens. We need to exercise our sense of agency—the power to fulfill our potential. Complacency can occur because of a general lack of momentum (experiencing a rut of a few days, weeks or months if one is inclined towards depressive episodes) or as a result of having stopped the behavior that generated the positive momentum in the first place. I can think of several instances during which I would be perplexed and frustrated by the lack of momentum or the results in my life. For instance, whenever I went through a period of not performing often enough at comedy clubs, I initially felt befuddled. On introspection, however, I concluded that I had simply not been reaching out to the club owners and show producers to let them know that I was in town and available to perform. A few emails later, I would find myself booked on some exciting shows. You may want to improve the quality of your sleep and yet be unwilling to give up that afternoon cup of coffee. Most of the time, wishing for something to unfold is not a sufficient prerequisite for that desired outcome to occur. The formula is quite simple: no input, no output. Applied to the two above examples: no emails, no booking; no giving up afternoon coffee, no sleep.

Expecting an output to magically emerge in the absence of an input is at best naive and at worst a form of self-sabotage. In World War I, the term "spike-bozzling" referred to the act of destroying enemy aircraft or equipment.[13] When we self-sabotage, we destroy our own "equipment" and capabilities to create a satisfying outcome. We self-spike-bozzle. (That sentence was a mouthful!) We all fall into the tempting trap of feeling saddened over things not working out the way we want them to instead of asking ourselves if we ever inserted the raw materials into the factory of life in the first place. Did I enter a dose of gumption, action and repetition into the formula? Or am I simply fretting over what "should be" while existing in a state of utter inertia?

Think about three outcomes that might currently be unsatisfactory in your life. For example:

1. Mediocre fitness
2. Average social life
3. Not speaking up at work

And now, for each of these three current outcomes, let's reverse engineer three inputs that could sway the outcomes in a different direction:

1. Mediocre fitness:
   a. Find one or more accountability buddies (friends who are interested in stepping up their own athleticism) with whom you can go to the gym or to sports classes once a week. At the time of writing this section, I personally have three accountability buddies I meet up with three times a week for different sports or wellness-oriented activities.
   b. Buy a pair of slick running shoes. While such a frivolous purchase seems like a splurge, the truth is that the proper outfit and equipment will motivate us more than some old and used-up supplies.
   c. Start listening to a podcast episode about health or fitness, or to a podcast whose host is an athletic person who occasionally talks about their commitment to physical and mental health. Look up relevant keywords to come across diverse options (as opposed to committing to one podcaster whose style might or might not resonate with your sensibilities).
   d. Set a daily goal of 10,000 steps. This step (no pun intended) may sound like a cliché—the goofy sitcom dad obsessively measuring his steps on his Apple watch. But walking is a simple yet powerful input that can enrich our lives, one step

at a time (pun intended this time). Especially during colder months when it's tempting to stay indoors and endlessly engage in brain-rotting activities, setting that simple goal can create momentum, especially if it means walking around the mall on a cold day.

2. Average social life:
   a. Say hello and have a quick conversation with at least one stranger every day. This could be at the grocery store, the gym (preferably not while people are working out), a conference or a party.
   b. Register for at least one event a month that you might not have gone to in the absence of this exercise (a comedy show, a cooking class, a bachata dance lesson, an improv drop-in session, etc.).
   c. Freshen up your wardrobe. While I used to dismiss the importance of this detail, I can now appreciate the importance of looking good in order to feel good and to be in a state of mind that is more conducive to social interaction. Your fashion choices also offer ample opportunities for the world's inhabitants to spark a conversation with you.
   d. Call one family member each day. You don't need me to remind you to call your parents, siblings, grandparents or even cousins, but you may sometimes require a gentle nudge to do so. A quick five-minute chat with a member of your

family is an effective way to connect. If you have a toxic dynamic in your family, you can ignore this step and focus instead on connecting with your chosen family.

3. Not speaking up at work:

   a. Have a nonwork-related conversation with one person at work every day. If you work in a large organization and go to a physical office, you can gain some bonus points by adding the challenge of saying hello daily to someone you do not know.

   b. Speaking at a meeting is challenging (trust me, I know that *very* intimately), so start by either asking a short question or sharing a brief comment or idea at every meeting. Prolong your contribution as you gradually desensitize yourself to the task. Naturally, aim to keep your comments to a length that will not annoy your colleagues . . . especially if the meeting is intruding into lunchtime. If you happen to be a fellow stutterer, you can ignore that last comment and . . . stutter on!

   c. Scout some public-speaking opportunities. That might include joining a Toastmasters club either at work (many organizations have their own) or outside. Honing your speaking confidence in a safe, supportive environment will empower you to scope opportunities at work, whether internally for colleagues or externally for clients.

d. Go to www.meetup.com and search for hobbies-based local meetups where you can challenge yourself to interact with people and discuss your shared interests.

In the absence of input (concrete behavioral steps), no amount of mindset or manifestation will bring about the momentum to start the changes that will blow your mind. And trust me, they will.

Chapter 8 takeaways

» Momentum is simultaneously scary and boring. It's scary because it requires doing something uncomfortable, and it's boring because it requires doing that thing over and over and over again.

» Your life today does not have to dictate your life tomorrow; radical change is possible.

» No input, no output: Expecting an output to magically emerge in the absence of input is at best complacency and at worst self-sabotage.

Meet Om Gupta, 19

At 19 years of age, Om is the youngest speechwriter, researcher and intern to ever join the government of India. This professional milestone almost never happened due to fear.

When he was about to graduate from high school, Om was perplexed by an existential question that permeates the minds of students around the world. His eyes clouded over with concern as he recalled asking himself: "What major will I choose in university?"

While he had the grades to apply for med school, a professional path people around him highly valued, Om admitted that he knew deep down that this was not the right path for him. What would his family and friends say when they found out that Om was far more interested in humanities than biology or science? In spite of that fear of judgment, he decided to follow his passion. A spark of confidence appeared in his eyes as he explained how he now writes speeches for politicians including Narendra Modi, the prime minister of India, a task typically done by people who are at least in their thirties or forties.

"Had I allowed that fear of judgment to get in the way, I would have been in a biology lab instead of in my current role in the government of India," Om shared with me, a wry smile tugging at his lip. According to Om, when we do what we know we wish to do, we are much more likely to excel. When, however, we simply do what society expects us to, we might end up having an average professional trajectory. Om knew that he did not want to be average. He wished to do something extraordinary. His posture straightened as he leaned forward and shared his belief that every single person has a unique selling point. "Why be average at what others want me to do when I can excel at something I want to do?" he asked rhetorically, his expression calm but convinced.

When asked about his strategies for getting over that fear of judgment to pursue his passion, Om had a very simple answer for me: self-acceptance. His shoulders relaxed as he explained that in his view, we must develop self-awareness instead of simply going with the flow of external expectations. He believes we must ask ourselves why we are currently doing the things we are doing? And should we be pursuing an alternative path instead? A thoughtful pause followed as Om clarified that by understanding the reason behind our actions, we can detect which of our behaviors are occurring simply because we are trapped by the fear of judgment. "Defeating fear can be easy," Om added. "It's just that many people do not know that fear is holding them back in the first place."

Om encourages people not to assume that we are the way that we are due to fixed personality traits. His hand rose slightly, as if emphasizing his point, as he discussed how we sometimes hold back due to the way we have been molded. We need to hone our self-awareness to overcome that self-limiting belief or obstacle.

The journey of conquering fear was of course not one that occurred overnight—it rarely does. A shadow of doubt emerged as he described the frightening repercussions of potentially not excelling. What would people say if he pursued his passion and failed? His fingers tapped rhythmically on the table as he spoke about how this fear can be exacerbated in cultures where people are apprehensive about the extent to which their shortcomings will impact their family and the people around them. In other words, in individualistic cultures, the person conquering fear might be mostly concerned with their own journey. But their counterpart in a collectivist culture, such as Om's, might have the added pressure of considering how their attempts to overcome fears could negatively impact the reputation of loved ones.

In spite of some setbacks along the way, Om strongly believes that deliberately overcoming his fear has impacted his life in the best way possible. His chest lifted slightly with self-assurance as he talked about how adopting the right mindsets and behaviors towards overcoming the fear of being judged has led to incredible growth and a sense of courage that has spilled over into other areas of life.

When asked about what he would like people currently facing fear to know, Om emphasized that we ought to do the things that we fear without overthinking the consequences. A flash of intensity appeared in his gaze as he shared that no matter if societal and parental expectations get in the way, he believes that "this is your life and you need to think about what you want to make out of it." According to Om, people are not responsible for your failure nor are they responsible for your success. His tone softened slightly as he left me with his sage parting words: "Do not get swayed by the wind!"

The inner stutter corner

Om's inner stutter was tied to the fear of what society would think or say about his choices, a fear that almost kept him from pursuing his true interests in the humanities rather than the more traditional path of medicine. This fear, rooted in societal expectations, interrupted his ability to make authentic choices, filling him with doubt and hesitation. Just as a physical stutter disrupts my flow of speech, Om's inner stutter could disrupt his self-expression, almost silencing his desire to pursue his desired path. His story reveals that even when he knew deep down that medicine wasn't the right fit, his inner stutter pushed him to question whether following his passion was worth the potential judgment from his family and community.

My journey parallels Om's in profound ways. Growing up with a physical stutter, I also faced an internal struggle, constantly worrying about how others would perceive me and fearing that my stutter would be negatively perceived by others. Often, I was also gravely concerned about how my own family perceives my "difference." This fear, much like Om's, made me question my potential and hesitate to speak up. Like Om, I had to confront the weight of others' judgments and expectations and move beyond it, recognizing that to live authentically, I needed to let go of fears rooted in how others might react.

For both of us, overcoming these stutters involved learning self-acceptance and understanding that the limitations imposed by fear, whether societal judgment or vocal hesitation, needed to be challenged. In facing our respective stutters, we found our voices and reclaimed the paths that fear had once gotten in the way of. This journey taught both of us that by working through that fear, we could create lives that felt congruent with our true selves.

Recognize your inner stutter, stop holding back and be like Om.

9.
Do NOT neglect this

It's up to you today to start making healthy choices. Not choices that are just healthy for your body, but healthy for your mind.

—STEVE MARABOLI

I consider this chapter to be one of the most important ones in the book. In order to adapt to the intense fluctuations that came with a hectic schedule of international keynote speaking, including higher highs and lower lows, I've had to hone mental wellness strategies to make this journey more prosperous, sustainable and well-balanced. This chapter is about sharing everything I've learned on this topic along the way. Let's begin.

One adjective that would adequately characterize my journey of the past few years is *wild*. When I say wild, I am not referring to the stereotypical lifestyle of reckless rock stars living *la vida loca*. I do, however, mean that the growth I have experienced has sprawled into diverse areas of my life in a dynamic and expansive manner. Just like the branches of an oak tree reach out in all directions while the roots anchor deeply, my personal growth gradually infiltrated various domains of my life. Since a journey of a thousand miles has been known to begin with a single step, I would like to invite you to experience one of the most influential steps I took: my first-ever stand-up comedy performance.

In the fall of 2016, my friend Dan told me that he had completed a stand-up comedy class at Second City. Growing up in Lebanon as a *very* socially anxious teenager, I derived great joy from escaping my ongoing angst and voraciously consuming stand-up comedy clips, in either video or audio format, on my third-generation iPod 3G. Feeling nostalgic yet? Whether it was the outrageous theatricality of Dane Cook, the cunning cleverness of the brave slap-survivor Chris Rock or the philosophical poise of George Carlin, my comedic taste as a teenager accommodated a wide array of performers.

My childhood friends Gabriel, Rami and Toufic like to recall an incident that occurred while I had them over to watch a comedy on TV in the living room. At a certain moment in the film, I suddenly picked up the remote control, pressed pause and told my friends I would be right back. A few moments later, they *allegedly* heard me laughing in my bedroom. Confused, they opened the door and caught me laughing to a stand-up comedy video on my desktop computer. Interrupting a comedy movie to go watch a stand-up comedy clip while my friends were waiting for me could surely be interpreted as a sign of the inevitability that my journey would intersect with the world of stand-up.

Years later, when Dan mentioned his stint with the stand-up comedy class, it occurred to me that stand-up comedy was a variation of the craft of public speaking that I had been honing over several years of work on my fear of public speaking through Toastmasters. That would have been during my final college year and after graduating. While comedy requires proficiency in constructing jokes by optimally combining seemingly innocuous setups with unexpected explosive punchlines, the performance itself is ultimately a form of public speaking. Maybe, just maybe, stand-up would constitute the next frontier.

A few weeks later, I signed up for a two-month introduction to stand-up comedy, a course that entailed a weekly three-hour in-person class at Second City, an improv and comedy school with locations in Chicago, New York and Toronto. After learning the basic anatomy of a joke, I began writing material both about my stutter and about a series of random observations involving cold-pressed juice, the genie from *Aladdin*, the swimming pool at the YMCA, Pablo Escobar and Hawaiian pizza. You might find my gastronomical leanings peculiar: I have my pizza with both pineapple *and* avocado. (I hope this confession won't permanently ban me from Italy or from your potluck. Maybe I am wilder than a rock star after all.) While the exercise of crafting jokes was intellectually joyous, nothing could have prepared me for the event of going up on stage. In one of the classes, our teacher, Canadian stand-up comedian Jim McAleese, reminded us that we would all be performing our "tight five," a five-minute set featuring the best material we had written, in an actual comedy club. The other students were eager to invite their family and friends to witness their first-ever stand-up comedy set, but I had absolutely no intention of telling a single soul. In fact, my family and friends found out that I had done my first-ever stand-up comedy performance a month and a half after that date, when I posted the video on my personal Facebook page. Also, I was terrified. Was I going to get severely stuck on a word for 45 seconds? Would the audience feel uncomfortable with me joking about my speech impediment? Will the jokes even . . . work?

Fast forward to the day of the show on December 16, 2016. The room starts to fill up, and I am experiencing a degree of nervousness I have never felt before. At one point, I recall looking at the exit sign and thinking, "I should just go . . ." Had I left, and I was legitimately considering doing so, my life might have looked completely different today. I sometimes wonder if I would still be working as a project manager in the marketing industry had I decided to leave the comedy club before performing that day. While one might think that stage fright would have subsided over the past few years, I can attest to the fact that the thought “I should go” has emerged in my mind before most of my public-speaking engagements. I still sometimes look at the exit sign of the comedy club or conference hall while stressing out moments before going up on stage, thinking, “I could leave right now!” On that cold day in 2016, I stayed and . . . I slayed. As soon as I went up on stage, it felt like I had entered a parallel dimension. This ephemeral version of myself was going to joke about his stutter in front of a room of complete strangers. I opened my set the following way: “I have a stutter . . . so if you have any plans in the next 48 hours . . . cancel them!”

The audience immediately responded with uproarious laughter. Turning a painful insecurity into a liberating moment of genuine connection with both the audience and myself remains one of the most significant milestones in my life. Former NBA player Shaquille O’Neal studied the link between humor and leadership in his doctoral dissertation, “How Leaders Utilize Humor and Seriousness in Leadership Styles.” (I am not making this up.) One of the key messages in his thesis was that humor can be used effectively to defuse tense situations and reduce stress in the workplace.[1] Unsurprisingly, Sigmund Freud, the founder of psychoanalysis, said that “humor is a means of obtaining pleasure in spite of the distressing effects that interface with it.” That is precisely what occurred during my first stand-up comedy performance. Indeed, as I continued my set with jokes about, for example, the absurd social situations

I experience as a person who stutters, the snob appeal of goji berries, Netflix being like a clingy ex and my ability to stutter in six different languages, the connection with the audience felt ecstatic till the end. In fact, it became glaringly obvious that humor was an exceptionally potent method for me to dissipate any sense of unease in the air.

In *Friends, Lovers, and the Big Terrible Thing*, the late Matthew Perry, globally known for playing Chandler in the iconic TV show *Friends*, spoke about using humor as a tool to defuse uncomfortable situations.[2] Whether it was in his personal life growing up in Canada and California or when interacting with Joey, Monica, Ross, Rachel and Phoebe on the show, he was known for his sarcastic sense of humor, quick wit and distinctive style of speech that emphasized parts of the sentence that would not typically have been emphasized. Can humor *be* any more effective?

I didn't know how it would happen, but I knew at that time that this was an experience I would be repeating. This simultaneously exhilarating and terrifying approach to conquering fear would become a hallmark of my transformational journey. However, when one goes from avoiding speaking almost entirely to stepping on stages in front of thousands around the world, one can expect that the many highs will inevitably be followed by the occasional lows.

As I've mentioned, I've often experienced high levels of anxiety and stress right before going up on stage. In fact, right before I delivered my keynote about conquering fears and building resilience at Bell Canada during their renowned mental health awareness campaign, Bell Let's Talk, I experienced a panic attack. "How am I going to get through this?" I thought. How ironic that the keynote speaker who has been invited to share his journey of overcoming obstacles was dealing with intense adversity mere moments before being called up to the stage. Leaning on a pranayama technique to regulate my breath that I had learned in yoga, I applied the 4–7–8 breathing method: inhaling through the nose for 4 seconds, holding the breath for 7 seconds and exhaling through the mouth for 8 seconds. This type of breathing has been shown to activate the parasympathetic nervous system and improve heart rate variability and psychological well-being.[3] While I remained somewhat anxious after the breathing, the increased sense of relaxation empowered me to successfully deliver an impactful keynote. It has also occurred to me that experiences like these actually make me qualified to deliver talks about overcoming adversity. Waiting for my name to be called on stages around the world, I often pace around backstage, at times feeling the dire need to use breathing techniques to inject some calm into my state.

Breathe in, breathe out

Meditation is simultaneously complex and simple. On the one hand, seeing that it represents the culmination of thousands of years of traditions and different schools of thought, it is complex. Whether it is the pursuit of nirvana in Buddhism or qi in Taoism, the path of contemplative prayer and union with God in Christian mysticism or the practice of Sufism in Islam, humans across cultures have sought to harmonize the relationship between the self and the world. The human problem that meditation attempts to alleviate is also a complex one: the inevitability of pain as we endure the difficult fluctuations of existence. While meditation does not promise to resolve obstacles, it can alleviate the emotional sequels of undesirable events through the cultivation of a nonjudgmental and mindful awareness of our sensorial experiences. On the other hand, meditation is simple in the sense that it is a minimalist approach for dealing with distress primarily using the power of the breath. Yet, it is not easy.

Here are two alternative scenarios illustrating the difference that meditation can make in one's life:

Scenario 1: Undesirable event X → Resistance → Emotional turmoil → Maladaptive behavioral responses that provide you with short-term relief while exacerbating medium and long-term pain → More emotional turmoil

Let's illustrate scenario one with a concrete example. Let's suppose you were hoping to get a promotion or a raise. You get rejected. Initially, you might resist reality as opposed to accepting it. It's normal, we all do it. "Why? Why did it not work out? Is it me? It has to be me," you might think. In cognitive behavioral therapy, practitioners often speak about the cognitive biases that can contribute to negative emotions and behaviors. Instantly taking responsibility for events that are beyond your control or blaming yourself for things that are not your fault is referred to as "personalization." According to American psychiatrist and psychotherapist Aaron Beck, other common patterns of distorted thinking include catastrophizing, all-or-nothing thinking, overgeneralization, mind reading, disqualifying the positive, "should" statements, emotional reasoning and fortune-telling. They are briefly explained in the following chart,[4] with some diverse examples and others that might be more relevant to you.

Cognitive distortion	Example
Personalization DEFINITION: Taking responsibility for external events outside of your control	DISTORTION: He didn't say hello to me at the office today. He must be angry at me. PLAUSIBLE ALTERNATIVE: He might not have noticed me or is overwhelmed by his own stressors now. It's not all about me.
Catastrophizing DEFINITION: Exaggerating the importance of negatives and focusing on the worst outcome possible	DISTORTION: No one will accept me because of my stutter! PLAUSIBLE ALTERNATIVE: Most people don't mind if someone has a speech impediment, and those that do simply do not have to be a part of my life.
All-or-nothing thinking DEFINITION: Viewing situations in terms of extremes (black-and-white thinking with no shades of gray)	DISTORTION: If my stutter doesn't go away, I will never be happy. PLAUSIBLE ALTERNATIVE: Even if I stutter my whole life, I will find happiness and joy in ways that have nothing to do with having a stutter. (You can replace stutter with whatever challenge or insecurity you might be dealing with.)

Overgeneralization DEFINITION: Jumping to conclusions based on a single data point	DISTORTION: That person I just spoke to was not very friendly. I bet everyone at the conference is the same. I might as well keep to myself! PLAUSIBLE ALTERNATIVE: I talked to one person out of hundreds of people. Everyone is different. It isn't reasonable to assume that this person is like all the rest. If I challenge myself and talk to other people, I might have pleasant interactions and make new connections.
Mind reading DEFINITION: Assuming you know what others are thinking, and often perceiving it to be negative, without evidence	DISTORTION: He's smiling while I talk to him; he must think what I said sounds weird or ridiculous. What a jerk! PLAUSIBLE ALTERNATIVE: What I said was humorous or maybe it reminded him of another story. Or he could just be smiling to be agreeable.
Disqualifying the positive DEFINITION: Ignoring or downplaying positive experiences, accomplishments or qualities	DISTORTION: I hate that I have a stutter. My life sucks. PLAUSIBLE ALTERNATIVE: Stuttering is one aspect of my life. While it comes with its challenges, I have a lot of other things to be grateful for. Who knows, maybe one day I'll find the positive in having a stutter.*

*And I did!

"Should" statements DEFINITION: Setting rigid and unrealistic expectations for yourself or others	DISTORTION: I haven't worked out in months. I have to start going to the gym every single day! PLAUSIBLE ALTERNATIVE: My body will need some time to adjust, so why don't I set the goal of going to the gym three times this week in addition to walking every day. I can revisit the ideal frequency of visits to the gym next week.
Emotional reasoning DEFINITION: Making decisions and conclusions solely based on how you feel as opposed to considering objective reality	DISTORTION: I feel so bad about how my presentation went. It must have been terrible. But I don't know why! PLAUSIBLE ALTERNATIVE: Multiple people complimented me about the delivery and content. They have no incentive to lie to me, nothing to gain from making it up. If they thought it was bad, they would most likely have said nothing!
Fortune-telling DEFINITION: Believing you can accurately predict the future, usually a negative outcome, without any evidence	DISTORTION: I just know that I'm always going to be shy. I always have been. Why should that change? PLAUSIBLE ALTERNATIVE: Many people succeed in life while being shy or introverted. But if I want to work on my shyness, there are many ways to do so, perhaps with a therapist who specializes in exposure therapy.

Such distorted patterns of thinking often lead to interpretations that elicit negative emotions. In order to deal with that uncomfortable state of mind, you might think, "I'd better pick up a case of beer on the way home, maybe some Häagen-Dazs, and I ought to rewatch *Friends* for the 47th time." After a long night of maladaptive coping on the couch, you wake up groggy the next morning and decide to skip the expensive gym class you had signed up for. They charge you a cancellation fee. You are disappointed by your behavior and decide to soothe yourself by ordering junk food through Uber Eats. The cycle continues and what was meant to simply be one undesirable event has led to a cascade of negativity in your life.

In Buddhism, the parable of the second arrow is about enhancing our capacity to handle difficulties in life. The Buddha asked a student, "If a person is struck by an arrow, is it painful? If the person is struck by a second arrow, is it even more painful?"[5] Whereas the first arrow represents the unavoidable pain (such as rejection), the second arrow represents the additional suffering we create through our reaction to it, such as rumination, self-blame or anger. While we cannot prevent the first arrow from striking, it is within our power to prevent the second arrow by not bringing emotional turmoil to the experience. In other words, while not getting that promotion is the first arrow outside of our control, all the subsequent counterproductive and unhealthy patterns constitute the second arrow, which, in theory, is avoidable.

If the above description sounds rather vivid, it's because I've been through this sequence before. Now, let's consider an alternative—scenario number two.

Scenario 2: Undesirable event X → Meditation → Mindful awareness and observation of emotional turmoil to create a healthy distance between yourself and the thoughts and feelings you experience → Adaptive behavioral responses that strengthen your resilience and ability to navigate these inevitable fluctuations → Emotional regulation

So, you got rejected. Ouch. When we face an event that we deem undesirable, our physiological alarm will go off. The minute we start feeling agitated is the moment that requires a mindful intervention. Similar to an intervention in which you might affectionately ambush a loved one who is going through a problematic addiction, a mindful intervention consists of lovingly ambushing ourselves with uncomfortable yet necessary self-awareness. If we are able to sit with our emotions and observe what our body is going through, we will experience a reaction without adding fuel to the fire. As American spiritual teacher Ram Dass would say, "Be here now."

Holocaust survivor and author Viktor Frankl is famously quoted as having said that "between the stimulus and response, there is a space. And in that space lies our freedom and power to choose our responses. In our response lies our growth and our freedom." Meditation allows us to widen that space so that we are more likely to respond than hastily and unhealthily reacting when things do not go our way. The optimal approach, of course, involves meditating dailyor regularly in order to hone, in a preparatory manner, the skill of observing our emotional turbulence through mindfulness awareness until the inner turmoil (inevitably) dissipates—as opposed to resisting it with a plethora of self-sabotaging mechanisms, including unhealthy habits. Depending on personal patterns, such habits might include overusing your phone and other technological devices and binge eating or consuming alcohol or other substances, providing temporary relief at the expense of your future self. To prevent ourselves from reaching unhealthy levels of reactivity that do not help us, a daily habit of meditation acts as a proactive and preventative method for optimizing our mental health.

More than once, in the days preceding a big speaking engagement, I have experienced fairly pronounced spikes in my anxiety level. It has been key to meet these fluctuations with proper mental wellness strategies, including maintaining my meditation and breathwork practices. While it may be tempting to abandon those techniques when we feel overwhelmed, the moments of high anxiety are precisely the ones that require these practices the most. Once, when I invited a friend to join me for a meditation class in the coming week, he responded saying, "I feel a bit too stressed at the moment with work and other matters. I'll get back to you in a couple of weeks to choose a class." Clearly, that friend would have benefited from both taking that class and honing a regular mindfulness practice that he could tap into on an ongoing basis. As Gandhi once said, "I have so much to accomplish today that I must meditate for two hours instead of one." As with all habits, it's best to start small. For instance, you could attempt this 31-day experiment:

1. Meditate for 2 minutes daily at the same time from Day 1 to Day 7.
2. Meditate for 3 minutes daily at the same time from Day 8 to Day 15.
3. Meditate for 4 minutes daily at the same time from Day 16 to Day 23.
4. Meditate for 5 minutes daily at the same time from Day 24 to Day 31.

After successfully completing the first month, you may decide to commit to a five-, 10- or 15-minute-long daily meditation. As I mentioned, I meditate for 15 minutes most mornings. While there are plenty of resources that I have personally used, including YouTube videos and various mindfulness apps with a plethora of guided meditations, you can get started by simply following this technique for observing your breath:

As you inhale through the nose, focus on the sensation of the air gently entering your nostrils.

As you exhale through the nose or mouth, focus on the sensation of the air gently exiting.

If thoughts pop up (and trust me, they will), your goal as a person who meditates is *never* to stop the thoughts from occurring. On the contrary, your goal is to be aware that the thought is happening, without overly focusing on the content (which, more often than not, is irrelevant) and to gently bring yourself back to breath awareness. Sean Finnell, the founder of Mindset Brain Gym, an excellent but now defunct Toronto mindfulness studio that I frequented, once shared the following analogy with me: If we equate experiencing a thought to the dumbbell coming down during a bicep curl, we can equate bringing our focus back to our breath with the act of lifting the weight towards our shoulder. Just as the main benefits of a bicep curl occur when we lift the weight, the main benefits of meditation occur when we manage to meet a thought with a gentle return to the breath, thereby consistently voyaging from the mind, where emotional pain is often amplified, to the body, where we can stay present amidst our senses.

According to what a barista at Toronto's Alternity café told me after I ordered my chaga mushroom latte, "You cannot feel your five senses in the past or in the future. You can only feel them in the present moment." For those of you who have tried to meditate and were not fans of that form of mindfulness, I would invite you to explore breathwork techniques such as the one popularized by Wim Hof.

The Wim Hof Method (WHM) focuses on a specific type of breathwork that involves taking a deep and somewhat fast breath through the mouth followed by a slower exhalation through the mouth, before returning to the inhalation. This type of cyclical breathing is meant to voluntarily induce hyperventilation as a way to increase oxygen levels while releasing carbon dioxide. According to Wim Hof, as well as enthusiastic practitioners from around the world, the breathwork positively impacts one's mental health in terms of depression, anxiety, mood, mental focus and pain management. With some research validating these effects as well as new studies that examine the benefits of both breathwork and

cold exposure (e.g., an ice bath or a cold shower), many are finding these techniques to be beneficial. In fact, researchers at Wayne State University have found that by generating a stress-induced analgesic response, the WHM may promote the release of opioids and cannabinoids in the brain, thereby creating a feeling of well-being, controlling mood and reducing anxiety.[6] Anna Lembke's research on dopamine (see Chapter 5) would validate the hypothesis that the voluntary exposure to discomfort which activates the internal mechanism of homeostasis creates a wave of "feel good neurotransmitters." Far from being a secret or a far-fetched fringe technique, the WHM has been adopted by many athletes including the tennis player Novak Djokovic, the UFC fighter Alistair Overeem and the American football player Steve Weatherford. In fact, Stanford University neuroscientist and world-renowned podcaster Andrew Huberman has spoken extensively about both cyclical breathing techniques and deliberate cold exposure. According to Huberman, "If you dread cold showers or a cold plunge first thing in the morning, you stand to benefit more, not less, from the long-lasting adrenaline and dopamine increase they trigger."

If neither of those approaches work for you, it's not the end of the world. There are other ways to instill moments of presence during our day. For instance, going on a daily walk and focusing on all the little sensorial details that we encounter also constitutes a very effective type of meditation, frequently referred to as "walking meditation." Some people experience such states of mind while running or working out. As long as we are creating opportunities to be mindfully aware of our bodily sensations, including our breath, on a somewhat regular basis, we are cultivating a sense of presence that can lower the likelihood of descending into needless negative spirals. In *The Body Keeps the Score*, Dr. Bessel van der Kolk discusses various therapeutic approaches and interventions aimed at healing the impact of trauma on the mind and the body. He discusses how mindfulness helps us reconnect with our bodies while also improving our ability to manage stress and promote well-being. In Dr. van der Kolk's words, "Mindfulness not only makes it possible to survey our internal landscape with compassion and curiosity but can also actively steer us in the right direction for self-care."[7]

I have noticed that while our thoughts are often distorted and divorced from reality, the breath can be a more reliable and trustworthy anchor. It's been said that "truth will set you free." If, given the plethora of cognitive distortions that we are susceptible to, our thoughts are often not true, then we can infer that thoughts will not set us free. The breath, however, is grounded in truth: We know the cool sensation of the air hitting our nostrils on the way up and the warm sensation of air on the way out. This tangible experience is free from mental distortion, making it a closer link to the truth. Therefore, since the grounded breath is closer to truth than our unpredictable thoughts are, it is more likely to set us free in the moment. Perhaps, instead of "I think, therefore I am," the French philosopher René Descartes should have said, "I breathe, therefore I am."

Anyone who has seen me right before a stand-up comedy show or a big speaking engagement knows that I need my quiet time. I will often be hanging out in the backstage area or the green room of a comedy club with my AirPods on, listening to a guided meditation that will get me out of my mind and into my body. Sometimes, in my first moment on stage, I take a deep breath to set a serene tone both for myself and for the audience. I then proceed to joke about that very breath with one of my opening lines by telling the audience that "I use a breathing technique [breath] to control my stutter [breath] so if anyone here is called Luke [breath] . . . I am your father." (For my younger readers, this is a *Star Wars* reference.) As Vietnamese Zen Buddhist Thích Nhất Hạnh has said, "Peace is every breath." So, let us breathe in and breathe out.

Why gratitude is actually badass

Robert Emmons, a leading scientific expert on gratitude, said that "you cannot feel envious and grateful at the same time."[8] Dr. Guy Winch, author of the book *Emotional First Aid*, stated that "gratitude is an emotion that grounds us and is a great way to balance out the negative mindset that uncertainty engenders."[9] In other words, an effective way to counteract uncertainty-induced negativity as well as feelings of envy and resentment is to incorporate gratitude into one's life. While gratitude might at times seem like a complex emotional state of mind, it's an attitudinal approach to life that can easily be brought about by listing a few things we are grateful for every single day. The things we list do not have to be extraordinary. In fact, whenever I have experienced phases of depression, my entries in my gratitude journal can be characterized as being more basic, in the sense that I am listing things like gratitude for being able to walk, take a deep breath and access food. Whenever I am going through happier periods, the entries can include more nuanced experiences, such as an amazing trip with my friends Aysan and Sharron, spending beautiful moments with my parents and my sister, Nathalie, or a specific professional accomplishment. Regardless of the type of phase I am going through, maintaining that "attitude of gratitude" has served as a healthy cornerstone for my overall mental wellness. In fact, making a list of things we are grateful for is arguably most effective when we least feel compelled to write it. It is precisely in those moments that we most benefit from deliberately shifting our focus from the negative to the positive. Hindu priest, entrepreneur and former monk Dandapani often refers to a saying that he attributes to his guru Sivaya Subramuniyaswami: "Where awareness goes, energy flows." This, of course, does not imply that negative events do not exist or that they are not painful to experience; rather, the philosophy is a kind nudge to deliberately focus us towards some of the positive aspects of our lives so that our energy fuels those realms further. In the book *The Untethered Soul*, author Michael Singer says that "to attain true freedom, you must be able to watch your problems instead of being lost in them. No solution can possibly exist while you're lost in the energy of a problem."[10] This practice, like meditation, is not about solving a problem or overcoming an obstacle in a measurable way, rather it helps accumulate mental wellness points that create a solid foundation, making it more likely that you will take action and conquer the inner stutter currently holding you back. It is difficult to think about our grander goals of self-actualization and unlocking our truest potential when we lack a sense of basic mental wellness. This would be the equivalent of putting cologne or perfume on before having brushed one's teeth. Similar to Abraham Maslow's hierarchy of needs (the psychological theory proposed in the 1940s that human motivation is built upon a hierarchical structure starting with basic physiological and safety needs, then progressing to psychological and self-fulfillment needs), I have found that a minimum threshold of mental wellness is often essential for personal growth. This foundational state, achievable through daily practices such as exercise, meditation, reading and journaling, creates the stability required to transform fear into action.

In terms of gratitude specifically, while I typically use *The Five Minute Journal*[11] because of its simplicity, there are countless options available out there including free-form journaling.

Here, word for word, is a typical entry from my journal:

Joze's journal, September 25, 2023

I am grateful for

1. The amazing gym class I took early this morning in Yorkville with my good friend Emile and his wife, Adriana. I also had an incredibly nourishing acai smoothie after the class. It was delicious!
2. Canadian Thanksgiving, which is coming up soon. I am grateful for the opportunity to spend a couple of days with my relatives in Oakville. Even though I personally do love city life, I deeply cherish time with Roger and his family in their beautiful tranquil neighborhood.
3. My real estate agent Aimee Chea who has been a joy to work with as I consider different condos in the city.

What would make today great?

1. Working on my stutter by asking for directions from 100 strangers, especially as I get ready for tomorrow's speaking engagement.
2. Finishing my shower with one minute of cold water.
3. Calling my grandparents to tell them about what I've been up to and vice versa.

Highlights of the day

1. I completed my exercise of asking for directions from 50 strangers. It was difficult but rewarding! I didn't have time to talk to 100 people this time.
2. I cooked up a surprisingly adequate stir fry today.*
3. I had a great conversation with my grandmother.

What did I learn today?

1. The one minute I spent in the cold shower immediately boosted my mood. I should make this a daily thing.
2. It's so important to appreciate my grandparents and the fact that I get to speak with them. They are full of wisdom and love.
3. We have to choose in life between pleasure that leads to pain and pain that leads to pleasure.

Does anything actually matter?

Everything in life is ultimately cosmically absurd and therefore actually meaningless. Yes, I can be a *lot* of fun at parties. Whenever I am at the comedy club and I'm about to go up and perform, I look at the audience and the stage, and I then think, "I'm . . . about to go . . . up there?!" Funnily enough, I've had that same exact thought even after hundreds of stand-up comedy performances over the past few years. And right after thinking it, I like to remind myself that this

* I *rarely* cook.

comedy club is located on a swirling rock in *one* galaxy out of two trillion in a universe that has a diameter of 92 billion light-years. While this moment feels personally meaningful, it is insignificant to the highest order in the grand scheme of things.

Injecting this strain of cosmic absurdity into the hormonal chaos of that discomfort rarely fails to reposition my appraisal of the moment that I am in. On having considered the nature of existence, I find myself smirking in the face of the absurdity, equipped with a healthy "f*ck it" mindset that is more conducive to courageously taking action. At times, we are coerced into this state of mind after experiencing a particularly difficult event in our lives.

On August 4, 2020, the port in the Lebanese capital of Beirut exploded following the detonation of tons of ammonium nitrate. Cyril Canaan, one of my childhood friends, was working in an office building in Beirut where leading Arabic-language daily newspaper *An-Nahar* is published. Sadly, Cyril did not survive. A year or so later, while I was stressing out about having to perform stand-up comedy at Awk.word, the main comedy club in Beirut that has pioneered stand-up in the Middle East, I glanced at a portrait of Cyril in the living room of my family home (we have a couple of them around the house) and was instantly reminded of the sheer insignificance of my discomfort in the grand scheme of things. The mere fact that I was in a metaphysical position to experience fear meant that I had the fortune of being alive. How easy is it to omit this crucial detail from our thoughts?

There is a popular concept in self-improvement circles that aims to get people to reconsider the language that they use when it comes to dealing with challenges. The idea is that instead of saying, "I have to go to the gym," one can say, "I get to go to the gym." This framework is about reminding ourselves that we are currently alive and in a fortunate position to take actions that many wish they could have taken. Jon Kabat-Zinn, the mindfulness teacher and creator of Mindfulness-Based Stress Reduction, said that “as long as you are breathing, there is more right with you than wrong with you, no matter what is wrong.” In alignment with both these sentiments, we can implement the following mindset shifts when it comes to conquering fears and doing uncomfortable yet growth-inducing actions:

I do not *have* to face that fear, I have the luxury of being able to face that fear.

I do not *have* to become the best version of myself, I have the luxury of being able to become the best version of myself.

I have found it key to always contextualize fear and discomfort with gratitude and appreciation for life itself. So, when might you start injecting gratitude into your mental wellness regimen? If this is a practice you already cultivate, carry on.

Walk the walk

I enjoy starting many of my days, especially during spring, summer and fall, with an hour-long nature walk. Plenty of studies have found that time in nature is an antidote to stress. It lowers blood pressure, stress hormone levels, nervous system arousal and anxiety while boosting immune system function, self-esteem and mood.[12] One does not need to read these studies to know, through direct experience, that spending time in nature is mentally healthy and beneficial. As an anecdotal side note, any time I have peacefully witnessed the waves of the sea or the ocean, I have been reminded of the inevitable fluctuations of life. Indeed, in those moments, I am primed to remember that all that goes up is inevitably followed by a down, and all that goes down is followed by an upward motion. Observing nature is also a way for us to remember that while we can sometimes feel alone, we are inextricably linked to the ecological world and the whole universe.

Okay, back to the walks. I have found that two types of walks may occur, depending on my mood:

1. A WALKING MEDITATION: a walk without any auditory stimulation (no music, audiobooks or podcasts), when I focus on my five senses and my experience of the natural world. I admit that many of my walking meditations have occurred because I forgot to charge my AirPods overnight.

2. AN "AUGMENTED" WALK: Whether I'm listening to music, an audiobook or a podcast, many of my walks tend to include some form of auditory stimulation. Some purists like retired Navy Seal and author David Goggins might argue that one should exercise without listening to music or other sources of stimulation, but I have found that sometimes, depending on the type of day, week or month I'm having, that stimulation offers a necessary incentive to get out in the morning. For instance, if I know that an episode of my one of my favorite podcasts has just been released, I can link the leisure of listening to that episode to the inconvenient yet necessary tasks that elevate my mental wellness, such as that daily walk, going to the gym, keeping my place tidy and clean and so on. While in an ideal world, one would be able to mechanically perform all these functions without such incentives, any

person who has gone through mental health challenges will agree that there are lesser harms in life. For example, if your decision is between starting the day with unhealthy snacks while scrolling through social media or going outside for a healthy "augmented" nature walk while listening to a podcast, the latter is a superior option.

Move your body

When we do not make ourselves sweat, the world makes us sweat. There are countless books, podcasts and YouTube channels that we can refer to when it comes to leveraging the unmistakable power of exercise on our mental state. Harvard Medical School published a paper stating that regular physical activity will lower your blood pressure and blood sugar; cut the risk of heart attack, stroke, diabetes, fractures, depression and dementia; and improve cholesterol levels and energy while increasing life expectancy.[13] The immediate positive effects of nature on our well-being also occur after we engage in almost any form of movement: gym workout, running, swimming, walking, dancing, rock climbing and yoga. And the list goes on.

As an international keynote speaker, I am grateful to have the opportunity to travel around the world to deliver my speeches to organizations and at conferences and educational institutions. I have come to believe that the amenities available in the hotel I stay at can influence not only my experience there but, more importantly, my presence on stage. So whenever the hotel selection is up to me, I prioritize establishments with elaborate gyms and swimming pools. In December 2022, I landed in Kuwait for a speaking engagement at Zain, a leading mobile telecommunications company in the Middle East. Because of the time difference between Toronto and Kuwait, I found it very difficult to fall asleep the night before my speech—as though the nervousness and excitement of an upcoming event weren't enough! While you might suggest that I could have taken a sleeping pill, I could not risk waking up feeling drowsy on the day of a speaking engagement. So, I tossed and turned all night in the otherwise extremely comfortable king-sized bed at Kuwait's stunning Grand Hyatt Hotel. When my alarm rang at 7 a.m., I was fully aware that I had not slept for a single minute. While it is not typically ideal, from a mental wellness perspective, to check our phones first thing in the morning, I decided to glance at my email in case any event-related announcements had arrived. And there were. Instead of speaking in the afternoon according to the original conference agenda, my keynote would now be happening at 9 a.m. instead. Oh, boy!

So I reluctantly got up and dragged myself to the fitness center. I felt like a zombie until I went into the pool. *Splash!* After a few minutes of swimming, I started feeling invigorated, and the fatigue gradually lifted with every stroke. It's no wonder that swimming has been known to release neurotransmitters, such as serotonin and dopamine, and hormones, such as endorphins, all of which improve the mood and produce a sense of euphoria.[14] By the time I was back in my room for my meditation, I knew I had dramatically changed my state of mind in less than an hour, thereby setting myself up for success before going up on stage. While we might not always have access to the perks we desire to alter our mood, we are often only a few movements away from feeling much better.

On the inescapability of tech

The fact that technology is a double-edged sword with both extraordinary benefits and nefarious consequences has been extensively documented over the past years. Whether it is from Cal Newport in *Deep Work: Rules for Focused Success in a Distracted World*, Adam Alter in *Irresistible: The Rise of Addictive Technology and the Business of Keeping Us Hooked*, Nir Eyal in *Indistractable: How to Control Your Attention and Choose Your Life*, Johann Hari in *Stolen Focus: Why You Can't Pay Attention—and How to Think Deeply Again* or Anna Lembke in *Dopamine Nation: Finding Balance in the Age of Indulgence*, there is a growing consensus that the incessant use of technology is causing an erosion in our ability to focus and have meaningful connections with others while also leading to unhealthy, addictive behavior. Some of my readers may confusingly frown upon hearing about addiction, considering it the domain of chaotic street dwellers. Whether we engage in the most harmful addictive behaviors, namely the compulsive consumption of alcohol and other substances, or the seemingly trivial ones, including social media, food or shopping, we are attempting to cover up pain with a temporary solution. In the words of physician and author Gabor Maté, "Not all addictions are rooted in abuse or trauma, but I do believe they can all be traced to painful experiences. A hurt is at the center of all addictive behaviors. It is present in the gambler, the internet addict, the compulsive shopper and the workaholic. The wound may not be as deep and the ache not as excruciating, and it may even be entirely hidden—but it's there."[15] I once had a conversation about this with my friend Layla, who shared that she had turned to alcohol and drugs in her youth to quiet the fear of expressing herself and the pain of not fitting in. "It's not because sh*t happened to you that you have to carry that sh*t with you forever," she told me—a bold reminder that whether it's substances, screens, shopping or snacks, many addictions begin as attempts to soothe what feels unbearable, unexpressed, or unresolved. While I encourage people facing more pronounced addictions to seek professional help (therapy will be discussed later in this chapter), there are a few effective techniques one can implement to start having a healthier relationship with the omnipresence of tech.

Here is a brief summary of some of the best practices discussed in the five books I mentioned above:

» TIME-BLOCKING TECHNIQUES: In *Deep Work*, Cal Newport recommends using time-blocking techniques to create dedicated periods for deep work with plenty of focus and no distractions. According to Newport, scheduling specific times for focused work in advance, in addition to eliminating (or minimizing) disruptions from our devices during these time blocks, empowers us to concentrate deeply and reduce our dependence on tech for ongoing stimulation.[16]

» TECH-FREE ZONES: In *Irresistible*, Adam Alter speaks about implementing "tech-free zones," which are designated times, similar to time blocking, *and* areas where digital devices cannot enter. According to Alter, establishing clear boundaries around the usage of our devices, such as banning smartphones from our bedrooms or adding screen-free activities to our calendar, allows us to gradually diminish our need for tech-induced stimulation while also creating more opportunities for meaningful in-person conversations and shared activities.[17]

» THE "10-MINUTE RULE": In *Indistractable*, Nir Eyal suggests using the "10-minute rule" to overcome distractions and alleviate the instinct to constantly check our digital devices. This simple yet effective technique involves responding to an urge to engage with a distracting device or social media site by waiting 10 minutes before succumbing to the temptation. By the time the 10 minutes are over, we might or might not still be experiencing the urge. Given the temporary nature of sensations, as explored when we discussed Vipassana meditation, it is likely that we will no longer feel the need to engage in that activity 10 minutes later. The purpose of this practice is to help people gradually regain control over their attention span while also breaking the cycle of compulsiveness when it comes to tech use.[18]

» MINDFULNESS: In *Stolen Focus*, Johann Hari speaks about the importance of mindfulness practices as a way to cultivate awareness of our thoughts, emotions and behaviors. Through this practice, we can become more aware of the triggers that seem to enhance our use of tech. A heightened awareness can not only help us make more intentional decisions about our interactions with technology, it can also lead us to a sense of control over our tech use and a healthily diminished dependence on tech as a source of stimulation.[19]

» THE "DOPAMINE FAST": In *Dopamine Nation*, Dr. Anna Lembke discusses the "dopamine fast," which is a temporary

> abstention from activities that stimulate the brain's reward system, including social media use, gaming or substance use. Through these voluntary pauses from dopamine-inducing activities, we are able to recalibrate our brain's reward pathways and lower our dependence on dopamine while also breaking the cycle of addiction to our digital devices.[20]

Clearly, all five authors, among many others, agree that creating a healthy distance between us and our digital devices is a crucial step that we must take for the sake of humanity. Whether the final objective is to break the addiction to tech, reduce screen time or drastically alleviate the negative mental health effects that many of us experience following excessive use of social media, is it clear that we need to mindfully craft our relationship with the otherwise revolutionary innovations that have elevated our lives in significant ways. In addition to my "digital detox" in Cartagena, discussed in Chapter 5, which was an unintentional experiment stimulated by optimal circumstances, I have also taken steps to proactively engineer these opportunities for cerebral recalibration. As well as occasionally using a lockbox to store my phone overnight, thereby avoiding it before bed and first thing in the morning, I have also attended events designated to fulfill this objective. Camp Reset, a four-day gathering in a traditional summer camp three hours north of Toronto, has one catch: Campers are forbidden to use technology for their entire stay. Reset co-founders initially attempted to solve their own dissatisfaction, induced by disconnection, isolation, loneliness and burnout.

Attending Camp Reset in September 2022, I not only experienced firsthand the psychological benefits of going on a four-day digital detox, but I also immersed myself in playful activities that were designed to facilitate spontaneity, humanity and genuine connection. As Irish playwright George Bernard Shaw said, "We don't stop playing because we grow old; we grow old because we stop playing." On leaving Bancroft, Camp Reset's beautiful northern Ontario location, I found myself less inclined to compulsively check my phone for incessant dopamine hits. However, those unhealthy tendencies can return a few days afterward in the absence of a practical daily framework that requires a weaning of our relationship with technology.

In *Atomic Habits*, the brilliant James Clear states that "the key—if you want to build habits that last—is to join a group where the desired behavior is the normal behavior." One of the ways that I have taken that advice to heart is by joining "focus sessions" on Zoom. An hour-long session that I joined, organized by my fellow speakers Nathalie Plamondon-Thomas and Denis Boudreau, leveraged the power of group accountability to focus on writing and included other speakers and entrepreneurs. I certainly wrote large chunks of this book during these sessions! I also occasionally use a website called Focusmate, which allows you to instantly connect with a stranger anywhere in the world who is also about to start a 25-, 50- or 75-minute-long period of productive work. When you make a commitment to a Zoom group or a like-minded stranger, you are significantly less likely to grab your phone for a social media check or step away from your desk to look at what's on TV or in the fridge. Whether you choose one or two daily deep-work sessions, ban tech from your bedroom, practice delaying gratification or join a focus session, the key is to start with what feels doable. If you plan to implement an occasional digital detox, the approach ought to be realistic and sustainable.

More than 100 years ago, Norwegian historian Christian Lous Lange presciently said that "technology is a great servant but a dangerous master." It is therefore up to us to renounce the servitude and become more masterful when managing our relationship with tech.

Is your dopamine earned?

Andrew Huberman, Anna Lembke, Simon Sinek and countless other thought leaders have spoken about the powerful role of dopamine in shaping our lives. Dopamine is a neurotransmitter made in our brain, and it plays a role as a "reward center" and in many functions including motivation, mood, memory, movement and attention.[21] Evolutionarily speaking, our reward system aims to motivate us to keep on doing the things that help us survive. For instance, eating and mating both feel good because our reward system wants us to take the actions that will enable us to survive and spread our genes onto future generations. And while the proximal cause of eating food or having sex might be driven by the fact that those activities feel good, the distal cause is that these activities feel good precisely because they advance our evolutionary goals as an individual organism and a species as a whole.

As modern humans who seek mental wellness, a key challenge entails figuring out the sources of dopamine that are most beneficial to us. Indeed, we ought to "swipe right" on the activities that energize us and "swipe left" on those that drain us. In my personal view, the dopamine that we obtain from the world can be categorized into two types, which I've coined: "earned dopamine" and "unearned dopamine." Whereas activities involving instant gratification such as eating junk food, compulsively checking our social media or binge-watching an entire season of *Ozark* first thing in the morning could be classified as *unearned* dopamine, going for a run, lifting weights, reading, meditating, taking a cold plunge or breathwork are all examples of *earned* dopamine. A through line that helps us distinguish between these activities is whether or not most of the pleasure is experienced during or after the task is completed. For example, scavenging through our social media apps for approval-induced dopamine through likes, comments or DMs tends to be characterized by a rush before and during the act but with increased anxiety and isolation after it. Conversely, stepping into an ice bath, exercising, meditating or reading will typically entail discomfort before and during the task, followed by dopamine-induced euphoria after its completion. Borrowing from Anna Lembke's framework, through our body's internal mechanism of homeostasis, I would state that unearned dopamine starts with pleasure and ends with pain, whereas earned dopamine tends to start with pain and ends with pleasure. I am not implying that the totality of our dopamine ought to be *earned*; such an objective would be overly stoic and would deprive us of many moments of joy, including tasting exquisite cuisine, watching a beautifully written TV show or staying in touch with the people in our lives who live in the four corners of the world. However, one thing is certain: Relying on unearned dopamine as the foundation of our mental wellness will lead us to experience burnout in addition to other nefarious mental health effects.

Ideally, we would engineer our lifestyle in a way that enables us to fill most of our "dopamine cup" with earned dopamine, and then top it up with unearned dopamine. Chronologically, this metaphor encourages us to obtain a healthy dose of dopamine through difficult yet rewarding activities first thing in the day—when our willpower is at its strongest—in order to maximize the dopamine in our cup, while topping up later, as needed, with distractions such as checking our social media or watching an episode or two of our favorite show in the evening. I have found that the more earned dopamine I accrue in the first hours of the day, the less inclined I feel about maximizing my dopamine intake through unhealthy ways throughout (and later in) the day.

While I was completing my bachelor of commerce at the Desautels Faculty of Management at McGill University, I learned the difference between "front-loading" and "back-loading" a project in a course called Operations Management. Front-leading is when most of the inputs are required at the beginning of a project, while back-loading is when the majority of the inputs are required towards the end of the project. Let's suppose you are enrolled in two courses with very different grading systems: Course A has one final exam worth 100 percent of your grade. Course B has numerous assignments in the first half of the semester worth 70 percent of the grade, to ensure that students grasp the core concepts, and a final exam worth 30 percent. In this example, Course A would be aligned with the back-loading approach whereas course B would be aligned with the front-loading approach. By treating our daily dopamine system as one that operates more effectively through front-loading with earned dopamine activities and back-loading with unearned dopamine, we ensure a healthier foundation that is sprinkled with some relatively inconsequential distractions towards the middle and end of the day.

Self-development author and speaker Brian Tracy wrote *Eat That Frog!* to encourage us to tackle our most challenging or unpleasant task first thing in the morning, thereby setting a positive tone for the rest of the day. By focusing on earning our dopamine healthily in those first hours, we are more likely to turn that frog into a prince.

Are you barking up the wrong tree?

In my journey, I have gone through, and continue to go through, ups and downs. When it comes to my stuttering-related challenges specifically, I have frequently run up against the same illogical fallacy: the expectation of a favorable output in the absence of an adequate input. For instance, I would marvel, with genuine confusion, when my stutter became a lot more severe during specific periods. These deviances from the norm would bother me, not because stuttering in itself is wrong (a belief I once held). Rather, they negatively affected my ability to express myself and communicate with others. Initially, I hypothesized that I could rectify these fluctuations by prioritizing my mental wellness through more regular fitness, meditation, reading, sleep and journaling practices. On strengthening the consistency of those useful practices, I often found that while my mental health improved, the lack of control over my stutter remained relatively similar. Therefore, I concluded that the only way to surmount the barrier would be to go through it; that is, to work on it directly. That would mean doing my speech therapy exercises, regularly connecting for support from other members in that program and practicing my speech techniques when talking to strangers and to friends and family. In other words, no amount of peripheral activity (e.g., fitness, meditation, reading), regardless of how positively it might contribute to overall mental wellness, could replace direct tactical action to resolve the problem.

In our current world filled with gurus promising extraordinary spiritual solutions, it is tempting to shy away from doing the difficult tactical work that will surgically yield the desired outcome. While realigning your throat chakra and visualizing your dream life might be effective for some people, they are not substitutes for taking action that is directly related to the challenge you need to tackle. In the same manner that I sought to miraculously improve my control over my stutter by doing push-ups or hitting the sauna instead of simply applying my speech therapy techniques, you might have your own peripheral habits that you lean towards. While going for a run can set you up for success neurochemically, overcoming a fear of public speaking will occur primarily in the context of repeating the act of public speaking once, twice, thrice and beyond. You can go for the run the day before your work presentation; however, you eventually still have to go up on stage. The shift that we seek will not usually emerge as a miraculous macro-moment. It will, however, occur through the deliberate process of interacting, through micro-moments of bravery, with the action we know we should be doing.

So, let's not beat around the bush, bark up the wrong tree or pray that we are one psychedelic experience away from a life-changing realization; the action we ought to take is often obvious. Having gone to the Amazonian jungle to participate in several ayahuasca ceremonies in an attempt to solve all my troubles, I was rudely awakened by the ineffectiveness of this psychoactive brew when it came to the specific challenge I was seeking to resolve. Desperate times do sometimes call for desperate measures. While such methods might work for some, I would encourage people to focus on identifying the more straightforward path, which often involves doing the thing that we have been resisting. In the words of Gary Keller and Jay Papasan, we must always do "the one thing" that will move the needle forward, as they argue in their book of that name. What is that *one thing* for you?

On therapy

Many ancient cultures regarded changes in mental health as omens, curses or signs from the gods. Ancient Greeks were the first to treat mental disorders as medical conditions; indeed, Plato, Xenophon and Aristotle found interests in areas that eventually coincided with the realm of psychotherapy.[22] In the 1500s, the Swiss scientist Paracelsus believed that the most common cause of poor mental health was an "emotional disconnect between a person and the world."[23] Although the Austrian physician Franz Mesmer, considered by some to have founded psychotherapy, treated his patients through hypnosis, and while the French physician Philippe Pinel has been credited with founding the field of psychiatry, it wasn't until Austrian physicians Josef Breuer and Sigmund Freud cocreated the "talking cure" for nervous disorders that modern psychotherapy was born.[24] But why, you might be thinking, does simply talking about our problems with someone, either a professional or a confidant, often make us feel better about ourselves and life in general?

American physician James Pennebaker developed the "written emotional disclosure paradigm," which refers to the importance of both verbal and written disclosure of feelings and thoughts.[25] It has in fact been shown that the expression of feelings improves our health.[26] Bruce Wampold, a professor of counseling psychology at the University of Wisconsin-Madison, is one of a great many authorities who says the evidence is fairly clear that psychotherapy is remarkably effective.[27]

Along my own journey, I have had positive experiences with therapy, provided I was working with a therapist that was right for me. (And do not hesitate to change therapists until you find one who appears to be a strong fit for you.)

While taking action to overcome a fear is an effective strategy for boosting our self-confidence, it may not directly address the origins of that fear. Moreover, taking action will not necessarily heal us from painful secondary outcomes created by insecurities we may have dealt with. For instance, working on my fear of public speaking does not help me when it comes to a fear of abandonment that might have intensified after years of negative reactions to my stutter. In other words, my public-speaking and stand-up comedy accomplishments have not prevented that fear from unhealthily showing up in my personal life sometimes. Ironically, a number of people have become motivational speakers because they have gone through adversity that does not simply go away overnight. While a person might have become vastly more skilled at managing the adversity, the trauma of that experience can linger. By talking to a therapist, we can work on processing these difficult emotions with the goal of replacing maladaptive mechanisms that strive to protect our inner child with healthy coping mechanisms that can empower us to thrive as well-functioning adults. In other words, experiencing a plethora of unbelievably positive milestones over the years does not imply that I have figured out all my sh*t. While milestones of professional and personal success can be achieved through the proper mindset and action steps discussed in this book, working on one's self-worth and other emotional obstacles requires separate work, possibly with the help of a licensed therapist as well as through other therapeutic modalities such as somatic work, which includes breathwork, movement, relaxation, massage and other practices.

Chapter 9 takeaways

- In order to deal with the inevitable fluctuations of life, we have to hone mental wellness strategies that can make our journeys on Earth more prosperous, sustainable and well-balanced.
- Meditation, gratitude, walking, contextualizing the relative insignificance of the moment, movement and a healthier relationship with tech all contribute to mental well-being.
- Therapy is not reserved for people going through severe obstacles; anyone can benefit from verbalizing their thoughts and feelings on a regular basis.

Meet Marisa Yovanovski, 26

Ever since she was a child, Marisa had been painfully shy. In middle school, whenever she had to make a presentation in front of her class, her teachers would tell her that she was speaking too quietly. Marisa always felt she was unable to articulate her thoughts in a manner that was clear and understandable to her teacher and classmates. Her hands fidgeted nervously whenever she stood in front of the class.

Unfortunately, the situation became worse in high school, to the point where she avoided going to class when her social anxiety was triggered. When she was at school, she still found a way to avoid social interaction. When the bell rung, she would wait in the classroom for a little while so that she'd be able to get to her next class without running into anyone in the hallway. When she was expected to hand a test back to the teacher, she'd time it so other students would also be returning their exams and no one would focus on her. Marisa kept her gaze fixed on the floor, avoiding eye contact with anyone. Whereas many students looked forward to eating in the cafeteria to socialize with their classmates, Marisa almost never ate there. Her posture tensed up whenever she thought about being surrounded by others. She would even return home or go to a friend's place to avoid being in a public setting.

The situation at home was not much different. When her parents were arguing, Marisa felt she did not have a voice or a creative outlet to express her thoughts and feelings. She felt trapped. In addition to dealing with social anxiety, Marisa experienced eating disorders, such as anorexia and binge eating. She had a lot of anxiety around body image, which also contributed to feeling self-conscious in social settings.

While in high school, Marisa had an unmistakable wake-up call. It started with her dating a guy who wanted her to attend social events with him. Adamant about continuing to avoid social situations as much as she possibly could, Marisa turned down every opportunity that came her way. Her voice wavered as she recounted how isolating it felt. As things got progressively worse, she started fearing that her condition would get in the way of her desire to go to university. Whenever she entered a social situation, she had panic attacks and agoraphobia. Her breath quickened as she remembered the overwhelming feelings. When she started having up to five moderate-to-severe panic attacks every day, she knew that she had to get some help. Marisa then checked herself into a hospital to get treatment.

At the age of 17, she started to learn coping skills, which included deliberately exposing herself to social situations. Seeing that she was afraid of being alone in public, the first step involved putting headphones on and simply going out for walks to get used to it. She then challenged herself to get a job as a cashier at a fast-food restaurant. At this new job, Marisa was expected to interact with customers as soon as they came in. Because it was her job, she built a sense of accountability around having to stay at the cash register. Her hands trembled slightly at first, but over time and with each interaction, she grew more confident. By exposing herself to her fear, Marisa gradually changed her relationship with it. Later on, Marisa got into breathing exercises and a meditation practice to further cope with her anxiety. She smiled softly as she described the peace that these practices brought her.

At the age of 18 and equipped with a promising toolbox of coping skills, Marisa enrolled in a university with 30,000 students. The transition to an environment made up of large lecture halls with hundreds of students, parties and a new job was not an easy one. In fact, she frequently returned home to get away from people and was always on her phone in order to cope with the anxiety. Unfortunately, her grades slipped a bit. She found herself at yet another crossroad, trying to feel comfortable with new situations, such as participating in group projects, starting conversations with other students and attending social events on campus. As she reflected on the struggles of that period, her expression grew serious.

Today, while Marisa still experiences fear occasionally, it is not what it used to be. Whereas in the past, she always considered the social aspect of an activity before turning it down, she now embraces challenging situations. In fact, not only did Marisa take her first international flight to England a few years ago (something that used to terrify her), but she now goes to retreats by herself, runs workshops and seminars, goes to parties alone and has even become a coach to help others overcome their obstacles. Her eyes lit up as she described the freedom she now feels.

When asked about what she would tell her old self or someone who is currently facing fears, Marisa said, "You're going to be scared to overcome it, but try to lean into the fear. As long as you're making the steps towards feeling better, you will feel better!" She nodded confidently as she shared this advice. She also spoke about the importance of developing a support system as opposed to attempting to do it alone. As a practitioner of mindfulness, Marisa always encourages people to tap into the power of the breath during moments of anxiety. Instead of dissociating, we can firmly feel our presence in the room through sensorial exercises, such as this five senses exercise: Focus on five things you can see, four things you can feel, three things you can hear, two things you can smell and one thing you can taste.

Try it now, dear reader.

The inner stutter corner

Marisa's inner stutter comes from the social anxiety and overwhelming fear that silenced her and made her feel invisible in situations that require interacting with others.

Like my hesitation to speak because of my stutter and the fear of judgment, Marisa's anxiety paralyzed her ability to engage socially. It manifested in her avoidance of social situations, constant self-consciousness and the feeling that she was unable to express herself confidently. Interestingly, I have always found that my experience as a stutterer was analogous to that of a socially anxious person. Indeed, we've both held back tremendously from interacting with other human beings out of fear of being judged by them.

In Marisa's story, her inner stutter affected her daily choices in school: avoiding the cafeteria, walking alone in hallways and timing her movements to avoid attention. In a similar way that a physical stutter can disrupt speech flow, her social anxiety disrupted her ability to function comfortably around others. By exposing herself to increasingly difficult social situations, such as taking a job as a cashier and enrolling in a large university, she eventually found ways to engage confidently. Marisa's journey has been a gradual process of finding her voice, building a roadmap of resilience and redefining her relationship with social fears, thereby transforming a once paralyzing inner stutter into a source of strength and positive impact through her coaching practice.

Recognize your inner stutter, stop holding back and be like Marisa!

10.

Things I wish I knew back then ...

To be yourself in a world that is constantly trying to make you something else is the greatest accomplishment.

—RALPH WALDO EMERSON

Sigmund Freud, the Austrian neurologist and father of psychoanalysis, said, "If youth knew; if age could." This quote refers to the ironic reality that young people tend to possess the ability and will to take action while lacking wisdom, while elders have the wisdom and yet may find themselves limited by ailments or other constraints. Fortunately, countless individuals have proven that age ought not to block one's realization of one's potential in life. In other words, it is never too late.

Whether it is Ricky Gervais, who became a famous comedian at 40; Susan Boyle, who reached global heights after her audition on *Britain's Got Talent* at 47; Colonel Sanders, who found success with Kentucky Fried Chicken at 65; Gladys Burrill, who completed her first marathon at 86; or Nola Ochs, who earned her doctorate in history at 98, the world is rife with inspiring examples of people for whom it was never too late to start. Whenever I'm asked to share insights I wish I'd known in the past, I prefer to frame them as "things I would tell my old self" rather than "things I would tell my younger self." This tweak in wording may seem minor, but its implications are significant. When I read articles where authors share advice they wish they'd known in their twenties, it often strikes me that this phrasing unintentionally implies the advice may not be relevant to readers who no longer consider themselves young. By instead thinking about our journey in terms of our "old self" and "new self," we avoid the ageist notion that meaningful transformation is limited to the early decades of life. This shift in language opens the door to continual growth and change, regardless of age. Indeed, whether you are 21, 31, 41, 51, 61, 71, 81 or 91, your potential can be further unlocked if and when you implement the mindset and behavioral changes in this book. Someone who beautifully demonstrates this adage is Katia Stern.

At age 40, Katia was a lawyer and a mother who had experienced over two decades of eating disorders, namely bulimia. She was constantly holding back because of the fear that others would judge the way she looked. More specifically, she felt painfully self-conscious about her body. She once asked her friend to take a picture of her, and as soon as she saw it, she cried for two consecutive weeks. While it was painful for her to accept that she did not like her body, it was the first step in realizing there was a gap between who she was and the person that she could become with the right mindset and action steps.

Naturally, we should strive to accept ourselves the way we currently are. However, if we feel frustrated by the gap between what is and what could be, we can use this information to guide our subsequent behavior in order to foster more optimal alignment in our lives. For Katia, this meant both changing her relationship with her body and starting to work with a fitness coach. Taking things to the next level, she boldly wrote down in journal, at age 40, that she would be competing in a fitness bikini competition that year. Immediately, self-doubt crept up in the form of negative and self-limiting thoughts. "Katia . . . you're a lawyer, you're a mother, you're 40 years old, for god's sake, you can't do this!" Then, after crossing out the goal from her diary, she started laughing as she realized that there was nobody else in the room. When I asked her why she had laughed, she replied that her fear of judgment was so massive that she was afraid someone might find out about this audacious goal.

That day, Katia decided she would sign up for the competition in Los Angeles. Expectedly, the journey was not a straightforward one. In fact, she often dreamed about not making it. By focusing on the end result and working with her coach, she started to see drastic changes in terms of health, vitality and fitness. "At 42 years old, I had the best body of my entire life. A woman's life isn't over when she's over 40!" she gleefully said. Setting that goal and working towards it was a major turning point in her life. Indeed, she decided to leave her law practice to focus on helping women improve their body image and self-love while also guiding them on the journey of fitness and mindset. At age 43, Katia was on stage at the Canadian National Bodybuilding Championship. At age 46, she became Mrs. Canada Classique. By age 50, she even started doing fitness modeling. What many didn't see was that this outward transformation was mirrored by an inner one. Katia had quietly overcome the eating disorder that had defined much of her earlier life, treating herself by working on her mindset.* She told me, "I take pride in my word; what I say, I own, even to myself." So, she made a promise and

* While Katia commented that she was able to treat herself when it came to her eating disorder, I would encourage readers who are experiencing such a disorder to explore professional help if necessary.

kept it. It had taken her over 15 years to reach that point, but she eventually discovered that change didn't have to be so hard. Her real breakthrough came when she realized just how much we underestimate the power of our beliefs. When I asked her what she would tell her old self and anyone who is currently experiencing fear, Katia spoke about the importance of falling in love with ourselves and with life. In her view, genuine self-improvement can occur only when it comes out of a place of self-love. Instead of seeking to change ourselves out of self-hatred or neediness, recognizing that we are lovable as we are can empower us to make the decisions that feel most aligned with the goals that will take us to victory.

Regardless of where we currently are in our lives, we can also learn from others who have previously navigated the complexities of existence. Who better to ask about the things they wish they had done differently than individuals who have reached the end of their lives? In her book *The Top Five Regrets of the Dying*, Australian palliative nurse Bronnie Ware speaks about the conversations she has with patients nearing the end. Here is a list of the top five things that her patients wish they knew in the past:

1. I wish I'd had the courage to live a life true to myself, not the life others expected of me.
2. I wish I hadn't worked so hard.
3. I wish I'd had the courage to express my feelings.
4. I wish I'd stayed in touch with my friends.
5. I wish I'd let myself be happier.

While all five answers are highly relevant to one's quest of crafting a fulfilling existence, 1, 3 and 5 are most relevant to the theme of this book. All three require cultivating a certain degree of courage while facing your inner stutter.

Indeed, gathering the courage to live a life true to ourselves requires being willing to risk judgment or rejection of our attempts at being authentic. For instance, when I first started to challenge myself to interact with people as opposed to avoiding them, I faced the reality that speaking more often inevitably meant I would have to stutter more often, too. In other words, I needed courage to deal with the reactions of others—reactions that had once shielded me from speaking. In your own life, you may have a fear of taking dance lessons, asking a question in front of hundreds or thousands of conference attendees or choosing a career path that your family members or friends disapprove of. Don't we owe it to ourselves to explore the full extent of our potential, regardless of how others might initially perceive us?

When it comes to expressing our feelings, many of us hold back in order to avoid the temporary discomfort, or emotional "ickiness" that we at times associate with being vulnerable. While we may love our parents, we may not yet have the courage to say the words "I love you." While we may be interested in a professional opportunity, we might resist seizing it. Yet, courage and action are the antidote to those moments of self-doubt. While we cannot guarantee that the outcome of the expression of our feelings will be the one we would prefer, living a life based on authenticity liberates us from the shackles of the "what ifs?" Never having to wonder about whether things would have turned out differently had we had the courage to express our feelings is optimal. In all honesty, dear reader, this is a truth that at times I find challenging. More than once, I have been in situations where I allowed certain words or feelings to remain unspoken,* causing ambiguity in my relationships.

Lastly, happiness is a complex idea and, while it is not the main focus of this book, conquering your inner stutter can bring about the well-being, purpose and positive emotions that we typically associate with it. In her 2007 book *The How of Happiness*, researcher Sonja Lyubomirsky stated that "happiness is the experience of joy, contentment or positive well-being, combined with a sense that one's life is good, meaningful and worthwhile." Letting ourselves be happy involves both being grateful for the things we have and acting in a way that will create positive and meaningful experiences in our lives. Achieving that is intricately tied to honing the courage to conquer our fears and become the best version of ourselves that we can possibly be.

Thankfully, we do not have to wait until we reach our final moments on Earth to derive actionable wisdom to start transforming our lives right away. This chapter will focus on the things I wish I knew back then. The following insights can be implemented to overcome the inner stutter at the individual, educational, organizational and societal levels.

It's okay to be different

It took me more than 25 years to understand that it's okay to be different. This realization was uncovered through the personal growth

* Coincidentally, filmmaker Josiane Blanc named the film that she made about my journey *Words Left Unspoken*.

journey I embarked on, but also because *society has become more accepting of differences.* We can all empathize with the idea that we ought not to hold back on account of factors outside our control. Growing up as a person who stutters, I despised being different. I despised the inability to say the words to express my thoughts and emotions. I would often wonder, "Why me?" While the societal shift towards greater acceptance and awareness of disability has certainly played a role in my transformational journey, I believe the agency of the individual to actively shape their own path is equally, if not more, significant. When I look back at my own journey, the successful milestones have not come from a suddenly accepting world or from my getting rid of what made me different. On the contrary, they occurred through both self-acceptance and changing my relationship with discomfort. If I could go back in time and talk to my old self, I would tell him, "It's okay to be different. Own what makes you unique."

In my opinion, efforts to create more welcoming spaces should be rooted in embracing what makes us unique while also empowering others to do the same. When guilt becomes the driving force behind these efforts, it can backfire. Well-meaning people who might have been supportive end up feeling pushed away. This leads to a culture where people walk on eggshells instead of engaging with genuine curiosity.

If the very programs meant to foster connection are making people feel excluded, it might be time to rethink the approach. A growth-based mindset acknowledges that we're all on a learning journey and that mistakes are inevitable when we're trying to better understand others' lived experiences.

Professor Loretta Ross has spoken about replacing public

"calling out" with the more inviting "calling in."[1] Calling out can alienate people and make them too afraid to ask questions or participate at all. Calling in, on the other hand, creates space for reflection and meaningful progress.

If the goal is to build environments where everyone feels respected, guilt won't get us there. It often leads to defensiveness. Curiosity will. By inviting questions and encouraging open conversations, we can build spaces that welcome all voices.

Allow me to share a personal story that illustrates the importance of being genuinely accepting of differences as opposed to it being performative.

Growing up in Lebanon, we had a weird birthday tradition that I always found incredibly silly and childish. Get this—whenever nighttime birthday parties took place near a swimming pool, all the guests conspired to throw the birthday kid into the pool with all their clothes on! Once that feat was accomplished, the rest of the party jumped in the pool, too.

Around the age of 14, I decided to celebrate my birthday with all my classmates at a neighborhood sports club. Even though I had always been shy because of my stutter, I'm grateful to have a large group of friends with whom I am still close. After a pleasant dinner by the pool, thc time was approaching for that dreadful tradition to take place. Ugh. What was I thinking, having my birthday party in a location where I was inevitably going to get completely drenched, with my clothes and shoes still on? I should have known better.

And then some time elapsed and I remained drier than the Sahara. In fact, nobody even acknowledged the tradition as they would have done at every other birthday pool party. Throughout the year, I had witnessed time and time again this boorish and senseless tradition. While a part of me was relieved to be off the hook, a significantly larger part of me was wondering, "Why am I not deemed worthy of being thrown into the pool?"

Did all my classmates equate my stuttering and the extreme shyness that resulted from it with oversensitivity? Did they simply assume I was dealing with enough obstacles without them having to impose on me this form of fraternal hazing? Did they not think of me as one of them?

Then Mark, one of my closest childhood friends, sensing the bittersweetness of my victory, yelled, "Joze! Why didn't anyone throw you in yet?" He rushed towards me and wrestled me until my inevitable descent into the pool. The water was cold, and my clothes and shoes made it hard to swim back to the surface. "What a stupid tradition," I thought, with a big smile on my face. You see, inclusion is not just about being treated with artificial niceness by everyone all the time. Inclusion is not about people walking on eggshells whenever they're around you out of the fear of offending or hurting you. Being included means you get thrown into the pool, too.

Overcoming the fear of being judged for being different becomes much easier in an environment that is genuinely accepting of differences. When people feel free to be curious and connect with others who are different, without hesitation or fear, it creates space for everyone to engage more fully with the world and unlock their true potential. The story demonstrates that the attempt to deliberately protect me only served to make me feel even more ostracized. That one person deciding to go against the grain and throw me into the pool was, ironically, the most effective ally in that scenario.

He single-handedly engineered an environment where the person who was *different* was able to feel like he was a part of the group. An organization that does not create such an environment might have its own *organizational* stutter. Similarly, a society that fails to make all its members feel like they are capable of prosperity has its own *societal* stutter. I tackle these topics of workplace culture in my speaking engagements at both organizations and educational institutions. As I've said, the best way to navigate these inner stutters is by identifying them, uncovering the unhelpful beliefs or biases that allow them to repeatedly occur and devising an action plan that generates opportunities to repeatedly face the obstacles. In doing so, not only are we unlocking our own potential; we may indirectly be inspiring others to overcome their own obstacles. Indeed, we all need the occasional reminder to give ourselves permission to show up authentically in the world. I know I do.

As we free ourselves from our own fear, our courage automatically inspires others, too. In the heartwarming film *Pay It Forward*, a young boy named Trevor McKinney is inspired by his teacher to impact the world through kindness. Trevor comes up with the idea of "paying it forward," where every person who receives one of his acts of kindness must then help three other people. His idea gains momentum and creates widespread positive change. Similar to the film's premise, when we face our fear and demonstrate our bravery out of a genuine desire to help others who are just embarking on their own journey of transformation, we inspire them to do the same. Therefore, although "paying it forward" is not the initial objective of challenging ourselves to conquer fear, it is an exceptional byproduct that positively influences the lives of family members, friends, our community and the world around us.

Use fear as a compass

Are you familiar with the author Mark Manson? He's best known for his self-improvement books with very *interesting* titles.* He also happens to be one of my favorite writers. On May 27, 2019, I attended his book signing at a major bookstore in downtown Toronto. There must have been 500 people there. After reading some passages from his book, he announced that he would like to spend the remainder of the time answering questions from the audience. As soon as I heard those words, my heart started to pound. The mere thought of potentially holding that microphone and speaking in front of hundreds of people caused a panic reaction to cascade. Ironically, at that time, I had already won public-speaking competitions and performed stand-up comedy. In other words, I was no stranger to speaking in public. Even though I had achieved milestones that my younger self would have deemed absurdly impossible, those breakthroughs didn't cause the fear or discomfort to disappear, or even to diminish. Far from it. In that instant, every past moment of triumph felt irrelevant, like it had never even existed.

Contrary to how in the past, the fear instantly dissuaded me from moving forward, my reaction that day was, "Uh-oh, this means I *have* to do this!" With a quiet smile, I put my hand up and locked eyes with the staff member walking around the room with the microphone. I was given the floor and started by telling Mark and the audience that my question was going to be full of s . . . suspense! I then told him that *The Subtle Art of Not Giving a F*ck* positively shaped the journey of growth I had embarked on over the past few

---

* You might be familiar with *The Subtle Art of Not Giving a F*ck.*

years.* *And it has.* On page nine, Manson writes that "the desire for more positive experience is itself a negative experience. And, paradoxically, the acceptance of one's negative experience is itself a positive experience." Applying these words to my situation in the bookstore, I had to decide between two propositions: waiting for the fear to go away and taking action another day in a hypothetical future, or accepting it, embracing its inevitability and choosing to act. Manson is also credited with encouraging readers to stop avoiding discomfort by choosing "the sh*t sandwich" that they like.† While almost every worthwhile endeavor, including overcoming your inner stutter, will require discomfort and sacrifice, we get to choose what challenge, or sh*t sandwich, to do or eat in order to become the best version of ourselves.

Right after speaking in the bookstore that day, I felt on top of the world. I had a similar experience at Ryan Holiday's lecture in Toronto in November of 2024, where I asked a question in front of almost four thousand people. I started that interaction by saying, "Ryan, I know you said that stoicism is easier said than done . . . but I have a stutter. For me, nothing is easier said than done!"‡ In both those instances, I was reminded that fear and action did not have to be mutually exclusive. Fear acted as a trampoline that propelled me forward. If we expect that one moment of triumph to automatically unlock the door for future success, we will never create the momentum required for ongoing growth and transformation. In other words, if you conquer your inner stutter or fear once, it

* You can watch the video of that interaction at www.jozepiranian.com/stopholdingback.

† Asking him a question was my sh*t sandwich that day!

‡ You can watch that interaction at www.jozepiranian.com/stopholdingback.

does not mean they are gone. It simply means that fear and action can coexist. Counterintuitively, it means that fear indirectly created action. Let's focus less on waiting for that breakthrough—that one moment that is going to change our lives—and more on cultivating micro-moments of bravery. In the words of Nelson Mandela, "Courage is not the absence of fear but the triumph over it."

Slay the dragon: once, twice and thrice

After delivering a keynote at a pharmaceutical company in Philadelphia, I had dinner plans with my friend Yeghiche Manoukian, who holds an executive position at a large enterprise. After covering a few superficial niceties, we dove into more substantial topics. Who needs small talk when big talk impatiently awaits, right? Having heard me speak at a conference in Madrid a few months earlier, Yeghiche (or Yeyo) told me that one of the quotes in my keynote stood out for him: "Through repeatedly exposing myself to the source of my fear, I manage to overcome it." That phrase had sparked a conversation between him and his executive coach, resulting in the following interpretation: There is a difference between overcoming and transmuting fear.

Yeyo continued by saying that while "overcoming" implies climbing over an obstacle or pushing it out of the way, the real goal ought to be *transmuting* fear by transforming it into its higher order. In other words, instead of simply overcoming massive fear, we ought to transmute it into massive courage or massive confidence. This reasoning is aligned with the popular quote from French chemist Antoine Lavoisier: "Nothing is lost, nothing is created, everything is transformed." My personal observations lead me to conclude that since fear must be repeatedly faced, it is technically not "overcomable." By mere virtue of our fear's tendency to constantly return, we can compare it to a dragon that must be slayed daily. However, while the act of slaying the dragon may not permanently eliminate it, it generates creative and momentous energy that drives us above and beyond the obstacle. I work on triumphing over my fear on a daily basis, through micro-moments of bravery, even when, *especially when*, I least want to. I have learned that I have to work on my fears every single day. Whether it is overcoming, conquering, transmuting or transforming, the fear doesn't stop and neither must we.

Chapter 10 takeaways

- It's okay to be different. Own what makes you unique. Through embracing our uniqueness and that of others, we create an environment where everyone can show up authentically and fulfill their true potential in life.
- Use fear as a compass that guides you where you need to go.
- Your fears might never stop, so why should you?

Meet Rachel Weinstock, 45

Rachel Weinstock, a Canadian teacher and author of *Be Who You Needed*, shared her personal journey of overcoming deep-seated fears that shaped her childhood. "I was afraid of being called ugly," she told me, her voice soft but sincere as her eyes briefly looked downward in recollection. This fear of being seen as different held her back for many years, shaping how she interacted with the world around her. Rachel observed that many of the students she taught dealt with similar fears. "Some kids hold back due to the fear of being called stupid, fat, ugly . . . the list goes on!" she said, her voice tinged with both empathy and frustration.

Rachel's journey of healing wasn't easy or linear. She spoke about her two decades of therapy, combined with reading positive literature, listening to podcasts and having vulnerable conversations with supportive people. "At first, it's truly difficult. Over time, however, it becomes easier," she said, reflecting on the process of sharing her vulnerability. I could relate. I used to dread telling people about my stutter, but now, the act of sharing that part of me feels more habitual and liberating.

Even after so much progress, Rachel revealed that certain moments can still trigger those painful memories. One such moment came years after she had been relentlessly teased for her appearance on the school bus. While working at an orphanage in Japan, a child there called her ugly. Her voice faltered as she recalled that moment, and her eyes clouded with the emotion of it. "I broke down," she said quietly, as if reliving that old pain. She realized that for much of her life, she equated not being seen as beautiful with not having worth as a human being.

But Rachel didn't stop there. By continuing her work

in therapy, she learned to confront the patterns that kept her stuck. She was determined to break free from them. "I felt like a gladiator in a ring with zero protection!" she exclaimed, frustration lining her words as she recalled the raw vulnerability of her past. She emphasized how crucial it is for adolescents, especially those struggling with insecurities, to feel safe and protected in those painful moments.

Her voice softened with compassion as she concluded, "There's beauty in everybody." This hard-earned truth carried a deep warmth, and I felt the truth of it resonate. Rachel ended our conversation by stressing that any tiny step we take towards replacing the negative patterns of our past with new, positive associations is a step in the right direction. Her words echoed my own belief in micro-moments of bravery. It is after all through these acts, whether we are confronting our own fears or empowering others to own their uniqueness, that we can create a world where everyone fulfills their potential.

The inner stutter corner

Rachel's inner stutter stemmed from a deep-seated fear of being bullied for being different, specifically, being called ugly. That fear took root early and shaped how she moved through the world. It wasn't just a passing insecurity; it was a story she told herself for years, one that made her hesitant to fully show up or be seen.

Like Rachel, I've had my own inner stutter with the fear of being judged for being different. Rachel's journey of healing wasn't straightforward, and neither has mine been. In her twenties, Rachel's past fear was triggered in a powerful way when a child at the orphanage in Japan called her ugly. That moment of breakdown reminded her of how deep her fears ran, and I've experienced similar moments where someone reacting negatively to my stutter can trigger old uncomfortable memories.

Rachel worked hard to heal, learning to challenge the patterns that kept her stuck. Through therapy, brave conversations and a commitment to growth, she began to replace those negative associations with new, positive ones. Like me, she's continued to face setbacks but always took the next step, no matter how small.

Today, Rachel's life is vastly different from the fearful place she once occupied. She's a teacher, author and advocate for self-empowerment, encouraging others to own their uniqueness. She believes that there's beauty in everybody, and her journey shows that by facing our inner stutter, we can all learn to embrace our worth and use our struggles to connect with others.

Rachel's story highlights the power of vulnerability and how the journey towards healing is about taking small, brave steps, a truth I've come to deeply understand in my own life. Recognize your inner stutter, stop holding back and be like Rachel!

EPILOGUE

Dr. Mark C., 76, is a dentist and a pilot. While his bachelor of science and doctor of dental surgery from McGill University led the way to dentistry, he was never supposed to become a pilot. In his youth, Mark's inner stutter was linked to a terrible fear of heights. In fact, anytime he was in a building or on a balcony on a high floor, he experienced a sense of panic. Looking over the edge would make him so nervous that he had to go inside immediately. And once inside, it was difficult for him to go back up to a high floor—anywhere. This fear even extended to climbing a ladder.

"What about traveling by plane?" I asked him when we met at an alumni event. He gave a small chuckle, admitting that he would intentionally select an aisle or middle seat in order to avoid looking outside the window and seeing how high up he was. "It became a hindrance, an impediment in my daily life and to doing things that most people would do so easily, without giving a second thought," he explained, with frustration in his voice. That is precisely how I felt about stuttering and my fear of speaking, seeing that everyone else around me appeared to be doing this basic act so effortlessly. In the same way in which I decided to conquer my fear of speaking through tackling the most extreme form, public speaking, Mark thought that maybe if he could learn to fly, he would defeat that fear once and for all.

Forty years ago, he met up with a flight instructor and joined him, as a passenger, on a flight in a small plane. His eyes widened slightly as he recalled, “I could feel the air beneath my feet on the floor of the aircraft.” When he was up in the sky, he became introspective and began to analyze why he was afraid of heights and flying. It occurred to him that he vehemently feared the lack of control. “If a car has a problem, you can pull over to the side of the road. If something goes wrong with a plane, however, you can’t do that!” He shrugged lightly, admitting that he had to come to terms with the lack of control, and therefore he embarked on his unlikely journey of becoming a pilot.

First, he learned the theory of flight and even built remote-control airplanes that he flew for years to better understand the mechanisms of planes. He then took a course in flying that involved 80 hours of “ground school,” the theoretical training, before stepping into a plane as a pilot. A faint smile tugged at his lips as he remembered one of his instructors telling him, “When you’re flying, height is your friend.” He then explained that if something goes wrong while you’re up in the sky, you have time to rectify the problem and land safely. His tone grew serious again as he told me that experiencing that same issue while being close to the ground would naturally be a far more challenging feat. When Mark explained that nuance, it struck me that similar patterns might occur in our mental health. Recognizing the issue while we’re way up in the air is the equivalent of recognizing the earliest sign of depression, anxiety or addictive tendencies way before the crash occurs. Conversely, recognizing the issue while we are already close to the ground is equivalent to depressive or anxious symptoms already set in motion. Resolving the issue at that point is far more difficult.

After ground training, Mark started to learn how to fly an actual aircraft with the aim of obtaining his pilot license; this part required 85 hours of flying sessions with an instructor. He leaned forward slightly, explaining that one of the requirements was the ability to recover the aircraft when in a spiral dive or when the aircraft is in spin. "A spin is a situation in which the airplane can no longer fly and the nose is pointing to the earth. You see the earth coming up quickly," he explained to me, his hands mimicking the dive motion as I attentively nodded. I admitted that it sounded like a very scary situation to be in. Mark gave me an empathetic look and agreed, sharing that in the first few classes as a passenger, he was as "white as a sheet" when the session ended. On telling his instructor that he did not believe he would be able to meet this requirement, he received wise advice that he has held onto since. "It's common to feel that way when you're a passenger," the instructor said. "When, however, you do it yourself, you have specific parameters to follow, and you can get through it." A proud smile appeared on Mark's face as he stated that he implemented all that he had learned and was able to successfully complete the entire training, including the dreaded spin.

If you are wondering, in case you somehow find yourself in that situation one day, here's what to do to recover from that nosedive:

1. You tilt the airplane's nose (the tip of the plane) downward so it's no longer pointing up.
2. You push the pedal on the opposite side to stop the airplane from spinning.*
3. Once the spinning stops, you speed up and pull the airplane back up into steady flight.

* If the plane spins left, press the right pedal. If it spins right, press the left pedal.

Mark's main fear related to a lack of agency over the situation, but by regaining control and following the specific parameters that he had learned, he could negotiate with the fear in a way that enabled him to take action and unlock his hidden potential. Overcoming the fear was a very emotional moment for him. "The day that I passed my flight test, my instructor gave me a set of wings that I still wear on my bomber jacket." Mark's eyes gleamed with pride as he shared that after all the steps he took towards achieving this goal and overcoming his fear, he was naturally extremely proud of himself. To put his achievement into context, from 50 people who started in his class, only three passed. By becoming an expert at his inner stutter, he combined learning and knowledge with taking courageous action. Similarly, as a dentist, he recalled starting implant dentistry 35 years ago, when that practice was completely new. While he initially had seen others do it, it was only through acquiring the knowledge and doing it himself that his confidence grew. Yet again, the action-oriented, bottom-up approach has proven its effectiveness.

When I asked Mark what he would share with his old self or with someone who is currently in the process of overcoming fear, he leaned back thoughtfully. When it comes to the fear of flying specifically, he said that people have it because they cannot stand the lack of control. He gave a firm nod as he recommended that those individuals learn about how an airplane flies and how it stays up in the sky, especially the fact that if the engine stops, the airplane does not sink like a stone. "The truth is that the airplane can fly for a long distance without an engine. Learn about it and you do not have to be fearful." This philosophy is consistent with the idea that we humans are informavores who can consume information, both actively and passively, so that we are better equipped to handle the challenges that come our way. Repeatedly showing our brain that we can overcome a challenge, as Mark did through his 85 hours of flight training, is a step that requires us to take courageous action. "My flight instructor told me that we learn from the mistakes that others made because we do not have the time to make them all ourselves," Mark shared with a smile. He is right. It is my hope that through reading this book, you have learned from the pitfalls that I experienced by allowing fear to dictate my life for far too long. You can learn from my mistakes, as well as from stories from both myself and others, concepts and calls to action to mitigate turbulence and to land safely at your desired destination.

We got through this. As we near the end of this book, I encourage you to reflect on the main ideas that were formulated over these ten chapters. We first looked at the redundancy of waiting for that perfect moment that might or might never come. Beyond being counterproductive, waiting is also a form of avoidance, which may be beneficial in the short term and yet is erosive of our potential in the long term. We avoid certain situations because we hesitate to take action, and that hesitation can be characterized as the inner stutter that gets in the way of realizing our purpose in life. Seeing that the inner stutter is typically the inaction following a specific form of fear (of judgment, of rejection, of failure, of success, etc.), we also examined the evolutionary origins of fear. As we looked back, we saw that humankind's response to fear served a crucial role in the survival of our ancestral lineage and concluded that we have the power to recognize the primitive tendencies of our Stone Age minds without succumbing to the pressures. Indeed, through desensitization and experimentation, we can show ourselves (and our brains) that we are capable of acting in the face of fear.

Far from being an endlessly overwhelming experience, the most challenging aspect of fear typically includes going through an initial moment of discomfort. Through micro-moments of bravery, we are able to tackle the inner stutter by turning fear into action one moment at a time. Seeing that we tend to overestimate the significance of the grandiose macro-moments and milestones in our lives, we looked at a realistic pie chart illustrating that most of our existence is spent in the micro-moments. It is through generating momentum and exposing ourselves to a plethora of novel data points while leveraging the fear of regrets to our advantage that we can acquire the adequate mindset for continuous growth. Indeed, through gradually exposing ourselves to the source of our fear, we can experience "surreal progress" in the sense that our realized milestones of success might start appearing absurdly impossible to our old self.

It's worth noting that it is in our nature to become complacent and to rest on our laurels once we have experienced some positive results. It is key to counteract that tendency by remembering that if we do not enter *input* in the factory of our lives, there will simply be no *output*.

But whenever we make taking uncomfortable action our primary focus, we risk burning out if we do not manage our mental wellness hygiene. Through mindfulness, gratitude journaling, exercise, wellness and therapy, we can make this journey of transformation one that is sustainable.

At the societal level, we can empower individuals to own their uniqueness and to turn fear into action so that they, too, fulfill their true potential in life. In today's world that increasingly emphasizes people experiencing a sense of belonging, it is important to keep in mind that the main focus of organizations, schools and society ought to be to create an environment where every human being, no matter their obstacles, can thrive and become the best version of themselves. Far from being an overnight trick, the journey outlined in this book is an ongoing process of using fear as a compass that will guide us towards growth, though at times it is uncomfortable. Moreover, we will have to repeatedly face that fear, once, twice and thrice, until we start believing, at a cellular level, that fear and action do not have to be mutually exclusive; fear and action can coexist.

The most important step to take after reading a book like this one is an action step. Whether or not you have already begun implementing these insights in your daily life, I cannot emphasize enough that the change you desire begins only when you start taking action. I am reminded of the following message I received from a person who was afraid of leading a workshop at work:

Hello Joze,

I wanted to share with you how much you have impacted me and inspired me. Last week during your keynote, I stood on your stage with my fear of public speaking. In that moment, I shared with you and everyone else that I was preparing for an upcoming workshop that I had lots of anxiety over. This morning as I got ready, I watched your YouTube video four times. I had also watched it a couple of times since I saw you last week. My workshop today was glorious! It went better than I could have ever expected and I really do believe you helped me explode through my fear!!! Thank you. Thank you. Thank you.

This person implemented the mindset shift and behavioral strategies discussed in my keynote speeches and in this book to overcome her fear. While familiarizing yourself with the ideas is one part of the equation, taking action is an irreplaceable element in the process of conquering fear. Whenever we are on the verge of starting to live differently, it is tempting to set unrealistic goals. Having read my story, you know that the change occurred in a radical yet rather gradual manner. Through one fear-defying action at a time, momentum brewed, thereby creating opportunities and milestones that my old self would never have fathomed. By using the takeaways at the end of each chapter as a behavioral reference point, you can begin implementing these changes in your day-to-day life.* Maintaining proper mental wellness habits will ensure that you do not needlessly exhaust yourself along the way. In fact, I would encourage you to build a supportive community for sustained personal growth. Whether this would be a public-speaking club, a meditation group or the Yes Way Joze Facebook group, we derive great benefits from aligning ourselves with communities that want us to thrive. In the words of James Clear in *Atomic Habits*, "You don't rise to the level of your goals; you fall to the level of your systems. Join a group where your desired behavior is the normal behavior and you'll rise together."

In conclusion, I would like to express my deep gratitude towards you, dear reader. As someone who has read plenty of self-improvement books over the years, I find it nothing short of surreal to have written a book of my own. Even more surreal is the fact that people are reading this book to accompany them on their own jour-

---

* You can also use the worksheets, created specifically for this book, that can be downloaded here: www.jozepiranian.com/stopholdingback.

ney of personal growth. I am grateful that you trusted me to be your guide over these ten chapters, and I wish you nothing but the absolute best on your journey. We all need inspiration sometimes, and I am at the top of the list of people who do. We are all in this together, fellow voyagers on the journey towards becoming our best selves.

In the same way that my old self would have deemed my current journey as absurdly impossible, your current self will deem your new journey rather unlikely. Equipped with the new insights, concepts and stories from this book, you now know that amazing things await you. Now, it's your turn to take a deep breath and walk through the fire.

ACKNOWLEDGMENTS

Writing this book reminded me that even if I don't stutter when writing, finding the optimal words to express the self is its own mountain to climb. I definitely did not do it alone.

To my family in my home country of Lebanon and all around the world, thank you for loving and supporting me along the way. I know I needed my mother's not-so-gentle nudges to keep on working on the book once or twice. To Mam, Pap and my sister, Nathalie, I love you. And to my Armenian ancestors whose resilient voices live in mine, this is for you, too.

To friends old and new, thank you for being you and for allowing me to be me.

To my editors and the entire HarperCollins team, thank you for believing in this story, and in me. You helped me turn my lived experience into written words for all to read.

To every person who stutters, hides or holds back due to fear: This book is yours, too.

And finally, to the old version of me who thought a stutter meant the end of a sentence.

Turns out, it was the beginning of a story.

NOTES

Introduction

1. Jieling Chen et al., "Post-Traumatic Stress Symptoms and Post-Traumatic Growth: Evidence from a Longitudinal Study Following an Earthquake Disaster," *PloS One* 10, no. 6 (2015): e0127241, https://doi.org/10.1371/journal.pone.0127241.
2. Daniel Liberto, "Anti-Fragility: Definition, Overview, FAQ," Investopedia, March 25, 2012, https://www.investopedia.com/terms/a/anti-fragility.asp.
3. Casey D. Calhoun et al., "The Role of Social Support in Coping with Psychological Trauma: An Integrated Biopsychosocial Model for Posttraumatic Stress Recovery," *Psychiatric Quarterly* 93 (2022): 949–70, https://pmc.ncbi.nlm.nih.gov/articles/PMC9534006/.
4. "Understanding Stuttering: Causes, Management, and Support," National Stuttering Association, August 7, 2024, https://www.westutter.org/post/what-is-stuttering.
5. "Understanding Stuttering," National Stuttering Association, https://www.westutter.org/understanding-stuttering.
6. Stuart Wolpert, "UCLA Neuroscientist's Book Explains Why Social Connection Is as Important as Food and Shelter," UCLA, October 10, 2013, https://newsroom.ucla.edu/releases/we-are-hard-wired-to-be-social-248746.
7. Ehud Yairi and Nicoline Ambrose, "Epidemiology of Stuttering: 21st Century Advances," *Journal of Fluency Disorders* 38, no. 2 (2013): 66–87, https://doi.org/10.1016/j.jfludis.2012.11.002.
8. "Myths About Stuttering," National Stuttering Association, August 7, 2024, https://www.westutter.org/post/myths-about-stuttering.
9. "What Is Stuttering," National Stuttering Association, https://www.westutter.org/post/what-is-stuttering.

Chapter 1: What are you waiting for?

1. Michelle Klotz, "Loss Aversion: Everything You Need to Know," InsideBE, May 16, 2022, https://insidebe.com/articles/loss-aversion/.
2. Archy O. de Berker et al., "Computations of Uncertainty Mediate Acute Stress Responses in Humans," *Nature Communications* 7, no. 1 (2016): 10996, https://doi.org/10.1038/ncomms10996.
3. Joel Cooper and Kevin M. Carlsmith, "Cognitive Dissonance," in *International Encyclopedia of the Social & Behavioral Sciences* (Elsevier 2015), 76–78.
4. John Montopoli, "Stuck in the Aftermath of Social Anxiety and Rumination," National Social Anxiety Center, June 20, 2016, https://nationalsocialanxietycenter.com/2016/06/20/stuck-in-the-aftermath-social-anxiety-and-rumination/.
5. Wendy Treynor et al., "Rumination Reconsidered: A Psychometric Analysis," *Cognitive Therapy and Research* 27, no. 3 (2003): 247–59, https://doi.org/10.1023/a:1023910315561.
6. Jocko Willink, "Extreme Ownership Quotes," Goodreads.com, October 20, 2015, https://www.goodreads.com/work/quotes/43458164-extreme-ownership-how-u-s-navy-seals-lead-and-win.
7. Mike Szydlowski, "Blowing out the Candles," *Columbia Daily Tribune*, September 13, 2017, https://www.columbiatribune.com/story/lifestyle/family/2017/09/13/blowing-out-candles/18826365007/.
8. Jayne Leonard, "Recognizing the Hidden Signs of Depression," Medical News Today, updated November 6, 2023, https://www.medicalnewstoday.com/articles/325513.
9. Greg Daugherty, "What Is Quiet Quitting—and Is It a Real Trend?" Investopedia, September 30, 2022, https://www.investopedia.com/what-is-quiet-quitting-6743910.
10. S.F. Dingfelder, "Old Problem, New Tools," *Monitor on Psychology* 40, no. 9 (2009): 40, https://www.apa.org/monitor/2009/10/helplessness.
11. Dingfelder, "Old Problem, New Tools."

Chapter 2: The appeal of avoiding

1. Martin Taylor, "What Does Fight, Flight, Freeze, Fawn Mean?" WebMD, May 19, 2022, https://www.webmd.com/mental-health/what-does-fight-flight-freeze-fawn-mean.
2. Taylor, "What Does Fight, Flight, Freeze, Fawn Mean?"

3. Taylor, "What Does Fight, Flight, Freeze, Fawn Mean?"
4. Taylor, "What Does Fight, Flight, Freeze, Fawn Mean?"
5. "10 Ways to Fight Your Fears," NHS Inform, June 13, 2024, https://www.nhsinform.scot/healthy-living/mental-wellbeing/fears-and-phobias/10-ways-to-fight-your-fears/.
6. "Indian Cinema Has Been Escapist Experience for Masses," *Business Standard*, May 25, 2017, https://www.business-standard.com/article/news-ians/indian-cinema-has-been-escapist-experience-for-masses-117052500584_1.html.
7. Olivia Guy-Evans, "Amygdala: What It Is & Its Functions," Simply Psychology, updated May 12, 2025, https://www.simplypsychology.org/amygdala.html.
8. Angela Haupt, "Why Is Everyone Working on Their Inner Child?" *Time*, April 6, 2023, https://time.com/6268636/inner-child-work-healing/.
9. Haupt, "Why Is Everyone Working on Their Inner Child?"
10. Haupt, "Why Is Everyone Working on Their Inner Child?"
11. Shulamith Lala Ashenberg Straussner et al., "Wounded Healers: A Multistate Study of Licensed Social Workers' Behavioral Health Problems," *Social Work* 63, no. 2 (2018): 125–33, https://doi.org/10.1093/sw/swy012.
12. Andrew Barkley, "7.1: Repeated and Sequential Games," in *The Economics of Food and Agricultural Markets*, Libretexts, February 27, 2020, https://socialsci.libretexts.org/Bookshelves/Economics/The_Economics_of_Food_and_Agricultural_Markets_(Barkley)/07%3A_Game_Theory_Applications/7.01%3A_Repeated_and_Sequential_Games.
13. Robert Waldinger and Marc Schulz, "What the Longest Study on Human Happiness Found Is the Key to a Good Life," *Atlantic Monthly*, January 19, 2023, https://www.theatlantic.com/ideas/archive/2023/01/harvard-happiness-study-relationships/672753/.
14. Marc Schulz and Robert Waldinger, "An 85-Year Harvard Study Found the No. 1 Thing That Makes Us Happy in Life: It Helps Us 'Live Longer,'" CNBC, February 10, 2023, https://www.cnbc.com/2023/02/10/85-year-harvard-study-found-the-secret-to-a-long-happy-and-successful-life.html.
15. Adam Hayes, "Law of Diminishing Marginal Returns: Definition, Example, Use in Economics," Investopedia, February 23, 2004, https://www.investopedia.com/terms/l/lawofdiminishingmarginalreturn.asp.
16. Tim Jewell, "What Causes Nervous Laughter," Healthline, updated May 31, 2023, https://www.healthline.com/health/mental-health/nervous-laughter.
17. Jewell, "What Causes Nervous Laughter."

18. Jia Jiang, "What I Learned from 100 Days of Rejection," TED Talk, Mount Hood, Oregon, May 2015, 16 min., 24 sec., https://www.ted.com/talks/jia_jiang_what_i_learned_from_100_days_of_rejection/transcript?language=en.

19. Michael Carey and Andrew Forsyth, "Teaching Tip Sheet: Self-Efficacy," American Psychological Association, 2009, https://www.apa.org/pi/aids/resources/education/self-efficacy.

Chapter 3: Why do you hesitate?

1. Tchiki Davis, "Why Self-Disclosure Powers Relationships," *Psychology Today*, March 13, 2023, https://www.psychologytoday.com/ca/blog/click-here-for-happiness/202210/why-self-disclosure-is-good-for-relationships.

2. Diana Paula Dudău, "The Relation between Perfectionism and Impostor Phenomenon," *Procedia, Social and Behavioral Sciences* 127 (2014): 129–33, https://doi.org/10.1016/j.sbspro.2014.03.226.

3. "'Psychology Works' Fact Sheet: Perfectionism," Canadian Psychological Association, September 18, 2020, https://cpa.ca/psychology-works-fact-sheet-perfectionism/.

4. Juliana Breines, "3 Ways Your Beliefs Can Shape Your Reality," *Psychology Today*, August 30, 2015, https://www.psychologytoday.com/ca/blog/in-love-and-war/201508/3-ways-your-beliefs-can-shape-your-reality.

5. Breines, "3 Ways Your Beliefs Can Shape Your Reality."

6. Breines, "3 Ways Your Beliefs Can Shape Your Reality."

7. Breines, "3 Ways Your Beliefs Can Shape Your Reality."

8. Sarah Maguire, "What Is the Baader-Meinhof Phenomenon?" *The Lighthouse*, July 23, 2020, https://lighthouse.mq.edu.au/article/july-2020/What-is-the-Baader-Meinhof-Phenomenon.

9. Maguire, "What Is the Baader-Meinhof Phenomenon?"

10. T.S. Sathyanarayana Rao et al., "The Biochemistry of Belief," *Indian Journal of Psychiatry* 51, no. 4 (2009): 239–41, https://pmc.ncbi.nlm.nih.gov/articles/PMC2802367/.

Chapter 4: Taming the tiger within

1. Jim Dobson, "French Spiderman Alain Robert Has Free Climbed the World's Tallest Buildings and He Is Not Finished," *Forbes*, April 26, 2020, https://www.forbes.com/sites/jimdobson/2020/04/26/french-spiderman-alain-robert-has-free-climbed-the-worlds-tallest-buildings-and-he-is-not-finished/.

2. Cassandra Willyard, "Fearless Woman Lacks Key Part of Brain," *Science*, December 16, 2010, https://www.science.org/content/article/fearless-woman-lacks-key-part-brain.

3. Jamshid J. Tehrani, "The Phylogeny of Little Red Riding Hood," *PloS One* 8, no. 11 (2013): e78871, https://doi.org/10.1371/journal.pone.0078871.

4. Tehrani, "The Phylogeny of Little Red Riding Hood."

5. Daniel T. Blumstein, *The Nature of Fear: Survival Lessons from the Wild* (Harvard University Press, 2020).

6. Mary Beckman, "Rejection Is Like Pain to the Brain," *Science*, October 9, 2003, https://www.science.org/content/article/rejection-pain-brain.

7. C. Nathan Dewall et al., "Acetaminophen Reduces Social Pain: Behavioral and Neural Evidence," *Psychological Science* 21, no. 7 (2010): 931–37, https://doi.org/10.1177/0956797610374741.

8. Leda Cosmides and John Tooby, "Evolutionary Psychology: A Primer," Center for Evolutionary Psychology, January 13, 1997, http://cogweb.ucla.edu/ep/EP-primer.html#Principle%205.

9. Deirdre Barrett, *Supernormal Stimuli: How Primal Urges Overran Their Evolutionary Purpose* (W.W. Norton & Company, 2010).

10. Gad Saad, "The Consuming Instinct: What Darwinian Consumption Reveals about Human Nature," *Politics and the Life Sciences* 32, no. 1 (2013): 58–72, https://doi.org/10.2990/32_1_58.

11. David M. G. Lewis et al., "Evolutionary Psychology: A How-to Guide," *The American Psychologist* 72, no. 4 (2017): 353–73, https://doi.org/10.1037/a0040409.

12. "What Is the Fight, Flight, Freeze or Fawn Response?" Cleveland Clinic, July 22, 2024, https://health.clevelandclinic.org/what-happens-to-your-body-during-the-fight-or-flight-response/.

Chapter 5: Act your way into new thoughts

1. "The History of Bill Wilson," Stepping Stones Foundation, July 10, 2020, https://www.steppingstones.org/about/the-wilsons/bills-story/.

2. "TIME 100 Persons of the Century," *Time*, June 14, 1999, https://time.com/archive/6735625/time-100-persons-of-the-century/.

3. Laurence Steinberg and Kathryn C. Monahan, "Age Differences in Resistance to Peer Influence," *Developmental Psychology* 43, no. 6 (2007): 1531–43, https://psycnet.apa.org/record/2007–16709–020?doi=1.

4. “Britain’s Scariest Roads Revealed,” BBC News, November 27, 2009, http://news.bbc.co.uk/2/hi/uk_news/scotland/glasgow_and_west/8382506.stm.

5. S. Rufus, “The 5 Ingredients of Shame,” *Psychology Today*, May 7, 2021, https://www.psychologytoday.com/ca/blog/stuck/202105/the-5-ingredients-shame.

6. Maria Miceli and Cristiano Castelfranchi, “Reconsidering the Differences between Shame and Guilt,” *Europe’s Journal of Psychology* 14, no. 3 (2018): 710–33, https://doi.org/10.5964/ejop.v14i3.1564.

7. Annette Kämmerer, “The Scientific Underpinnings and Impacts of Shame,” *Scientific American*, August 9, 2019, https://www.scientificamerican.com/article/the-scientific-underpinnings-and-impacts-of-shame/.

8. Zawn Villines, “The Effects of Fat Shaming on Health,” Medical News Today, updated November 28, 2024, https://www.medicalnewstoday.com/articles/effects-of-fat-shaming.

9. Villines, “Effects of Fat Shaming on Health.”

10. Theodore Roosevelt, speech at the Sorbonne, Paris, April 23, 1910, https://www.presidency.ucsb.edu/documents/address-the-sorbonne-paris-france-citizenship-republic.

11. James Grout, “The Roman Gladiator,” *Encyclopaedia Romana*, updated April 7, 2025, https://penelope.uchicago.edu/~grout/encyclopaedia_romana/gladiators/gladiators.html.

12. Julia Zimmermann and Franz J. Neyer, “Do We Become a Different Person When Hitting the Road? Personality Development of Sojourners,” *Journal of Personality and Social Psychology*, September 2013, 105(3): 515–30, https://pubmed.ncbi.nlm.nih.gov/23773042/.

13. Elisabeth Schubach et al., “Me, Myself, and Mobility: The Relevance of Region for Young Adults’ Identity Development: Regional Identity,” *European Journal of Personality* 30, no. 2 (2016): 189–200, https://doi.org/10.1002/per.2048.

14. Jonathan Look, “Why Travel Is Important Today More than Ever,” *Forbes*, September 24, 2018, https://www.forbes.com/sites/jonathanlookjr/2018/09/24/why-travel-is-important-today-more-than-ever/.

15. R. Mickens, “Why Is the Earth Habitable?” American Museum of Natural History, accessed May 8, 2025, https://www.amnh.org/exhibitions/permanent/planet-earth/why-is-the-earth-habitable.

16. Mark Manson, “What Is Self-Improvement?” July 20, 2017, https://markmanson.net/self-improvement.

17. Manson, “What Is Self-Improvement?”

18. Saul McLeod, "Operant Conditioning: What It Is, How It Works, and Examples," Simply Psychology, updated March 17, 2025, https://www.simplypsychology.org/operant-conditioning.html.

19. "Motivation," *Psychology Today*, accessed May 8, 2025, https://www.psychologytoday.com/ca/basics/motivation.

20. "Motivation," *Psychology Today*.

21. Stefan Falk, "Understanding the Power of Intrinsic Motivation," *Harvard Business Review*, March 8, 2023, https://hbr.org/2023/03/understand-the-power-of-intrinsic-motivation.

22. Marie Dacey et al., "Older Adults' Intrinsic and Extrinsic Motivation toward Physical Activity," *American Journal of Health Behavior* 32, no. 6 (2008): 570–82, https://www.researcgate.net/publication/5410706_Older_Adults'_Intrinsic_and_Extrinsic_Motivation_Toward_Physical_Activity.

23. Robert Matthews, "How Long Is a Moment?" *BBC Science Focus Magazine*, October 10, 2019, https://www.sciencefocus.com/science/how-long-is-a-moment.

24. Lisa Marie Basile, "5 Health Benefits of Ice Baths," Goodrx, August 23, 2024, https://www.goodrx.com/well-being/alternative-treatments/6-ice-bath-benefits.

25. Hedy Marks, "Stage Fright (Performance Anxiety)," WebMD.

26. Terry Gross, "In 'Dopamine Nation,' Overabundance Keeps Us Craving More," NPR, August 25, 2021, https://www.npr.org/sections/health-shots/2021/08/25/1030930259/in-dopamine-nation-overabundance-keeps-u-s-craving-more.

27. Anna Lembke, "Dopamine and the Pleasure–Pain Balance," Society for the Study of Addiction, February 8, 2023, https://www.addiction-ssa.org/dopamine-and-the-pleasure-pain-balance/.

28. Jacqueline Sperling, "The Social Dilemma: Social Media and Your Mental Health," Mass General Brigham McLean, March 29, 2024, https://www.mcleanhospital.org/essential/it-or-not-social-medias-affecting-your-mental-health.

29. L'Oreal Thompson Payton, "Americans Check Their Phones 144 Times a Day: Here's How to Cut Back," *Fortune*, July 19, 2023, https://fortune.com/well/2023/07/19/how-to-cut-back-screen-time/.

Chapter 6: Micro-moments of bravery

1. Matt Cutts, "Try Something New for 30 Days," TED Talk, March 2011, 4 min., 12 sec., https://www.ted.com/talks/matt_cutts_try_something_new_for_30_days/transcript?language=en.

2. James Clear, "Identity-Based Habits: How to Actually Stick to Your Goals This Year," December 31, 2012, https://jamesclear.com/identity-based-habits.
3. Clear, "Identity-Based Habits."
4. "Vipassana Meditation," Dhamma.org, accessed May 8, 2025, https://www.dhamma.org/en/about/vipassana.
5. "Vipassana Meditation," Dhamma.org.
6. Steward T.A. Pickett et al., "The Ontogeny of Theory," in *Ecological Understanding* (Elsevier, 2007), 97–115.
7. Melanie Hopkins and Scott Lidgard, "Gradualism," Oxford Bibliographies, August 30, 2016, https://www.oxfordbibliographies.com/display/document/obo-9780199941728/obo-9780199941728–0072.xml.
8. "How to Foster a Growth Mindset in the Classroom," American University School of Education Online, December 10, 2020, https://soeonline.american.edu/blog/growth-mindset-in-the-classroom/.
9. Thomas Nagel, "What Is It like to Be a Bat?" *The Philosophical Review* 84, no. 4 (1974): 435–50, https://www.sas.upenn.edu/~cavitch/pdf-library/Nagel_Bat.pdf.
10. Frank Jackson, "Epiphenomenal Qualia," *The Philosophical Quarterly* 32, no. 127 (1982): 127–136, https://doi.org/10.2307/2960077.
11. "Sonder," The Dictionary of Obscure Sorrows, https://www.dictionaryofobscuresorrows.com/post/23536922667/sonder.
12. Angela Lee Duckworth, "Grit: The Power of Passion and Perseverance," TED Talk, April 2013, 2 min., 53 sec., https://www.ted.com/talks/angela_lee_duckworth_grit_the_power_of_passion_and_perseverance/transcript?language=en.
13. University of Queensland, "Nature v Nurture: Research Shows It's Both," May 19, 2015, https://www.uq.edu.au/news/article/2015/05/nature-v-nurture-research-shows-its-both.
14. Michael D. De Bellis and Abigail Zisk, "The Biological Effects of Childhood Trauma," *Child and Adolescent Psychiatric Clinics of North America* 23, no. 2 (2014): 185–222, https://doi.org/10.1016/j.chc.2014.01.002.
15. Tom Huddleston, "How Michael Jordan Became Great: 'Nobody Will Ever Work as Hard as I Work,'" CNBC, April 21, 2020, https://www.cnbc.com/2020/04/21/how-michael-jordan-became-great-nobody-will-ever-work-as-hard.html.
16. Huddleston, "How Michael Jordan Became Great."
17. Huddleston, "How Michael Jordan Became Great."

Chapter 7: From moment to momentum

1. Joshua B. Miller and Adam Sanjurjo, "Is It a Fallacy to Believe in the Hot Hand in the NBA Three-Point Contest?" *European Economic Review* 138 (2021): 103771, https://doi.org/10.1016/j.euroecorev.2021.103771.
2. Miller and Sanjurjo, "Is It a Fallacy to Believe in the Hot Hand in the NBA Three-Point Contest?"
3. Tristin Hopper, "Malcolm Gladwell Got It Wrong: 'Deliberate Practice'—Not 10,000 Hours—Key to Achievement, Psychologist Says," *National Post*, April 12, 2016, https://nationalpost.com/news/canada/malcolm-gladwell-got-it-wrong-deliberate-practice-not-10000-hours-key-to-achievement-psychologist-says.
4. Andrew Huberman, "How to Increase Your Willpower & Tenacity," Huberman Lab, Scicomm Media, March 20, 2025, https://www.hubermanlab.com/episode/how-to-increase-your-willpower-and-tenacity.
5. Sonia McDonald, "Rewiring the Brain for Change," Human Resources Director Australia, December 4, 2013, https://www.hcamag.com/au/specialisation/change-management/rewiring-the-brain-for-change/139474.
6. Sara Bernard, "Neuroplasticity: Learning Physically Changes the Brain," Edutopia, George Lucas Educational Foundation, December 1, 2010, https://www.edutopia.org/neuroscience-brain-based-learning-neuroplasticity.
7. Harry Haroutioun Haladjian, "Informavores: Beings That Produce and Consume Information," *Psychology Today*, March 28, 2019, https://www.psychologytoday.com/us/blog/theory-of-consciousness/201903/informavores-beings-that-produce-and-consume-information.
8. "Barbara Fredrickson," Pursuit of Happiness, April 29, 2014, https://www.pursuit-of-happiness.org/history-of-happiness/barb-fredrickson/.
9. Catherine M. Pittman and Elizabeth M. Karle, *Rewire Your Anxious Brain: How to Use the Neuroscience of Fear to End Anxiety, Panic and Worry* (New Harbinger Publications, 2015).
10. Pittman and Karle, *Rewire Your Anxious Brain.*
11. Suzanne Rowan Kelleher, "This Is Your Brain on Travel," *Forbes*, July 28, 2019, https://www.forbes.com/sites/suzannerowankelleher/2019/07/28/this-is-your-brain-on-travel/.
12. Thomas Gilovich and Victoria Husted Medvec, "The Temporal Pattern to the Experience of Regret," *Journal of Personality and Social Psychology* 67, no. 3 (1994): 357–65, https://psycnet.apa.org/doi/10.1037/0022–3514.67.3.357.

Chapter 8: Will you stand up for your life?

1. "Biography of Eleanor Roosevelt," Archives.gov., April 8, 2008, https://georgewbush-whitehouse.archives.gov/history/firstladies/ar32.html.
2. Lauren Boone, "How Eleanor Roosevelt Faced Her Fears and Raised the Bar for All First Ladies," *MSNBC*, August 22, 2023, https://www.msnbc.com/know-your-value/out-of-office/how-eleanor-roosevelt-faced-her-fears-raised-bar-all-first-n1307067.
3. Boone, "How Eleanor Roosevelt Faced Her Fears and Raised the Bar for All First Ladies."
4. "Human Rights Day—Women Who Shaped the Universal Declaration," United Nations, accessed May 8, 2025, https://www.un.org/en/observances/human-rights-day/women-who-shaped-the-universal-declaration.
5. Daniel Coyle, *The Talent Code: Greatness Isn't Born. It's Grown. Here's How.* (Random House, 2009).
6. Coyle, *The Talent Code*.
7. "Resilience," American Psychological Association, accessed May 8, 2025, https://www.apa.org/topics/resilience.
8. Elaine Shpungin, "4 Ways to Boost Your Resilience," *Psychology Today*, October 13, 2023, https://www.psychologytoday.com/us/blog/peacemeal/202108/4-ways-to-boost-your-resilience.
9. Shpungin, "4 Ways to Boost Your Resilience."
10. C. F. Valenzuela, "Alcohol and Neurotransmitter Interactions." *Alcohol Health and Research World* 21, no. 2 (1997): 144–48, https://pmc.ncbi.nlm.nih.gov/articles/PMC6826822/.
11. "What to Know about Systematic Desensitization," WebMD, June 17, 2021, https://www.webmd.com/anxiety-panic/what-to-know-systematic-desensitization-therapy.
12. "What Is Exposure Therapy?" WebMD, April 15, 2015, https://www.webmd.com/mental-health/what-is-exposure-therapy.
13. Paul Anthony Jones, *The Cabinet of Linguistic Curiosities: A Yearbook of Forgotten Words*, Second Edition (Elliott & Thompson, 2019).

Chapter 9: Do NOT neglect this

1. Shaquille O'Neal, "How Leaders Utilize Humor and Seriousness in Leadership Styles" (PhD diss., Barry University, 2012).

2. Matthew Perry, *Friends, Lovers, and the Big Terrible Thing* (Flatiron Books, 2022).

3. Andrea Zaccaro et al., "How Breath-Control Can Change Your Life: A Systematic Review on Psycho-Physiological Correlates of Slow Breathing," *Frontiers in Human Neuroscience* 12 (2018): 353, https://doi.org/10.3389/fnhum.2018.00353.

4. Suma P. Chand et al., "Cognitive Behavior Therapy," in *StatPearls* (StatPearls Publishing, 2025).

5. Anja Tanhane, "Miyanda Therapy and Training," Mindfulness Meditation, October 4, 2014, https://mindfulnessmeditation.net.au/arrow/.

6. Julie O'Connor, "Novel Study Is First to Demonstrate Brain Mechanisms That Give 'The Iceman' Unusual Resistance to Cold," Wayne State University, February 28, 2018, https://today.wayne.edu/news/2018/02/28/novel-study-is-first-to-demonstrate-brain-mechanisms-that-give-the-iceman-unusual-resistance-to-cold-6232.

7. Bessel van der Kolk, *The Body Keeps the Score: Brain, Mind, and Body in the Healing of Trauma* (Penguin Books, 2015).

8. Robert Emmons, "Why Gratitude Is Good," *Greater Good Magazine*, November 16, 2010, https://greatergood.berkeley.edu/article/item/why_gratitude_is_good.

9. Christopher Littlefield, "Use Gratitude to Counter Stress and Uncertainty," *Harvard Business Review*, October 20, 2020, https://hbr.org/2020/10/use-gratitude-to-counter-stress-and-uncertainty.

10. Michael Singer, *The Untethered Soul: The Journey Beyond Yourself* (New Harbinger Publications, 2007).

11. *The Five Minute Journal* (Intelligent Change, 2013), https://www.intelligentchange.com/products/the-five-minute-journal.

12. Jim Robbins, "Ecopsychology: How Immersion in Nature Benefits Your Health," Yale Environment 360, January 9, 2020, https://e360.yale.edu/features/ecopsychology-how-immersion-in-nature-benefits-your-health.

13. "Exercising to Relax," Harvard Health Publishing, July 7, 2020, https://www.health.harvard.edu/staying-healthy/exercising-to-relax.

14. Seena Mathew, "Swimming Gives Your Brain a Boost—but Scientists Don't Know Yet Why It's Better than Other Aerobic Activities," *The Conversation*, July 27, 2021, https://theconversation.com/swimming-gives-your-brain-a-boost-but-scientists-dont-know-yet-why-its-better-than-other-aerobic-activities-164297.

15. Gabor Maté, *In The Realm of Hungry Ghosts: Close Encounters with Addiction* (Knopf Canada, 2008).

16. Cal Newport, *Deep Work: Rules for Focused Success in a Distracted World* (Grand Central Publishing, 2016).

17. Adam Alter, *Irresistible: The Rise of Addictive Technology and the Business of Keeping Us Hooked* (Penguin Press, 2017).

18. Nir Eyal, *Indistractable: How to Control Your Attention and Choose Your Life* (BenBella Books, 2019).

19. Johann Hari, *Stolen Focus: Why You Can't Pay Attention—and How to Think Deeply Again* (Crown Publishing Group, 2022)

20. Anna Lembke, *Dopamine Nation: Finding Balance in the Age of Indulgence* (Dutton, 2021).

21. "Dopamine," Cleveland Clinic, September 6, 2023, https://my.clevelandclinic.org/health/articles/22581-dopamine.

22. Jim Haggerty, "History of Psychotherapy," Psych Central, May 17, 2016, https://psychcentral.com/lib/history-of-psychotherapy.

23. Haggerty, "History of Psychotherapy."

24. Haggerty, "History of Psychotherapy."

25. Didem Acar and G. Dirik, "A Current Paradigm: Written Emotional Disclosure," *Psikiyatride Guncel Yaklasimlar—Current Approaches in Psychiatry* 11, no. 1 (2018): 65–79, https://dergipark.org.tr/tr/download/article-file/598344.

26. James W. Pennebaker et al., "Disclosure of Traumas and Immune Function: Health Implications for Psychotherapy," *Journal of Consulting and Clinical Psychology* 56, no. 2 (1988): 239–45, https://psycnet.apa.org/record 1988-27259-001?doi=1.

27. Susan Dominus, "Does Therapy Really Work? Let's Unpack That," *The New York Times*, May 16, 2023, https://www.nytimes.com/2023/05/16/magazine/does-therapy-work.html.

Chapter 10: Things I wish I knew back then . . .

1. Loretta J. Ross, "Don't Call People Out—Call Them In," Ted Talk, Aug 4, 2021, 2 min., 14. sec., https://www.youtube.com/watch?v=xw_720iQDss.

INDEX